CONTEMPORARY AMERICAN JEWELRY DESIGN

Ettagale Blauer

VNR VAN NOSTRAND REINHOLD
New York

To Toby Davis, who showed me the way to Rhinebeck.

Copyright © 1991 by Ettagale Blauer

Library of Congress Catalog Card Number 90-44214
ISBN 0-442-00362-5

Printed in Hong Kong by Excel Printing Company

Van Nostrand Reinhold
115 Fifth Avenue
New York, New York 10003

Chapman and Hall
2-6 Boundary Row
London, SE1 8HN, England

Thomas Nelson Australia
102 Dodds Street
South Melbourne 3205
Victoria, Australia

Nelson Canada
1120 Birchmount Road
Scarborough, Ontario M1K 5G4, Canada

16   15   14   13   12   11   10   9   8   7   6   5   4   3   2

Library of Congress Cataloging-in-Publication Data
Blauer, Ettagale.
    Contemporary American jewelry design / Ettagale Blauer.
        p.   cm.
    ISBN 0-442-00362-5
    1.   Jewelry—United States—History—20th century.   I. Title.
NK7312.B5   1991
739.27'0973'09045—dc20   90-44214
                                                                    CIP

The cover shows the work of Tony Papp (p. 42), Mary Lee Hu (p. 54), Harold O'Connor
(p. 61), Carrie Adell (p. 83), Eric Russell (p. 108), Caroline Strieb (p. 108), Vicki Eisenfeld
(p. 147), and Marne Ryan (p. 162).

Contents

Preface

The Phenomenon of Studio Goldsmithing

When the history of art in the 1980s is written, much of it will be etched in gold. This is the time of the contemporary goldsmith, an artist who chooses to work in precious metals rather than oils or marble.

The contemporary jeweler-as-artist has only recently become a recognized force. With rare exceptions, the whole field is little more than thirty years old. But it is only within the past fifteen years that these jewelers have entered the jewelry mainstream.

The phenomenon of contemporary goldsmithing embraces an eclectic group of artists, each with a unique vision, each taking a personal path to jewelry producing. They have as little relationship to the typical, mass-produced jewelry as a champagne maker has to a bottler of orange soda. They approach a piece of art, not a piece of metal. The work is personal and a perfect expression of the "back to the land" movement that spawned it. Many of these goldsmiths were looking not merely for a way to make a living but for a way to make a life that was worthy of living.

Running a business while trying to remain a creative metalsmith at the same time is the ongoing challenge. The jeweler—artists have solved or resolved these often conflicting needs in slightly different ways and in a beautiful variety of techniques and styles. Their methods, their growth, and their work are discussed here.

When I first began covering jewelry in 1972, the presence of these jewelers was a delightful surprise to me. Until then, I thought jewelry was all circle pins, class rings, and strands of graduated pearls. This is a personal book; I know these people, some for more than fifteen

Facing page:
Stuart Golder at his loom
in Cincinnati, Ohio.

ix

years. My selection encompasses the best examples of the various methods and styles that exemplify the world of contemporary jewelry making today.

With the exception of the teachers profiled, all the jewelers whose work is shown make a living from their jewelry. I make a crucial distinction between them and others who sell their work but do not derive their living from it. The latter form an elite group that sometimes helps sharpen the cutting edge of contemporary goldsmithing but is usually more self-indulgent than those who must satisfy enough of the marketplace to be self-supporting.

Techniques are inherent in the work and form a natural part of the text. Contemporary handcrafted jewelry embraces techniques as old as written records and as new as space technology. American goldsmiths also reach across cultures, wedding traditional handcrafting methods to contemporary design. The vocabulary of jewelry making today includes the Japanese techniques of *mokumé* and *shakado;* the five-thousand-year-old technique of granulation; reticulation; marriage of metals; and handweaving. Enameling is used to "paint" jewels, the closest the jeweler comes to working at the artist's canvas.

The book traces the growth of the craft fairs and craft galleries, the most important venues for the exhibition and sale of contemporary jewelry. These fairs used to be as innocent as the jewelers themselves. Both the goldsmiths and the fairs have changed, grown up, and become much, much more businesslike. Much of that early charm is gone but so, too, are craftspeople who weren't capable of filling the orders they wrote.

The craft galleries are the strongest supporters of this work and have labored at great cost to promote the work of contemporary goldsmiths. With rare exceptions, these galleries date from the early 1970s.

My own vantage point includes not only my experience covering this movement for the past fifteen years but my perspective of the entire jewelry market—from mass-produced work, to period jewelry, to the world of gems, including the techniques, the materials, even the mines from which these metals and stones come.

Introduction

Studio Goldsmithing Today

DEFINING THE MEDIUM

What is contemporary American jewelry? Does it fall comfortably into a "period" description such as Art Deco or Edwardian? Is it what you see when you walk into a jewelry store?

For the most part, the answers are "no," and "no." There is no one style to contemporary jewelry. It may be geometric or organic, spare or ornate, Bauhaus or Baroque. And as for jewelry stores, they are more often marked by the *absence* of contemporary American jewelry, which is found most often in craft galleries or specialty retail shops.

Some call it "studio goldsmithing." That's a good start on a definition for it implies, correctly, that this work is created in an individual jeweler's workplace. Ironically, the term it really deserves, *designer jewelry*, has been co-opted. In the world of American marketing, *designer* is synonymous with *signature*. Mention contemporary jewelry to anyone not familiar with the work shown here and the response is, "Oh, you mean like (insert any well-advertised designer name)." Designer-name jewelry is available through major retailers; it has as much to do with design as Bill Blass has to do with the chocolates sold under his name. It is, rather, a convenient marketing method aimed at making one product stand out from myriad others that look just like it. This has become necessary in fields where all the products have the same ingredients, look alike, and do their job equally well.

In the American jewelry world, from the individual studio goldsmith to the biggest of the mass producers, the raw materials are the same, principally gold and silver. It is how those raw materials are used that spells the difference in the product.

The typical manufacturer is selling a commodity with a certain intrinsic value. The lowest expression of this thinking is the chain

1

Gayle Saunders. "The Strength Within" brooch. 14k colored golds, 18k yellow gold. (1987)

maker who sells his product by the pennyweight. Selling by weight is ingrained in the industry and has been promoted aggressively, to the point where it has poisoned the minds of the jewelry retailer and ultimately the consumer and blinded them to the possibility of buying design ideas and originality.

Retailers want their jewelry to be easy to sell, easy to price, easy to understand. They key in on the messages presented by the marketers with the biggest budgets: diamonds are forever, nothing else feels like real gold. Small wonder they ask, "How much does it weigh?" But that kind of approach has led to the soul-destroying 50-percent-off sales (and the 80-percent-off sales). When you're selling weight, and hence price, the only advantage one retailer has over another is a lower price. With merchandise nearly always on sale, consumers have learned to wait for even lower prices before making their purchases.

Studio goldsmithing suffers from none of these problems. Each piece makes its own design statement, not just in materials used but in style and workmanship. Though there is intrinsic value in the metals and stones used, this is only part of the equation. Original design and fine craftsmanship make up the rest of the price, although this jewelry is often no more expensive, ounce for ounce, than mass-produced pieces. That is a function of its more limited manufacture and distribution. Sold largely through craft shows and a limited number of craft galleries, contemporary jewelry sidesteps the need for expensive advertising campaigns. Most contemporary goldsmiths sell as much as they can make. Their market is driven not by demand but by supply.

PERIOD DESIGN?

While "modern" design in furniture denotes the stripped down, Danish-blond look of the 1950s, contemporary jewelry shares a sensibility rather than a look. Unlike the great, and not so great, jewelry periods of the past, contemporary jewelry cannot be conveniently labeled. The look is as diverse as the artists themselves. But the best of the jewelry may be recognized for its artistic content. It is art in gold, art in silver, art in titanium. A piece ornamented with granulation may not be labeled Etruscan revival any more than a cloisonné brooch fits into any Chinese dynasty. Jewelry of the 1970s and 1980s resists compartmentalizing.

Tony Papp. Brooch. Marriage of metals: nickel and sterling silver. (1988)

*Marci Zelmanoff.
Earrings. Sterling silver,
oxidized copper, bronze.
(1988) (Photo by Bob
Barrett.)*

There have, however, been periods of a year or two when a particular technique emerged. Marriage of metals, mokumé gane, as well as titanium and its sister metals, niobium and tantalum, each enjoyed a period of intense exposure and experimentation. Once the flurry of interest was over, these techniques and materials became part of the jeweler's palette, to be brought forth when needed, just as a commercial jeweler sets amethysts one year and sapphires the next.

Why do certain metals or metalworking techniques suddenly appear everywhere and all at once? In fashion, the direction often comes from the fabric makers. In jewelry, the impetus often stems from a crafts teacher sharing knowledge or through a workshop given by a master teacher to a roomful of teachers who, in turn, carry it back to their classrooms. From there it ripples out in a hundred directions, but like the ripples in a pond, the strength of the originator is diffused, sometimes becoming an indistinct echo. Too many of those learning the technique simply swallow it whole; nothing is added.

PUSHING THE MEDIUM

While gold and silver remain the principal metals used by contemporary jewelers, these jewelers distinguish themselves within the larger jewelry community by their willingness to try other materials. The most dynamic and dramatic such experiment was the craft community's discovery of niobium, titanium, and tantalum, known collectively as the refractory metals.

Although these naturally occurring metals have been known to science since the 1700s, their use in the space program brought them to commercial feasibility. They enjoy two extraordinary physical properties: tremendous strength combined with light weight and extremely high melting points. This was the ideal combination for use in shields on space vehicles and in other forbidding environments.

But the same combination of strength and lightness also makes the metals attractive to jewelers. Because the metals can be colored through an electrolytic process, they have tremendous appeal to craft jewelers looking to add color to their pieces without using either gemstones or enamel. With refractory metals, the colors achieved are permanent, durable, and flow through the metal; the back and front are equally attractive. Moreover, the colors achieved are the classic jewel tones: a range of red to violet, rich greens, and blues. Jewelers soon learned how to control the colors by varying the electrical current used. Finally, the raw material is so inexpensive compared with gold, or even silver, that it is sold by the pound rather than by the ounce.

These benefits are counterbalanced by formidable obstacles. The chief drawback to the refractory metal is the difficulty it presents in using conventional jewelry-making techniques. Because it cannot be fabricated at the bench but instead requires commercial-scaled equipment, most jewelers use it very simply, letting the look of the metal carry the message.

One of the first proponents of refractory metals was Ivy Ross, whose company, Small Wonders, was in the forefront of the craft jewelry movement. In her workshops, she brought this new material to the attention of other jewelers. Ross's designs offered the first hint of her originality; she invented new forms of the material, such as her titanium wires, then created new ways to manipulate them, and finally thought of new ways to set them into jewelry. The result was pieces that were totally revolutionary in many ways yet comprehensible to the more traditional jewelry community. I believe this combination—her use of colored diamonds, for example, in combination with titanium— established the new metals faster and more widely than would have happened otherwise. Although Ross went on to a career largely outside of the jewelry world, her influence was considerable.

The titanium group spread through the craft world like a chain letter, and not surprisingly, the quality of the work soon became diluted. It was taken up, it seemed, by everyone who ever turned hand to metal. Because most metalsmiths were limited by the difficulty in working the metal, the problem of proliferation was heightened by a sameness to the designs. Very few emerged from out of that pack. One of the best was Susan Sanders (then known as Susan Portner), a jeweler from Alexandria, Virginia. Sanders combined brilliant, varicolored geometric sections of titanium that she sandblasted and then set into 14k gold. The resulting pieces had a wonderful appeal: the jewelry was precious yet contemporary, bright yet tailored. It perfectly straddled the two jewelry worlds of craft and tradition. In time, Sanders gave up her titanium work in favor of more conventional 14k gold because the explosion of poorly designed titanium jewelry made it too difficult for buyers to appreciate the quality of her work.

Tamiko Kamata Ferguson, however, has stayed with it through the years, persisting in offering the most beautifully controlled patterns of titanium. Her ability to color the metal exactly as she wants it is unique among those who work this material. She can place dot patterns or subtle stripes exactly where she wants them and controls her colors with precision. This expertise is combined with original shapes and forms, bringing titanium back to a place of honor in the jewelry firmament.

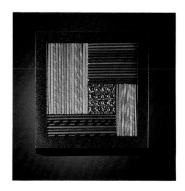

Ivy Ross. Brooch. Sterling silver, 14k gold, titanium wire, irradiated colored diamonds. Winner of the "Diamonds Today" Award, 1981.

Ivy Ross. Brooch. Sterling silver, niobium. (1982–1983)

The studio goldsmith relishes technique; it's a challenge rather than a burden to make a better clasp, to shun ready-made, commercial findings, to create a unique gold alloy. The subtleties of matching gold to colored gemstones may result in an effect that's visible only to the goldsmith, but for many, that's reason enough to do it.

PERSON TO PERSON

The contemporary goldsmith expects more from the customer than money; jewelry is worn intimately, in touch with the body. Since the piece is an expression of the person who made it, there is an expectation of the type of person who chooses it. In many cases, customers and jewelers become friends; this one element alone distinguishes the contemporary or craft jeweler from his commercial counterpart. These jewelers often know the ultimate customer, usually through the sale of a one-of-a-kind piece at a craft fair or during a one-person show at a gallery where the artist and the public meet. These events—assuredly commercial but also social—reinforce the relationship between the artist and customer, customer and gallery, gallery and artist. Because the gallery deals with the money, the customer and the artist may center their relationship on the creative aspects of the transaction.

This relationship was once the cornerstone of commerce. A person needed or wanted an object, he approached the maker, a conversation ensued, a design was made, a price was set, the deal was struck. In time, the maker delivered the item.

While today wealthy consumers can custom order home furnishings, clothing, and jewels, goldsmiths bring this special relationship within the reach of someone with as little as two hundred dollars to spend on a modest ring or a pair of earrings. One piece leads to another and over time, as the consumer becomes more affluent and more comfortable with this special process, the work ordered becomes more important. It takes a strength of conviction in one's own taste and style to work in collaboration with a goldsmith. Of course, much of the work is purchased through a go-between without that special relationship. But

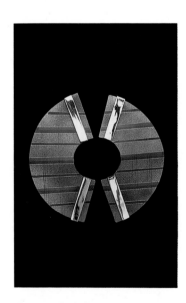

Susan Sanders. Earrings. Sandblasted titanium and 14k gold. (Early 1980s)

just knowing the name of the maker is a way of bringing the two to-gether.

Once every woman of modest means was her own dressmaker; she chose the fabric and the pattern and then fitted herself exactly. Every-thing she wore was unique—a one-of-a-kind outfit. With the coming of the industrial revolution, the sewing machine, and the garment indus-try, most women had to be content with buying their clothes, like their jewelry, off the rack (only the rich could afford a dressmaker). When products are mass produced, they must appeal to a mass audience. The small, personal shop gave way to the anonymous, large chain store and department store. Volume was everything. In recent years, however, there has been a return to the small store, the boutique, the neighbor-hood specialty shop. And the craft gallery takes its place in that circle, offering both personal attention to the customer and a venue in which handmade jewelry may be viewed and purchased.

The process by which the jewelry reaches these shops is unique; it is an outgrowth of the 1960s, the back-to-the-land movement, the baby-boom generation. The story of contemporary American jewelry is as much about marketing as it is about manufacture, and in that sense, it is quintessentially American.

Tamiko Kawata Ferguson. "Galaxy" neckcuff. Titanium; brushed oxidation. (1981)

Chapter 1

Craft Shows

ORIGINS OF THE CRAFT SHOWS

Like the stock market, the marketing of contemporary crafts started under a tree, but there the similarity ends. For while the objective of the stock market was to make money trading on the production of unseen and unknown people who labored far away, the craft fair was intended to bring creator and consumer face to face. Both halves of the equation were remarkably innocent of the processes that were needed to bring them together, a reflection of the 1960s when the emerging world of crafts began to make itself known to the mass-market-oriented American consumer.

The hippie ethic was at its height in the 1960s—a reaction to the bland, homogenized world that itself represented an attempt to forget the horrors of the second World War. The hippie, flower-power rebellion took the form and gentle spirit of nonviolent protest. But in a land where little white gloves reigned supreme and Lawrence Welk set the musical agenda for middle America, brightly colored tie-dyed clothing, long hair, the Beatles, and a general belief in expressing love for one's neighbors were such radical ideas that it was feared they could threaten the very foundations of American society. Fitting in was a highly desirable goal as well as the accepted norm. Anyone who chose a different path, who wanted to stand out from the crowd, threatened to upset the very safe status quo. Most adults of the time had first-hand memories of what it meant to survive during the Depression. Security was a precious gift and one that was worth the sacrifices required to achieve it. A better way of life and a college education were the dreams one had for one's children.

For those who did not experience the Depression it was impossible to understand the fear its memories bred. To many of the younger generation, who stood to benefit the most from their parents' work ethic,

Facing page:
Terry Foltz-Fox. "Moon Dance" neckpiece. Marriage of metals: sterling silver, copper, nickel, chemically oxidized brass. (1988)

the idea of working for the same company for forty years, for any company, was appalling. As the world around them became more standardized and gray, they wanted most of all to express their personal feeling, their individuality, their creativity. Precisely because they were unconcerned about their basic, daily needs, they were free to satisfy one of the most original and American of ideas, the pursuit of happiness. Many sought that satisfaction in a most American way: they moved out of the cities and back to the land.

For most, it was the first time they had lived on the land; these were the children of the cities and that post-war phenomenon—the suburbs. They sought out places where they could live cheaply, in harmony with nature, and as differently as they could imagine from the way they had been raised. It was the era of free love, natural childbirth with a midwife in attendance, organically grown foods, and weddings in meadows. Fathers took equal responsibility for the care and education of their children. They were there from the beginning, turning up in hospital delivery rooms along with their wives or "significant others."

But how to sustain themselves, how to earn money? What kind of work would allow them to sidestep the mind- and soul-numbing corporations yet put food on the table? Handmade objects were the answer that arose simultaneously in cottages and cabins from California to the New England woods. Lovingly made, oddly shaped, amateurish at every turn were those first candles, wooden cradles, and spoon jewelry. Mothers who had saved every cent to put their sons and daughters through college in the expectation they would become doctors, lawyers, accountants, teachers, or at least diligent vice-presidents of insurance companies found themselves with an overabundance of vividly colored twisted candles and tie-dyed shapeless clothing. For the makers, these products also established a way of reinforcing a cashless society. Bartering for products and services freed them even further from the consumerism they were so determined to escape. Those objects, no matter how ungainly, had a ready market—other like-minded people of their

Joseph and Smadar English. Necklace. 22k gold, aquamarine crystals, and pink sapphires. (1991)

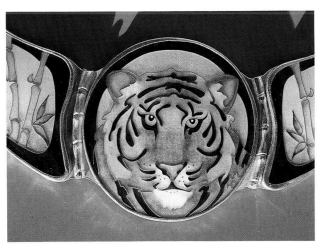

Thomas Farrell. "Ed's Kite" brooch. Enamel on copper with fine silver; constructed setting of 14k gold and sterling silver. (1985)

Merry Lee Rae. Neckpiece. Detail of cloisonné enamel and 18k gold tiger worked across several panels. (1979)

generation moved by the same desires and same beliefs who had not actually made the move back to the land. They could express their own rebellion, albeit more modestly, by buying the products of those brave enough to go all the way. The craft movement now had means and motive, maker and buyer. What was missing, however, was opportunity, the venue at which these two could come together. And so was born the craft fair.

By moving the point of sale from the studio to the craft fair, these creators decisively set the course for the marketing of crafts in America, a course that was instantly different from the world of the art gallery. From the beginning of the commercially viable craft movement, it has been the constant, intimate contact between creator and consumer that has given shape to the product and the flow of the products in these media. Although this book specifically embraces the world of the contemporary American jeweler, the same process was at work in the other fine-craft media of glass, clay, wood, and fiber. But jewelry has always occupied a unique category within the craft world because its materials have intrinsic value. The finished work of a fine glass-blower, ceramicist, fiber artist, or woodworker may be valued at any price, but the cost of the sand, clay, yarn, and wood doesn't compare with the price of an ounce of gold or silver.

The contact between maker and consumer gave craftspeople control over the sale of their products as well as their creation. It side-stepped that most American institution—advertising—relying instead on the ability of the product and its maker to speak for themselves. Astonishingly, through the two decades to be considered here, this has remained the rule. For while the craft shows as well as the number of craft makers have grown to astounding numbers and a level of sophistication impossible to imagine just twenty years ago, their success flows on its own, very much apart from the mainstream of American consumerism. They continue to attract the faithful among both wholesale and retail buyers. Advertising is directed to special interest publications, read by an increasingly knowledgeable public. No matter how successful a craft show, it cannot compete on an equal basis with mass marketers in the mass media.

ON THE ROAD TO RHINEBECK

As Kleenex is to tissues and Xerox is to photocopies, Rhinebeck is the standard by which all craft fairs are judged. Yet the show did not begin in Rhinebeck, New York. It began with a group of craftspeople gathering in the ski town of Stowe, Vermont, in 1965, moving through the years to Mt. Snow in 1966 and then to Bennington, Vermont in 1969 before arriving in Rhinebeck in 1973. It remained at Rhinebeck through the glory years, moving to its present venue at West Springfield, Massachusetts, in 1984. Each move changed the show, sometimes reflecting the growing sophistication and business needs of the craftspeople, sometimes reflecting the politics of the show management.

Some still mourn for the very earliest days at Mt. Snow when for twenty dollars, a craftsperson earned the right to a space inside the Snow Lake Lodge. It wasn't an assigned space, neatly marked out by show management. Craftspeople lined up at the door, ran in, and set up a space. If three people wanted to use electricity from the same two-outlet source at the same time, a committee was formed to decide how to handle the demand.

For those who couldn't afford twenty dollars, there were five-dollar spaces just outside the lodge. And for three dollars, you got a tailgating space; you backed your car up to the lodge in the parking area and sold right out of the car. When the car was empty, you went home.

Bennington, considered the real predecessor to Rhinebeck, housed the show for four years at Bennington High School. Those who couldn't fit or refused to tolerate the crowded and stifling gymnasium found spaces out in the field, under trees if they were lucky.

RHINEBECK

The Northeast Crafts Fair arrived in the charming upstate New York town of Rhinebeck in the summer of 1973. It was the right event, in the right place, at the right time. The town of Rhinebeck evokes Sleepy Hollow, yet it's within easy reach of New York City. Located about ten miles from historical Woodstock, the town that gave a name to a whole generation, it offers a captive audience in the form of weekending, affluent families. The 2½-hour drive or 2-hour train ride made it possible for wholesale buyers to come up from New York for the day, shop the show, and return that same evening after a pleasant day in the country. The Dutchess County Fairgrounds provided room for just 450 exhibitors, which kept the show at a comfortable, walkable size.

One of the secondary delights of doing Rhinebeck was the pleasure of seeing the best of all the crafts media. Jewelers were not segregated in one area but mixed within the other types of work. At the wholesale level, jewelry buyers could shop the whole show and come away not only with their work done but with a good sense of what was going on in the larger craft world. Goldsmiths, fiber artists, woodworkers, potters, and glassblowers could all be seen at their exhibits spaced throughout the show. There was plenty of time to walk the aisles and, even subliminally, absorb what was going on with the other media even if you were focusing on jewelry only. The craftspeople were on the receiving end of a constant flow of compliments and appreciation of their work. These comments were not being wasted on hired help; it

The Rhinebeck Craft Show, 1980. A flute maker in one of the exhibit tents at the Dutchess County Fairgrounds. (Photo by Jason Lauré.)

was a requirement of the American Craft Enterprises (ACE) shows that the originator of the craft be present in the booth.

To be sure, the jewelry exhibits were concentrated in the more secure areas of the Rhinebeck show. The intrinsic value of jewelry and its supreme portability have always made it more vulnerable to theft than, say, a handwoven tapestry or a large ceramic vase. But while the show remained at Rhinebeck, it was arranged in a careful mix of media, giving the sense of walking through a large and particularly wonderful home.

Some 275 of the exhibitors showed in big yellow and white striped tents; the rest were in concrete-floored, tin-roofed, barnlike sheds. When it rained, the dirt floors in the tented areas tended to get muddy, sometimes even flooded out. And when the sun beamed down, the tin roof heated up fiercely. But the work! The work was wonderful. This was the heyday of the jewelry craft movement. Each June, as I approached the first jewelry booth, I wondered, would it be as exciting this year? Was there anything miraculous left to create? And each year, I would start scribbling in my notebook in delight. The jewelers had reinvented the wheel once again. The work was brilliant, the techniques astonishing, the artistry both personal and approachable.

A walk down the aisles revealed a *Who's Who* of the best in the craft jewelry world, or at least the part of it that had heard about Rhinebeck from another jeweler, or a teacher, or a relative. There was always a sense of being let in on a secret cache, a treasure chest of delights.

Part of the reason for the quality of the show was the jurying system, instituted at the second Rhinebeck event. Much to the surprise of the organizers, who had moved the show to Rhinebeck to take advantage of the spaciousness of the fairgrounds, more people applied than there was room for. A jurying system seemed the only way to allocate

Sydney Lynch. Brooches. Sterling silver, 24k gold foil. (1990) (Photo by R. Bruhn.)

spaces. As the show grew out of its amateur status, becoming a more businesslike event, it emerged under its own banner, American Craft Enterprises, described as the marketing subsidiary of the American Craft Council (ACC). The relationship between the two has always been edgy, but there is no question that ACE is a money-making operation and as such, has become the tail that wags the dog. ACC, at that time, could not even envision having a profit-making show as part of its operation. Indeed, its charter as a non-profit organization made it mandatory that the show be spun off under its own banner.

The pressure to grow was immediate. And with the institution of the jurying system, there was now a growing group of craftspeople who faced each year not knowing if they would have the opportunity to show and sell their work at this venue. Not since the days of waiting for their scores on the SATs did these young people wait so anxiously for the mail. "Are you in?" was the question in the air.

The craft movement, and the show, was becoming a phenomenon. The location at Rhinebeck, so remarkably right, exposed the show to the view of editors from New York as well as a growing number of collectors who loved the thrill of searching for that special object as much as they loved the object itself. While buyers were not likely to share the secret of their source, retail customers loved nothing better than to bring their friends to Rhinebeck to shop the show on the public days. Attendance grew into the tens of thousands.

ACROSS THE ROAD

Though it had seemed, when the show was moved from Bennington to the Dutchess County Fairgrounds, that there would be room enough for all who wanted to participate, Rhinebeck immediately became a sold-out show with 2000 craftspeople competing for fewer than 500 spaces. The supply of craftspeople multiplied faster than the booths to accommodate them. Entrepreneurship being the American way, show-people sprang up like mushrooms after the storm, ready to take in the best of those who were closed out of ACE. Since it was sometimes mere chance that saw one craftsperson accepted and another rejected, the competitors created their own jury and came up with a quite respectable show, albeit one that was totally exposed to the elements. In 1981, Richard Rothbard's Craft Market America was printing its own little catalogue, issuing its own badges, and doing its best to keep up the quality.

These efforts notwithstanding, these shows were more usually known by such ironic names as "Rhineject" or "Salon des Refusés," or, ethnically, "Rhinedreck." Names aside, the existence of these shows pointed up the obvious: there were many more craftspeople looking for places to show their work, and someone would find a way to take in as many of them as possible.

One group of enterprising jewelers made a place for themselves across the Hudson river in Kingston. Housed in a series of rooms at the Holiday Inn was one of the most elite group of "rejects" imaginable, among them Gayle Saunders, Marci Zelmanoff, Ross Coppelman, Marsha Zion, Thomas Farrell, and David Yurman. Some, in fact, had not even bothered to apply for the ACE Rhinebeck show but instead had thrown in their lot at the last minute with some like-minded jeweler friends. A private guard gave this gold-oriented group a better sense of security and an atmosphere they felt was more suited for their high-priced work. They profited more from a clientele derived from their own mailing lists than the high-volume traffic offered at the fairgrounds.

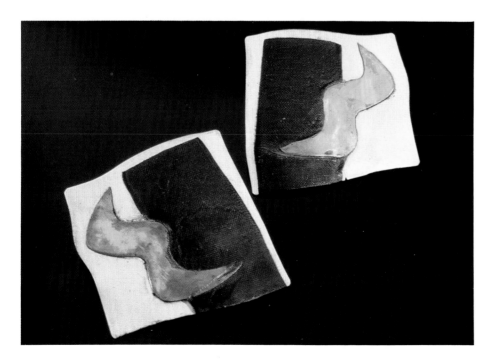

*Marci Zelmanoff.
Earrings. Sterling silver,
oxidized copper, brass.
(1988)*

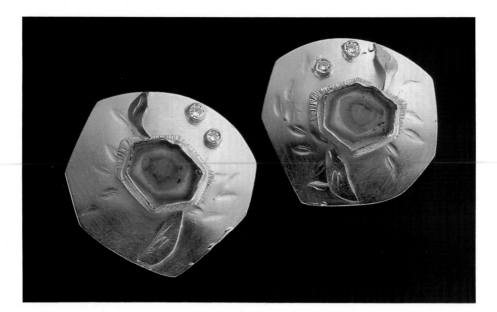

Stephani Briggs. Earrings. 18k and 22k golds, watermelon tourmaline, diamonds. (1988) (Photo by Mark Rockwood.)

THUMBS UP?

For just a moment all the elements were in harmony. The marketplace and the craftspeople and the buyers had achieved a perfect balance. Hardly was this balance achieved when the very success of the Rhinebeck show changed the attitude of the craftspeople. For some, this was the only major event they exhibited at during the entire year. Having just found their way to running a business, they were faced with the yearly gamble of the jurying process. Although jurying was meant to assure the quality of the show, it is a process fraught with potential for error. Even if it works perfectly, however, craftspeople's ability to display their work at their major business venue remains a question mark each year. ACE, having nurtured and cajoled and demanded professionalism from the exhibitors, had to find a way to give them some security. And so was born the five-year option. For craftspeople whose track record showed they were steady producers of viable crafts, a five-year opportunity to exhibit, sidestepping the jurying process, was made available. This alleviated their anxiety, but as it solved the one problem, it created another: with a number of spaces now reserved in advance, there were fewer places for newcomers. The very freshness and energy that had marked the show before was in jeopardy. To solve this problem, the show was moved once again—this time to West Springfield, Massachusetts.

"THE BIG E": WEST SPRINGFIELD

In 1984 the wonder that was Rhinebeck, the whole grand and glorious era, came to an end when the ACE show was moved to the exhibition grounds at West Springfield, Massachusetts. To many, it was the last craft show, certainly the last one with a strong sense of the spirit that brought these craftspeople together in the first place. More and more, the shows had become big business, while at the same time clinging to the jurying system. The results were often uneven. But there was no question about the major problem concerning the move to the unknown site at West Springfield: would the savvy retail customer, and even the wholesale buyer, be willing to make the trip? And, would the loss of the country fair atmosphere that prevailed at Rhinebeck change the show beyond recognition? The retail customers certainly voted with their feet, although the wholesale buyers persevered.

Rhinebeck is a pleasant 2½-hour drive from New York City. The town is charming, the fairgrounds easy to reach, the "folksiness" at just the right level. West Springfield is a tedious and ugly 3½-hour trip on tough highways, and at the end of the road lies an exceedingly unpleasant exhibition space. Adding to the general sense of loss at having had to leave Rhinebeck was the distinct scent of livestock in the air. The exhibition grounds are home to various agricultural events— sheep, cattle, and horses are housed in these same buildings. This fact, combined with the summer heat, makes the atmosphere unpleasant and even unhealthy. These back-to-the-land artists never expected to be showing their fine work in spaces that were more often used for cattle shows. Ironically, in the beginning, although it seemed enormous, according to show organizer Carol Sedestrom the event only housed 600 exhibitors, a twenty percent increase over the 500 at the last Rhinebeck event. It was not to remain so. The pressure to increase in size was ever present, with more and more young (and old) craftspeople emerging every year.

From that modest beginning, the show surged in size to 800 participants two years later and then to more than 950—a third of them jewelers—in 1990. It wasn't the size alone that changed the nature of the event and the experience. The charm had been left in Rhinebeck. First time visitors to West Springfield were like shell-shocked veterans who couldn't grasp the changed nature of the war. And for those who hadn't read all the information before the event, the new arrangement of booths came as a revelation: no longer would the media be mixed in that artful, seemingly haphazard manner. There were just too many aisles to walk. From now on, the jewelry and accessories would be found clustered together at one end of the show while the decorative goods—ceramics, glass, and wood—could be found elsewhere. Now the visitor simply encountered one jeweler after another, with nothing in-between to refresh the eye and the mind. The loss was palpable. The quality of the exhibitors began to change as well. With hundreds of jewelers, for example, it became more difficult for any one line to stand out. Sheer quantity numbs the eye. And with quantity came a diminution of quality. Those who work in the simplest ways offer lower-priced lines that are easy to grasp. The higher-priced work becomes more difficult to sell to buyers who haven't the time to learn just what makes one piece worth twice as much as another, seemingly similar piece.

Kathryn Gough. "Circles & Stones" cloisonné enamel neckpiece. Afghan beads, Dieter Lorenz stone, druzy quartz. (1989) (Photo by Tommy Elder.)

BALTIMORE

Two years after the move to Rhinebeck, ACE initiated another show, this one in the heart of downtown Baltimore. The difference in venue, and the timing of the show (it takes place in February), indicated the rapidly changing nature of the event. Baltimore is the center of a huge metropolitan population. The show itself, within easy reach of Baltimore's renewed harbor district and the city's genteel yet sophisticated population, had to invent its own, instant history. Without the physical restrictions of Rhinebeck, it was free to grow, and grow it did. In 1987,

Sydney Lynch. Brooches. Sterling silver, 24k gold foil. (1990)

an infamous year in show history, the Baltimore show grew by 350 exhibitors—virtually a whole show's worth of craftspeople. With 850 exhibitors housed in the vast sprawl that is the Convention Center, the show still attracted far more applicants than it could accommodate.

And bowing to the rapidly changing nature of the event, the planners set aside an entire section for exhibitors who sell only to wholesale accounts. Some craftspeople find their work unsuitable for selling in the environment of the "public days." Others can't afford to be out of their workshops for the additional days required. This factor, in addition to the sheer size of the show, resulted in a four-division event: at one end in the largest hall are the jewelers and clothing makers who stay for the entire show; next to them is a similar group that disappears after the trade buying days, leaving a gap that must perplex those who attend on the public days; next comes an enormous space devoted to decorative objects, followed by a smaller group of decorative makers selling only to the trade. This group likewise disappears after the trade days. This arrangement has the considerable benefit of keeping each of the two groups, fashion and home, in adjacent halls. When the wholesale firms depart, the public is left with only those who wish to sell directly. Over three days, as many as 35,000 people flood in to see, touch, try on, and purchase crafts.

FEEDBACK

The crafts shows not only brought the work and the audience to one common ground, they gave the goldsmiths a chance to catch up on their friendships, to share ideas, to swap tips on technical matters, to simply enjoy being in the company of a community of craftspeople. These like-minded people are widely dispersed around the country, and the craft shows provide one of the rare occasions for them to get together. Unlike commercial jewelry shows such as the Jewelers of America show held in New York or the Pacific Jewelry Show in California, the Rhinebeck show was organized both as a business venue and a celebration of craft. An opening night preview, when no selling was permitted, was structured so the artists could walk around the show and see everyone else's work. Following the wholesale days, a day off was devoted to a picnic where they could renew these important professional friendships. Having refreshed themselves both physically and mentally, the craftspeople were able to plunge into three hectic retail days. Here, over a long weekend, the jewelers saw their work reach the hands of the ultimate consumer. There's no jury that can compete with the buying public.

With a consuming mentality structured by the mass-market producer, the public was, and still is, in a perpetual state of being educated. "Where do you get these things?" customers will ask a jeweler whose battered fingers betray the signs of hand labor. "You actually make them yourself?" The concept of dealing with a real artist is captivating and certainly an important part of the exchange. But the acid test is always the one that rules in the marketplace: "How does it look on me?" Here is the customer with the jewel in hand, draping a necklace around her neck, trying on an earring. And as the process takes place, the jeweler can see what works and what doesn't, and immediately begin to adjust designs to make them more wearable. For many jewelers, the retail days provide a living workshop, the logical final element in the design process. Trying things on family and friends at home is useful, but it can't compare with a customer saying, "I like this, but the catch is too hard to open."

Goldsmiths who brought only major work quickly learned that it was vital to have some less "important" pieces as well. It is always easier for a woman to buy a pair of earrings than a major necklace or ring. The woman who walked away empty-handed wasn't likely to return. The one who bought a pair of earrings would become the repeat customer, gaining in confidence and ready to make a greater commitment to the jeweler the following year. And she brought her friends with her. During the years that the show was at Rhinebeck, the built-

Left:
The West Springfield Craft Show, 1985. Jeweler Paul Morelli's exhibit. (Photo by Jason Lauré.)

Right:
Ross Coppelman. Pin/ pendant. Boulder opal, fancy colored and white diamonds, pearls, 22k gold. (1989)

Kyle Leister. "Blossom" brooch. Sterling silver, 14k pink, yellow and green golds, pink tourmaline, freshwater pearl. (1986)

in market of New Yorkers with summer homes in the region guaranteed this kind of return customer. Relationships grew between maker and consumer, to be renewed year after year. The craft show was a living laboratory for every element of the jewelry world: designer, consumer, gallery owner, and editor. While most searched for new ideas with their checkbooks, I did the same with pen and notebook in hand. And we always came home filled up with beautiful ideas and a sense of discovery. The jewelers, who retreated to their many corners of the United States between shows, had once again absorbed some wonderful new, or very old, technique.

The balance between wholesale and retail days gives jewelers two equally important and different kinds of business. Wholesale orders translate into months of work leading up to the crucial Christmas selling season. Retail selling days mean cash in hand, to be used to buy materials to fill those wholesale orders and to live in the coming months.

It was not only the loss of the Rhinebeck venue that spelled an end to the charming days of the craft fair for the jewelers and their customers. Pressure to change was coming from another direction entirely: another show manager had appeared on the scene.

BUYERS' MARKET SHOWS

Even the explosive growth of the ACE shows still couldn't contain the number of people who clamored for spaces. The charming little shows across the road now had a new champion, and if ever there was a clear-eyed realist, Wendy Rosen was it. With her Buyers' Market shows (for wholesale buyers only), Wendy Rosen acknowledged that crafts had become a business, and she set about to take in as many people as she could. She opened up first in 1982, in Baltimore, where she staged a hotel show with 82 exhibitors. In 1990, that show took on circus-like proportions, moving into the cavernous Convention Center in Atlantic City with 1200 exhibitors. She moved the show again after that one time in Atlantic City, searching for the right location and the right date. And the craftspeople trooped along.

When ACE moved the Rhinebeck show to West Springfield, Rosen offered the outcasts—as well as a growing legion of craftspeople who wanted to bypass the uncertainties of the jurying process—an alternative. She staged a show in the Civic Center in Springfield, just across the river. Here, another few hundred showed their work in a building that was much more pleasant than the "Big E." The quality was good, the venue easy to reach for those who had already driven to the ACE show, and accessible by special buses for those who hadn't. And Springfield was in fact where people stayed and had dinner anyway.

But within two years, Rosen had outgrown the Civic Center and made a quantum leap to Boston, where she took over the Bayside Center and expanded her show to 800 booths. While crafts were still the focus, the show was beginning to feel more like any commercial gift show. The specialness was a growing victim of each move and each expansion in the number of exhibitors.

Now the tail began to wag the dog. ACE, the leader in the field, responded to Rosen's move out of the Springfield area by expanding *its* show to 800 exhibitors. The decision was based purely on marketing, rather than a reflection of the number of craftspeople looking to become exhibitors. Carol Sedestrom, who started out as a craftsperson herself but who has been directing these ever-growing shows for ACE for more

The Buyers' Market craft show at the Springfield Civic Center, 1985. Jeweler Patricia Daunis talks with author. (Photo by Jason Lauré.)

The Buyers' Market craft show at the Springfield Civic Center, 1985. View of exhibits. (Photo by Jason Lauré.)

than fifteen years, felt obliged to expand the show in order to attract enough buyers. Ironically, this was not a problem when there was only one show, housed in Rhinebeck.

The two events coexist uneasily, although as ACE expands, it embraces work quite different in concept from its original vision. But the two events emanated from quite different motivations. ACE was established as the marketing arm of the American Craft Council to exercise some direction over the Rhinebeck show, which had simply grown helter-skelter. It needed oversight, and as it grew too big for the space allotted to it, it needed a neutral body to make the thumbs-up decisions. Sedestrom, herself a craftsperson, knows firsthand the joys and dilemmas of selling work in an open tent.

Rosen came out of the advertising business and, from the first, saw the crafts field as a promising business opportunity. Ironically, although she appeared to be the upstart when she started her first show in 1982 in a hotel in Baltimore, she has not had to compromise any of her own beliefs. The shows for her were, are, and always will be, business. She analyzes her exhibitors by how many square feet they occupy and how many accounts they serve, and she looks at her buyers as money machines. In the first couple of hours, she sees them hitting a show, walking it quickly, dropping off material for the exhibitor to read, and then returning to write an order before they are shut out by their competitors. The orders are written largely, she says, *before* the buyer leaves her shop. "You drop paper and then you fill in a couple of new pieces. You don't start the order in the booth because you don't have enough time. In our marketplace, everything is switched. In most markets, supply is bigger than demand. In this market, there is more demand than supply."

Walk down the aisle of any large craft show and the results are on display: there is a sameness to the work that defies the logic of showing in a crafts setting. It may indeed be made by hand, but it might just as well have been stamped out by a die strike machine. There is no embellishment, no attempt to build upon the basic technique. The effort is directed at quickly producing a lot of flashy, low-priced work. These quick-buck workers turn out earrings by the hundreds because earrings can be fashioned with a bit of wire pushed through a hole. No jewelry-making skill is needed. You will search long and hard before you find a pair of post and clutch earrings; they don't know how to attach a post.

Their enthusiasm for titanium epitomizes the process and the problem. This space-age metal, dull gray in its natural state, can be electrolytically charged to achieve a range of vivid jewel tones: purple, green, blue, red. It's cheap, it's light in weight, and when used with integrity it results in totally new, exciting, and affordable jewelry. When it was fresh, it was special. And then came the flood. Like gold or silver, the basic building blocks of the jeweler's profession, titanium without artistry is boring. But it's also vivid. The combination proved deadly as booth after booth offered nearly identical work—not a few pieces at a time, but dozens.

It shouldn't be surprising that so many of these manufacturers are in business, but it is stunning to realize that ACE sees its role as finding places for them. Carol Sedestrom, who sees the flood of applications for the crafts shows on a daily basis, views ACE's recent collaboration with the Boston Gift Show, for example, as an appropriate expression of concern. "We are interested," she says of the Boston Gift Show, "be-

Tamiko Kawata Ferguson. Necklace, bracelet, and earrings. Multicolored niobium, sterling silver; electro-oxidation. (1985) (Photo by Mitsuya Okumura.)

cause we feel there are a number of people who exhibit with us who have solved their production problems; they produce a more middle-of-the-line market. There are people in our shows who need to move onto a bigger market. We need to set up the pipeline for the new, young, inexperienced. Some of these people have been waiting two or three years to get into that show. I became totally overwhelmed that there are lots and lots of small makers of objects that are looking for a place to sell their work. Because they are not coming from colleges, they are not coming from the craft tradition, they don't know about American Craft Enterprises.

"I was amazed at the entrepreneurial activity out there in the world . . . and at the absolute lack of places for people like these to show their work. It's a real education for me to realize how many people there are out there, how many of them aren't coming from the track that we know."

But what about the notion of the craft fair as a place to show wonderfully original work? The dilution of the quality of work at shows such as Springfield carries with it a second dilemma for individuals who still want the craft shows to function as they did in the past: they are competing against production work, rather than like-minded craftspeople. And the choice is plain: produce or get out. Stephani Briggs, one of the younger, up-and-coming jewelers says, "The change is a big concern for me. I am not interested in doing the production anymore. I am concerned about ACE, the direction. How much commercialism is included; there are people who are just manufacturers. At Springfield there's so much negative feeling—the location—the buyers don't like going there. The environment in Springfield is embarrassing. It's an agricultural fair." This is a widely held belief. Craftspeople, many of whom are among the most health-oriented people in the country, who seek out organic vegetables and shun meat, who take every opportunity to prevent pollution and care for the environment, are expected to show their work in a building that many call a health hazard. Because ACE has expressed its satisfaction with the facility at West Springfield, the only option for many jewelers is to leave the show, and that they are doing. The numbers aren't large, but some of the most creative people are among them.

The progression of shows from new, to healthy, to overblown, is at the speed of light. Whole business lives are lived out in a decade, leaving in their wake the somewhat shattered participants. For those with the real thing, its value will remain intact; the rest is little more than costume jewelry—entirely disposable.

THE NEW YORK ARMORY SHOW

The four regional shows staged by ACE (Springfield, Baltimore, Minneapolis, and San Francisco) are structured to sell at both the wholesale and retail levels, although the wholesale far outweighs the retail in terms of income. But the retail business is crucial to many jewelers, and not only for the ready cash it provides. This contact with the customer brings the whole relationship between maker and buyer back to where it was at the beginning, under a tree in Vermont. When the Northeast Craft Fair was moved from Rhinebeck to West Springfield, the greatest loss, other than the environment, was the retail customer. The sophisticated metropolitan New York area customers were missing, having turned instead to the myriad craft events offered to them within their own area. This was reinforced by the appearance of a new craft fair at the old Dutchess County Fairgrounds timed to coincide with the ACE show in West Springfield; it is called the Craft Fair at Rhinebeck, capitalizing on the allure of the town.

The retail customers who do attend the Springfield show, and there are thousands of them, are New Englanders and that difference is felt in terms of what they buy and how much they spend. In 1987, ACE announced a new show in New York City. This was not just tacit recognition of that loss. It was specifically meant to make up for it, according to Carol Sedestrom, who at the time called it "a more convenient show location for previous Rhinebeck visitors who did not follow the show to Massachusetts." But that description was totally at odds with the reality of the new show: limited to just 100 exhibitors, it offered New Yorkers the upper level in terms of style and price of crafts today. The show was built around one-of-a-kind or limited edition work, which naturally restricted both its scope and the type of clientele. Also, such a small number of exhibitors in no way could replace the 500 who showed at the last Rhinebeck event.

Instead, the show provides a brief exposure for craftspeople who often don't appear at larger fairs and allows the New York customer a chance to view and purchase some of the best crafts being made today. Housed in the 7th Regiment Armory on Park Avenue, it occupies what is considered a most prestigious show space in the city. The look of the show is itself a departure: uniform, elegant exhibit booths are provided by ACE and arranged in oblique rows, giving the sense of walking through a museum rather than a country fair.

Some of the craftspeople for the first event, in 1987, were invited to participate by ACE; the others won spaces through the jury system. The cost of the event, three times that of a regional craft show, acts as its own, economic, jurying element. By no means does it keep out bad work, especially work that reveals a basic problem in the artist's eternal search for an individual statement. In too many instances, the work is technically fine but without direction. Often, the maker errs on the

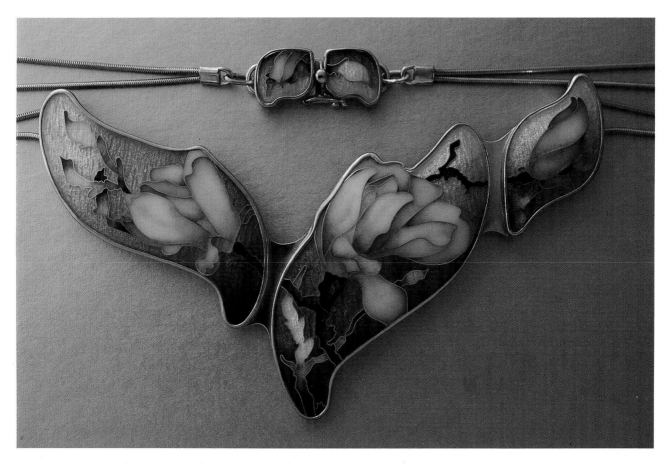

Merry Lee Rae. Cloisonné neckpiece in panels. (1982)

side of excess; in this show, minimalism doesn't seem to be a trend or even an option.

By their very presence, the New Yorkers who attend give this show an air of success and importance. Here, where there's a craft show of considerable quality available on an almost weekly basis, and free to boot, some 9000 people pay seven dollars each to attend. During the five years the show was held (it closed after the 1991 event), it provided a unique showcase for high-end craft work.

UPSCALE MARKETING: THE NEW ART FORMS SHOW

Even more elite than the Armory show is the New Art Forms show held at the Navy Pier in Chicago each September. Established in 1986, the show differs from all the others in that the exhibitors are the galleries and not the makers. While contemporary jewelry is only a small part of the work shown, it is being introduced to a discerning and affluent public. The goldsmiths whose work is shown there like the idea of having an interested and informed salesperson on the front lines. It is a relief for the artists who feel that at some point they must step away from the marketplace. Barbara Heinrich, who is represented at the show by the Susan Cummins Gallery, says, "The show has really set new standards for our field. People come from all over the country to buy there." Although artists sell their work through many galleries, at the Chicago show, an artist may be shown only by one gallery. With just 70 galleries exhibiting, there is an opportunity for showgoers to spend time at each booth. Patricia Faber of the Aaron Faber Gallery says the show attracts "the best educated group of shoppers I've ever met. They're collectors, they understand technique, they know names. It's a very savvy group of people." To ensure the quality of the overall event, the show manager, Lakeside Group Expositions, juries the exhibition.

The jury, and its role in the marketing of American crafts, is an unresolved phenomenon. Like the jury system in general, it is a very imperfect method for making choices in a democratic society.

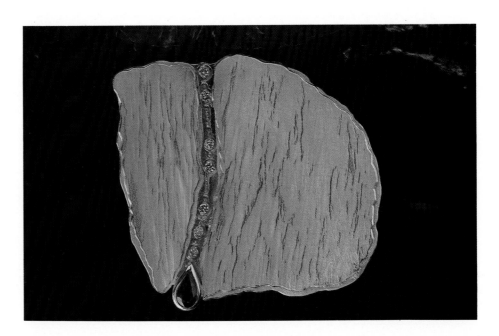

Barbara Heinrich. Brooch. 18k gold, diamonds, sapphire. (1990) (Photo by Tim Callahan.)

The American Craft Enterprises jurying process: Five slides are shown to the jurors simultaneously and are judged according to a weighted rating system. Example shown is jewelry by Vicki Eisenfeld. (Photo by Bob Barrett.)

EYE, THE JURY

Marketing, in its myriad forms, remains an all-consuming issue for craftspeople. The constant growth in size of both the ACE events and the Rosen shows, plus the proliferation of shows, from the sidewalks of New York to the fairgrounds of Rhinebeck, guarantee that a quantity of crafts is available to the public on an almost constant basis. Yet those who look to the ACE shows to uphold a standard of craftsmanship find themselves increasingly surrounded by lesser work. And even given the changing level of products offered, they must still depend on a jury to determine whether they will have a venue in which to offer work each year. Has the jurying system succeeded in this formidable task?

Although I have never juried a show, I have observed a typical jury at work, judging the jewelry entries for an ACE show. I found the process brutal. The jurors, one for each medium in the show—ceramics, fiber, wood, metal, glass, leather, jewelry—are chosen by the craftspeople from the previous show. All the jurors judge all the categories, one category at a time. Each entrant submits five slides of the work to be offered. The successful candidate is obliged to display the same work in the booth that is shown in the slides. So far, so good. But a few problems are obvious immediately. Good slides make for good entries. Sometimes, the work looks better in the slides than in the flesh.

But poor slides, truly miserable slides, make it virtually impossible to judge the quality of the work. At best, two-dimensional slides are only a second-rate substitute for three-dimensional work. The texture, the roundness, the weight, the colors, simply the size, are all just shadows of the reality. The materials used—is something gold or vermeil, glass or ceramic, 14k or 18k—may be surmised or not. So, in actuality, there is a silent category at the shows—photography.

The importance of judgment, especially poor judgment, is immediately apparent. Any number of pieces may be shown in each slide, but if there are too many, the work is too small to be "read" by the jurors. If the jewelry is photographed against a busy background, a background of the same color, or on a model, it can be difficult to see. If all five pieces are virtually identical, the jeweler appears to have little to say. If the five are too diverse, the jeweler appears unfocused. Even the fact that the slides are projected and therefore enlarged is a potential problem. Work that may be two inches across is now five or ten times that size; the proportions are lost along the way. But nearly all of these problems are easily corrected the second time out—or could be if there were any feedback to the candidate, and that really is too much to ask of any organization deluged with applications.

The more significant problem is the jurying process itself. As each candidate's five slides are projected—nice and big, well lit, and easy to see—the judges view them in silence. All the candidates' slides are viewed once, without any ratings being assigned. As soon as the first viewing is completed, the process is repeated, and the jurors see them all again. This time, each candidate is rated via a numbering system. In order to force the jurors to make a love–hate decision, there is no middle to the system, no safe harbor where everything would be judged "so-so." The system offers scores of "1," "2," "5," or "6." There is no "0"—that is considered "psychologically damaging." Each set of slides

Marne Ryan. Earrings. Oxidized sterling silver, 18k gold, rutilated quartz. (1990) (Photo by Tony Ward.)

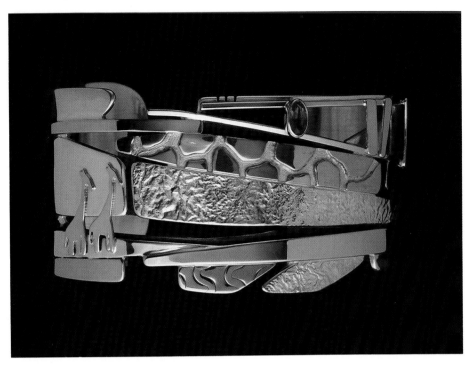

Kyle Leister. "Giraffe" cuff. Sterling silver, copper, nickel, 14k pink and yellow golds, citrine. (1989)

is on the screen for five seconds during each of the two viewings. During the second viewing, the jurors look, they decide, pencils circle numbers, the decision is made.

Unless one of the jurors asks a question, the five-slide sets click by relentlessly. When a question is asked, the slides linger on the screen. Usually, the question pertains to the materials being used. These are answered by the monitor reading from the candidate's entry card. But the special knowledge of the medium, the province of the juror whose medium is being judged, is lost to the panel. There is no discussion about originality, about other slides that echo the work in question, no discussion about the virtues of a given set of slides. Each juror's vote carries equal weight; the jeweler on the panel is deemed as worthy of judging woodwork as the leather artist is of judging goldsmithing and no more worthy to judge jewelry.

The history of the medium in question—who of these candidates is the originator and who the imitator—is not discussed. The fact that candidates are permitted to enter more than one set of slides makes it difficult to know if similar work is a copy or just the same person again. In the desire for both impartiality and egalitarianism, the jurying system has lost the basic element of connoisseurship. And this, in part, explains the unevenness of the shows.

In the jewelry category, there is an additional problem: work made of paper, clay, ceramics, glass, and plastic is mixed in with work of gold and sterling. Fashion jewelry or fine jewelry, it's all shown indiscriminately. The eye is constantly forced to readjust to different types of work, not just in style but even in intent.

While all this is going on, the candidates wait. In December, ACE informs all the successful candidates that they have space in the show

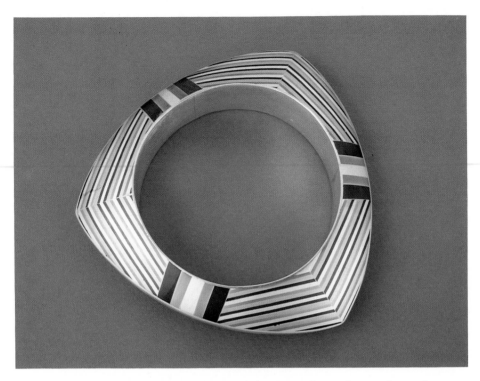

Terry Foltz-Fox. Hollow form bracelet. Marriage of metals: sterling silver, copper, nickel, chemically oxidized brass. (1987)

or shows to which they have applied. But the Baltimore show is at the beginning of February. The candidates obviously must have enough work ready long before the notice comes in. Some hedge their bets by applying to other shows as backups, especially the Rosen shows, for which the process is more one of renewing a contract than a crapshoot.

In an effort to alleviate the anguish of the veteran exhibitors, ACE instituted an option system. Anyone who had been approved by juries for five years was guaranteed booth space for a number of years, the actual number varying between those who show during the wholesale-only days and those who do both wholesale and retail. But it seems that every solution comes with built-in problems. Here, the problems are twofold. First, the option was taken up by the exhibitors in huge numbers—in such numbers, in fact, that they virtually wiped out the spaces for newcomers. Then, having achieved the space, some craftspeople found that they were unable to take on any new accounts because their production for the year was already committed. In some cases, exhibitors who no longer needed their booths were obliged to occupy them while others who could have used them were locked out.

Second, as the option years rolled by, the exhibitors got out of the habit of competing. After as many as five years without having to be juried, they found themselves scrambling for new slides, making work that would perhaps photograph well or catch the eye of the jury, and competing in a virtually new arena. With the flood of applications—typically 2000 for the Baltimore show, for example—someone's business could be put into jeopardy during a ten-second glance at months of effort.

Given this kind of uncertainty and anxiety, it's not surprising that craftspeople are constantly looking for new ways to market their work and to exert some control over the process. A few jewelers have opened their own shops, sidestepping the show process entirely. Others have shops and still enter shows, keeping one foot in each camp. The need for marketing venues continues. If crafts were ever to take their place among mainstream products, the situation would be alleviated, but that is not going to happen. For a brief moment, in the 1980s, it looked as if it might. Jewelers were making fair inroads into the commercial jewelry shows and achieving some success in reaching out to the traditional retailer. But the moment has passed. Most craft jewelers have retreated, back to the craft shows, to galleries, to mail order. Contemporary American jewelry continues in all its strength and diversity, but it marches to its own beat.

A CHANGE IN ATTITUDE

Along with the increase in the sheer number of exhibitors, the nature of the work seen at craft shows has changed. This is not surprising, in and of itself. But with the emphasis on ever-bigger events, and with costs increasing, albeit more modestly at these shows than at those held in union-run facilities, many jewelers have found themselves pressured to make production lines. Many have shifted away from one-of-a-kind work or limited editions to production work.

The change is not merely in the quantity of merchandise but in the very nature of the design ethic in back of it. This stems from the explosion of craftspeople onto the marketplace. The progress of organic growth has been replaced by a need for instant gratification. Rather than nurturing their artistry and improving techniques as they work, today's craftspeople come out of jewelry classes with technique in hand and a line to sell a week later. Eschewing the labor-intensive, elegant work that employs marriage of metals, mokumé gane, reticulation, or granulation, they embrace roller printing and cookie-cutter methods of achieving quick, bold results. This is the generation *after* Woodstock; for them the back-to-the-land movement might have happened in the *1860s*.

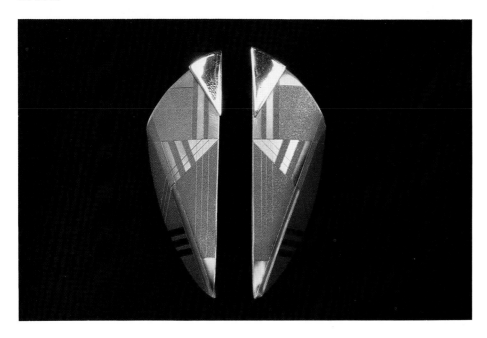

Susan Sanders. Earrings. 14k gold, geometric panels of textured titanium. (Early 1980s)

Chapter 2

Craft Galleries

Like pioneers in other fields, contemporary jewelers have had to create not only the physical reality of their jewelry but often new ways to sell their work. Their work, viewed as alien by the retail jewelry shops that should have embraced it as something exciting and traffic-stopping, instead was shunned as different, difficult, "a problem." In response, the jewelers turned to the phenomenon of the craft fairs and to the small number of craft galleries.

Through the years, the three partners—jewelers, galleries, and craft fairs—changed. They grew, they shifted focus, they redefined their roles in the craft world. Against this constantly changing marketplace, the goldsmiths have had to balance their dual roles, spiritually welded to the craft world yet undeniably tied to the intrinsic value of their basic materials.

From the beginning, jewelry has been viewed apart from the other crafts. Galleries and shops that handled the decorative products for the home, such as clay, glass, fiber, and wood, were often not equipped to deal with the different demands posed by jewelry, which is smaller, highly reflective, and more valuable per square inch. Display requirements were different, security was invariably more of a problem, and valuing the work for its artistic merit as separate from its inherent material worth further set it apart.

Few galleries were able to be equally successful with all the crafts; often, jewelry became the orphan of such shops. At the same time, those galleries that embraced jewelry exclusively, because they understood it and believed in it as an exciting and viable alternative to conventional jewelry, found it extremely difficult to finance their beliefs.

Only a handful of visionaries in the United States have successfully created galleries that either represent all the crafts well or that can be supported by jewelry alone. These gallery owners/directors are as creative and devoted to their vision as are the craftspeople whose work

Facing page:
Merry Lee Rae. Brooch.
Cloisonné enamel on
sterling silver. (1989)
(Photo courtesy of Aaron
Faber Gallery.)

they show. They have to be in order to persevere. The personalities of these individuals are stamped upon their galleries as clearly as the signatures of the work they sell. Each brings something different to the mix of business acumen and artistic endeavor, and in the process moves the craft in new directions. At the galleries, work may be viewed everyday; craft fairs are here today and gone in two days.

The relationships between the galleries and the artists they represent are complicated, sometimes difficult, sometimes joyous, never static. There is the always delicate moment when a gallery owner must tell an artist the new work isn't up to the old or that the work has become too predictable. There is the equally delicate moment when an artist must tell a gallery that someone else is better able to represent the work and that the relationship is over. Marriage and divorce, separation and reconciliation, and property settlements play a similar role in the relationship between artist and gallery as they do between husband and wife. Striking a balance, and maintaining it, is a tightrope act that must be performed.

From the beginning, the galleries introduced the public to the written word, offering price lists of the works on display, along with descriptions of the materials and techniques used. Postcards sent to a carefully cultivated mailing list of clients and editors served as invitations and enticements, with their sumptuous, full-color photographs of new work. Biographies of the artists were made available, establishing the important connection between the creator and the creation.

Why were the galleries so willing to disclose this information when traditional retail stores went out of their way to keep the jewelers invisible and unavailable? Traditional jewelry designers—those who work for Bulgari and Cartier, for example—do not make the pieces they design: these pieces, usually cast, are made by teams of workers; each specializing in a different skill. Since the jewelry made for these stores is in the style of the store, the designers become interchangeable.

Contemporary jewelers, on the other hand, offer work made by their own hand and in their own style. While galleries are the expression of the tastes of their owners, within that framework the customer finds work expressing many different styles and design ideas. The actual work is the reflection of the design sensibility of the creators. One cannot be substituted for another, as if they were generic house designers. These craftspeople are complete workshops unto themselves. From design sketch to fabrication, stone setting, and polishing, they *are* the workshop. And while many of the jewelers do employ helpers for part of their production, all of them spend time making the jewelry that bears their names. The finished design is a product of the original idea transmuted by the physical process of fabrication. There is a serendipitous discovery of design during the making of the piece.

The gallery owner or director (often the same person) receives comments by customers and potential customers on a daily basis. The best design proving ground is often the public. Jewelry gets tried on—or doesn't. Customers express a desire for a similar piece but with a different gemstone; or a bigger one, or smaller one. Since the contemporary goldsmith makes everything by hand, or with a minimum of machine assistance, the requests may inspire rather than impede the design process. The gallery also provides the kind of customer contact for the goldsmith that is not available to those who sell entirely at wholesale shows and trade fairs. The gallery provides the permanence that jewelry buyers prefer. The retail days at craft fairs provide excite-

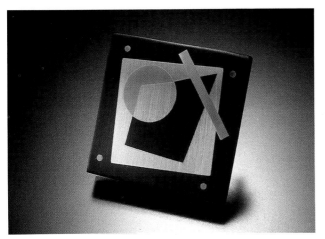

Tony Papp. Brooch. Marriage of metals: sterling silver, nickel silver, brass with patina. (1988)

Marne Ryan. Collar. Oxidized sterling silver, 18k gold, bezel-set fancy-colored diamonds. (1989-1990) (Photo by Tony Ward.)

ment and customer contact, but they cannot offer the ambience, the quiet, and the security of a gallery. The "important" sale—whatever that means to each customer—is made in the store.

A few galleries are an expression of the artist's desire to market his own work directly to the consumer. Given the uncertainties of exhibiting at juried craft shows, some jewelers prefer to take their chances in a local market. The overhead is higher, certainly, but so are the profits, since the same work they were selling at wholesale now carries a retail price tag. Contemporary jewelry is virtually always sold at the price first established for it by the shop owner. This price is a realistic reflection of the price paid for it, the overhead, the profit margin, advertising, and the like. Also built into the price is the cost of holding that jewelry until it is sold. That cost includes insurance, alarm systems, security guards, showcase space; the longer the piece is held, the greater these costs become. Often, these costs are shared by the maker of the piece since a great deal of work is in the store on consignment, a form of loan from the maker to the seller. The gallery owner has the right to sell the piece but does not own it. The maker of the piece may take it away for a show in another gallery or for a customer in another city. When work is on consignment, the jeweler bears the continued cost of financing the metals and gemstones that were used to make it, as well as his own labor and overhead. It is to the benefit of both maker and gallery to see that the work sells sooner rather than later, and it is to that end that the gallery's promotional activities, the staging of one-person or theme shows, are directed.

AARON FABER GALLERY
New York City

It began on the mezzanine of a jewelry exchange on the corner of Fifth Avenue and 47th Street, in the heart of the jewelry district in New York. Here, in this most commercial jewelry center, Edward Faber, his wife Patricia Kiley Faber, and a soon to be "divorced" partner, Efrem Aaron, first showed contemporary goldsmithing in 1974. They could not have chosen a less likely environment. On the main selling floor below, dealers with the blood of buccaneers coursing through their veins bargained with customers, both sides consumed by the process of establishing a sales price based strictly on weight and measure. Meanwhile, up on a balcony the size of a handkerchief, perhaps ten feet by ten feet, the Fabers showed handmade, contemporary goldsmithing heavy with artistic intent. But there was a common cord tying them together—the materials. At both venues, the jewelry was made of precious metals. (In those days, few contemporary goldsmiths used gemstones in their work.)

The space was tiny, but the shock waves that rippled out were considerable. The Fabers shrewdly and assiduously courted not only collectors but also the press, and this smallest of galleries had an impact far beyond its size. In reality, its size was an issue only in comparison to the vast acreage of art galleries. It was appropriate in that venue where the "booths" that comprised the jewelry exchanges, then and now, are barely large enough for two people to work side by side. But the jewelry and the people populating those other spaces were all of a kind; the Faber Gallery ventured into brave new territory. Within three years, the Fabers' operation moved to its current address, a comfortable store on 53rd Street, just off Fifth Avenue and across the street from the Museum of Modern Art. In 1986, the American Craft Museum moved into its new building just down the street.

While New York may be the fashion capital of the United States, its role in the contemporary jewelry movement has been minor, thanks in no small part to the cost of real estate. The movement had to overcome the entrenched 47th Street jewelry mentality that had seeped into the consumer's mind: weights, measures, and considerable glitz are the hallmarks of commercial jewelry. At a handful of galleries across the country, artistry and subtlety, technique and design were being offered, and these qualities are not easily quantifiable.

The regular shows given by such galleries for their goldsmiths emphasize the artist rather than the materials or even the shop. In the world of commercial jewelry, this is unheard of. At traditional jewelry retailers, such as Cartier and Van Cleef & Arpels, the jewelry is identified as a product of the store selling it; the style that of the purveyor rather than the maker. At the galleries, the makers' names are exalted; moreover, the customer can actually meet the maker, discuss the jewelry, and in general become a patron of the arts rather than just a shopper. It proved to be a heady experience for a small group of women who found their personalities and styles expressed in this jewelry.

While similar scenes were being played out in key galleries around the country, the Faber Gallery, and briefly Byzantium, had the special advantage of being in the media center of the United States. It was easy for the editors from *Vogue* or *Harper's Bazaar* or *Women's Wear Daily* to visit these galleries. These editors and others frequently made use of the jewelry in their pages. This exposure expanded the audience from the handful of people who actually saw the shows to the hundreds of thousands across the country who read these publications.

At the same time, I had started to show this jewelry in the heretofore ultra-conservative pages of *Jewelers' Circular-Keystone*, the most closely read of the jewelry trade publications. Whatever the story I was illustrating, I included handcrafted pieces alongside the most traditional offerings from 47th Street manufacturers. In most instances, this was the retailers' first exposure to this jewelry, though most of it was being made in their own hometowns, in the out of the way, small

Earl Pardon. Neckpiece. Sterling silver, 14k gold, enamel, shell, blue topaz, ruby, garnet, amethyst, hematite; constructed. (1988) (Photo courtesy of Aaron Faber Gallery.)

towns of America. But these jewelers would never have made it through the front doors of those stores; they needed the "Good House-keeping" seal of approval that *Jewelers' Circular-Keystone* gave them.

SCULPTURE TO WEAR AND ARTWEAR
New York City

There was no pattern for any of these craft jewelry shops to follow when they plunged in. Some succeeded on sheer grit, others with the help of publicity, still others through high visibility. In the latter category was Sculpture to Wear, a tiny but high-profile gallery housed in The Plaza-in New York. Virtually all of the artist–jewelers shown there were well known, among them Picasso (Pablo, not Paloma), Braque, and Calder. But there was one very unknown: Robert Lee Morris. By the time Sculpture to Wear closed in 1977, five years after Morris's work was first shown there, it had launched his career and introduced him to a small but influential group of customers. Perhaps more important, it had brought him to the attention of the fashion press.

Morris, self-described as a pure product of the 1960s, has carved out a specific slice of the contemporary jewelry market for himself. Through his Artwear shops in New York, which feature his own jewelry as well as that of dozens of other artists, he is part of the trend-setting

Robert Lee Morris. Belt. Brass and copper helix. (1980)

Robert Lee Morris. Bracelet. Gold-plated brass. (1981)

fashion scene. His jewelry designs for major fashion designers have given his work an even wider audience. And finally, through his close connection with the major fashion magazines, his work and his name have become known to a national audience. But when it all started, less than twenty years ago, there was no way to predict that any of this would happen. Then, Robert Lee Morris was just another rebellious young man wanting above all not to live the way his parents lived. Unlike most other rebellious young men of the Woodstock generation, he has succeeded on a major scale.

Yet in his beginnings, Morris represents the craft movement at its purest. When he came out of Beloit College in Wisconsin in the late 1960s, he was "full of ideas, very revolutionary. When I hit the real world after college, I was determined to try and live—to be true to myself. There was a generation gap between our parents who were for the war and the children who were against it." For Morris, that gap may have been more palpable than for most of his generation—for he was raised as an Air Force brat, spending his preteen years in Japan and his high school years in Brazil. Somehow he came out of that unusual experience as a typical, all-American product of his time, and he shared the aspirations of the back-to-the-land movement. It was, he recalls, "the beginnings of craft communes. The spirit of William Morris was alive again. It was the notion of living by my hands."

He began, with a small group of like-minded friends, on an abandoned farm in Wisconsin. Each person made crafts of some kind; Morris taught himself to make jewelry with some tools he found on the property. The whole group then gathered up what they had made and set up their own little craft show. When the farmhouse burned down, Morris and a friend moved to Vermont and opened a shop. They did what they knew how to do, and what they *had* to do, to make money. "I taught my pal everything I knew about jewelry making." It couldn't have been much. "This was before I knew how to solder." The friend made his share of the money by caning chairs; Morris painted signs for shops in town. And he read jewelry books, especially "the how to make jewelry book by Thomas Gentille." The rest, the history and the success, all grew from those small beginnings. What is unique about Morris is not that he has remained the same person he was then, but that he has managed to create a business employing sixty people. And although he now works all the time to turn out the various collections he is committed to do, he still approaches each design, each object, one at a time. It is a testament to the spirit of the 1960s that he, and a few others like him, have managed to sustain that sense of direction. That he does it in the middle of one of the most frenetic parts of New York rather than in the woods of Maine or Vermont is a function of his personality.

When I first profiled him in 1975, Morris demonstrated how he raised a silver bracelet from a piece of metal. That cuff is still in his line today, but with a difference: it has also become a signature piece made by Morris for fashion designer Donna Karan. Morris's association with various fashion designers, most notably with Karan, has given him an exceptionally high visibility within the circle of women who follow fashion devotedly. Three hundred stores sell his designs, most of them now cast and made in metals ranging from 18k gold to gold-plated brass.

He sees his jewelry as communicating "a very intense, focused worldview—making powerful allusions to ancient history, myth and legend, drawing on shapes and symbols that evoke strong, emotional responses. Most of all, I am interested in the way my art connects to humanity, how it makes people feel. I want people to fall in love with my pieces and, in falling in love, to discover something new about themselves."

Just as contemporary goldsmithing remains a thing apart from the commercial jewelry world, Morris and his group represent yet another stream separate from the rest of what is being made today. It is another alternative, in this instance, an alternative to contemporary goldsmithing as well as to traditional fine jewelry. It is not costume jewelry, though it relates strongly to fashion. It may in time prove to be period jewelry, strongly identified with this era.

The support Morris provides for himself and his artists through his galleries enables this work to survive. When artists are driven to open

Robert Lee Morris. Belt.
Gold-plated brass. (1980)

their own shops in order to have a place to show their work, they acknowledge that their work is largely separate from most jewelry sold today. This need for creative marketing places the contemporary goldsmith in a unique category of American jewelry.

The artist in control of his destiny remains the ultimate issue for all goldsmiths at work today. So much of what they do, and what they are about, is out of their control. It is perhaps inevitable that they would look to their own galleries as a way of being masters of their own marketing. But as will be discussed in the examples of Doug Steakley and Tony Papp, galleries by their very nature burden the owner with a whole other range of problems. For some goldsmiths, such as Susan Reinstein, these problems can be kept in check. Others continue to grapple with them, searching for a balance that seems ever so slightly beyond their grasp.

CONCEPTS
Carmel, California

While the Faber Gallery grew out of a desire to show the work of contemporary goldsmiths, the equally renowned and venerable Concepts Gallery in California was the expression of one jeweler's need for a viable venue in which to show and sell his own work. When Doug Steakley and his wife Jackie started Concepts in 1976, it was out of necessity rather than preference. Steakley was a goldsmith turning out both jewelry and holloware, but when it came to exposing his work to the public, he found "There was no other place to show."

Originally Steakley thought he would do his metalsmithing in a studio space in the Carmel Valley and establish Jackie in the shop to sell it. But almost from the beginning, he was showing both Scandinavian work and the work of jewelers who were friends from his college days. Once the gallery was established, it all changed very quickly. "We started showing more and more the work of other people." By 1986 Steakley had stopped making his own jewelry entirely, a direct result of the need to devote all his time to running the gallery. In that same year, he opened a second store in Palo Alto, down the coast from Carmel, and by his own reckoning "became more a gallery person." With fifteen employees, Steakley had no choice but to be a manager, shunting between the two stores.

The question of viability for a contemporary jewelry gallery is one that remains unanswered even after fifteen years. Gallery owners continue to struggle to support these businesses. Steakley's choice of Carmel, a town that even by California standards exists outside of the rest of American life, may have put an added burden on him—but perhaps not. It was for him the easiest, the clearest choice to make. It provided the opportunity to enjoy the ideal lifestyle. "I found Carmel when I was young and a hippie and lived in the Haight. It was about 1968, after college. I came to Big Sur, to folk festivals. When I went to graduate school, I knew I was going to move to Carmel. I always knew where I wanted to be."

Carmel is in essence a shopping mall in the form of a town, bordered by the Pacific Ocean on one side and demarcated by abruptly rising hills. Here, Steakley has persevered in offering only fine, contemporary goldsmithing in a kind of cultural desert.

He has paid heavily for that decision. As with most gallery owners, Steakley finds "It's really a difficult business to support." That was true even when the only other competition was traditional jewelry stores. In the years since he opened, other stores carrying contemporary jewelry have opened in this tiny shoebox of a town. And although the principal activity in Carmel revolves around shopping, it tends to be more trendy or name-brand oriented. In Steakley's shop, all there is to see and buy is contemporary goldsmithing, along with a few holloware pieces. After all these years, this work still has not earned a place in the consumer's mind as a logical alternative to ordinary jewelry.

After the years of expansion and growth, Steakley has returned to his roots. He sold the store in Palo Alto in 1990 and is back to one shop, two employees, and the role he prefers, that of goldsmith. He has not, however, abandoned his driving need to upgrade the world of the contemporary goldsmith. He served as president of the Society of North American Goldsmiths (SNAG), a time-consuming position, and staged the largest SNAG conference ever, in San Francisco in 1990. In many ways, he expresses the best of the contemporary American craft jeweler: concern for his product, concern for his colleagues, concern for his medium.

OTHER NOTABLE GALLERIES

There remain only a handful of successful jewelry galleries in the United States, and like Concepts, they are the personal expression of owners who have a passion for the work and a willingness to back it. In some cases, they subsidize the work—either directly, with money from other sources, or indirectly, by selling other kinds of work. Faber, for example, has become one of the foremost purveyors of vintage wrist watches and also sells diamonds and colored gemstones. The wonderful Works Gallery in Philadelphia, owned by Ruth and Rick Snyderman, is a full-scale craft store, carrying the best of ceramics and glass as well as jewelry. This delightful gallery, located in a small row house, gives customers the feeling of walking into a home. Pieces are displayed decoratively, and there is a sense of discovery as one climbs the steep and narrow steps from floor to floor. Rents in Philadelphia being substantially below those of New York, the Works has the luxury of being able to spread out, albeit vertically.

Quadrum Gallery, located in The Mall at Chestnut Hill, a suburb of Boston, is the brainchild of Cynthia Kagan. There, a veritable *Who's Who* of contemporary jewelry is on display. The secret to this gallery's success lies not only in the educated eye of the owner but in the well-informed salespeople. Brochures are readily available on each of the artists being shown, and there is an enthusiasm, a genuine sense of helpfulness on the part of the staff, that could be used as a template for other galleries.

There are relatively few jewelers whose work is regularly seen in New York, simply because of the high costs involved in maintaining a showcase for it. A gallery must have a fair representation of any given individual's work, and this limits the number of people whose jewelry may be on display. Unlike a museum in which 90 percent of the work is hidden away, a gallery must display at least several pieces by each jeweler all the time, especially since nearly all of the work being shown is on consignment.

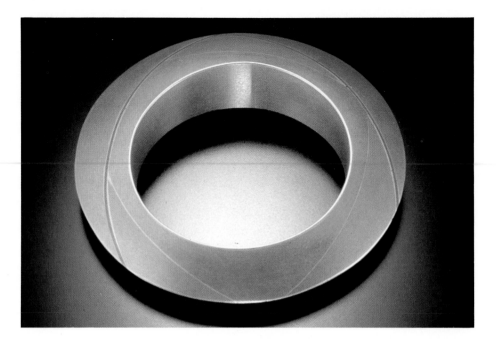

*Tony Papp. Bracelet.
Marriage of metals:
bronze, sterling silver,
nickel silver, mild steel.
(1988)*

The scarcity of venues in New York led Tony Papp, a highly skilled and talented designer, to open his own gallery in the upscale shopping area of Trump Tower. But the extraordinarily high cost of keeping it going, combined with a low volume of traffic, made this a short-term venture. Papp's gallery opened with much fanfare and the appearance of both Donald Trump and Papp's well-known father, producer Joseph Papp, in 1986. Two years later, it was closed. He would have kept it open, he says, "even if it was just breaking even—for selfish reasons. I wanted a place for my work to be shown." Papp didn't limit his gallery to just his own work, however. He carried a considerable range of work from a number of known and up-and-coming jewelers, exhibiting their work prominently along with his own. In addition, he says, "I wanted to be responsible for my own displays and for the care of the work." That's a constant worry for goldsmiths. As the work is handled, tried on, and put away, it's subject to far more wear and tear than it would ever receive in the hands of the ultimate customer. Most jewelry galleries' insurance companies require that all, or nearly all, of the jewelry be put in the safe each night. In the process, it is handled at least twice each day. Customers, or even salespeople, who aren't familiar with a clasp may damage it. Then, the piece is returned to the goldsmith for repair at his or her own expense. For most jewelers, a certain amount of consignment is unavoidable. Very important pieces, the kind that draw attention and are promotable, are too expensive to be bought on speculation. However, the goldsmith is obliged to make them on speculation, with the hope and expectation that they will generate publicity and eventually be sold.

While it was open, the Tony Papp Gallery gave the impression of the little engine that could. It stood up against the most elite of the traditional, high-jewelry firms yet wasn't in any way in competition with them. The customer heading for Buccellati or Harry Winston's little annex, or Asprey's of London, all of them located within the same area, was unlikely to be in the market for Papp's subtle marriage of metals designs or for the work of the myriad other artists he carried. It was a ray of sunshine in the midst of all that glitz—but the economic realities of gallery owning could not be ignored.

The Susan Cummins Gallery in the charming town of Mill Valley, a half-hour's drive from San Francisco, offers one of the largest selections of contemporary jewelry along with contemporary art and ceramics. The consistent eye, vital to the success of any gallery, is the shared vision of owners Beth Changstrom and Susan Cummins.

The location of a gallery has less to do with its success than do the energy and skills of the people who own and manage it. Both Ornament and Santa Fe East in Santa Fe, New Mexico, thrive in a town that appears to be consumed by Native American jewelry. Joanne Rapp's The Hand and The Spirit in Scottsdale, Arizona, competes successfully in a town that also offers myriad silver and turquoise jewelry.

Helen Drutt, who was established in Philadelphia for some fifteen years before opening an upstairs gallery in New York, has persevered in offering her own vision of contemporary jewelry along with contemporary art.

All of the jewelry/craft galleries mentioned, as well as others in various parts of the United States, have established personal contact with many of their customers. They consider the job of educating the public to be part of their ongoing responsibility and to this end regularly stage one-person shows to present an artist's current work. Often, they also do retrospectives, much in the manner of museums. In each case, the work is described in brochures and folders. All of these activities serve to create a bond between the maker and the customer, especially for those clients who become serious collectors. They also illustrate how very different a jewelry gallery is from a jewelry store.

The importance of the individual who is in direct and personal contact with the customer is crucial; often, it is the gallery salesperson who nurtures these relationships, especially in the case of collectors for whom buying contemporary jewelry is far more than a fashion statement. These collectors follow the careers of the jewelers as faithfully as any art patron and direct their collecting according to a particular game plan. Unlike art collectors, however, they offer highly personal and visible expression of their patronage by wearing the jewelry they buy.

Many of the collectors have a shopping list of jewelers whose work they want to own. One young lawyer buys one piece from each artist as she can afford it; another collector buys almost across the board, having work from the broadest spectrum of jewelers, often upgrading to better work as she can afford it or as the jeweler matures. Collectors attend the best of the craft fairs, searching out jewelers whose work may not be represented in their hometown. Freddi Miceli, well known to many of the jewelers whose work she collects, keeps a scrapbook of photographs to document the work she has bought. Using the craft gallery as the connection, she works closely with goldsmiths, commissions pieces, and has collected enough pieces to stock a fair-sized gallery. It began, she recalls, about 1970 when she first saw the work of Glenda Arentzen. "I had never seen gold sculpted like that, textured like that. I feel that people who are well dressed, but without jewelry, are like a home without a plant or a child in it." For Miceli, the pleasure of owning the jewelry is just part of the process. "One of the most joyous things about collecting contemporary art is getting to meet the person who made it. I have such reverence for what that person has created." Miceli is now in partnership with Svetlana Dymski in the New York gallery called Artium.

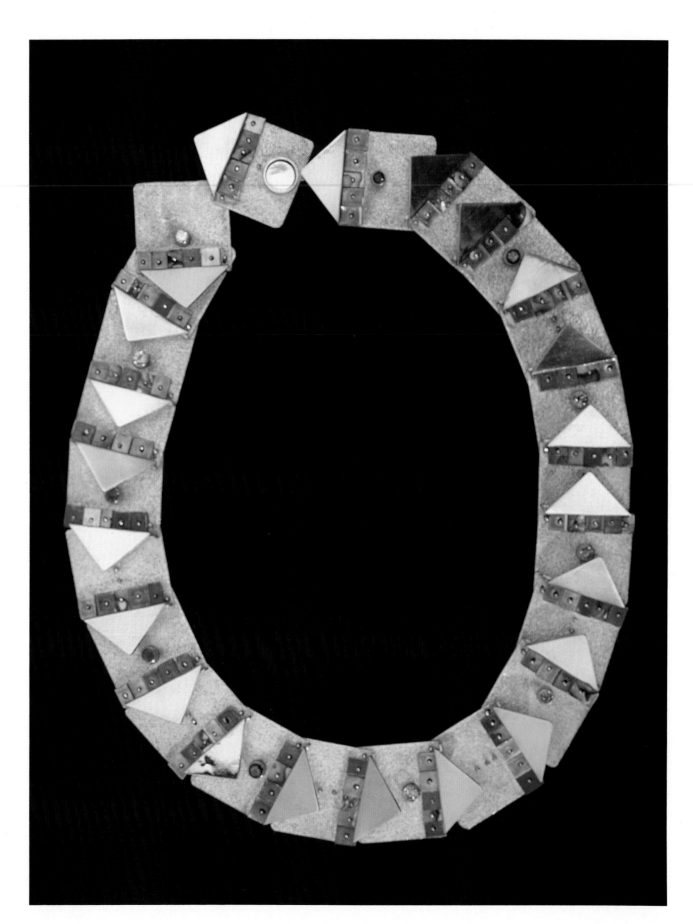

Chapter 3

Teachers

While the education of the public is in the hands of the galleries, the education of the goldsmiths is the domain of the metalsmith teachers. Although a number of the goldsmiths best known in the field carved out a road to success through experimentation, trial and error, and the occasional workshop, an equal number came up through a more formal educational system. Partly because the field is still quite young, a rather small number of teachers has played a significant role in setting standards, guiding artistic inspiration, and giving the students the necessary technical base to carry out their ideas and find their own voices.

The ideal teacher acts as a guide and mentor, not an example to clone. The role is demanding and difficult for it requires nurturing of the student and a surrender of the teacher's ego; yet at the same time, enough of the teacher's ego must remain to show how the artistic voice can be expressed through the medium of metal. Few teachers manage that balance. Comments from former students are rarely lukewarm. Most look back to their college years either with intense admiration for their teachers or bitter anger toward an authority figure who wasn't able to overcome his own artistic frustrations.

Sometimes the student is placed in an adversarial position by a teacher who feels threatened by the emerging talent. Occasionally a renowned visiting professor, here for a term and then gone, takes advantage of the students as a ready source of labor to work out his own ideas under the guise of education. There are egos on both sides—developed and developing. The process, as experienced by many of the goldsmiths profiled here, appears as diverse as the number of teachers and students caught up in it. It is not unusual for students to work initially in the style of their teacher; learning does come from imitating one who has mastered a skill, and the metal techniques can be learned through various artistic interpretations. The problem lies in the inability of the student to go beyond the teacher's voice or in the inability of

Facing page:
Earl Pardon. Neckpiece.
Sterling silver, 14k gold,
enamels, garnet,
amethyst. (1988)

Earl Pardon. Bracelet. Sterling silver, 14k gold, shell, ruby, garnet, blue topaz, spinel. (1988) (Photo courtesy of Aaron Faber Gallery.)

the teacher to demonstrate a general rather than a literal way to apply the method.

There is a difference between teaching a specific technique, teaching the vocabulary of jewelry-making skills, and teaching a way of thinking about jewelry. Workshops offer those already trained as metalsmiths a chance to pick up a new technique taught by someone who has spent years perfecting it. Undergraduate and graduate degrees in metals have broader aims.

EARL PARDON
Saratoga Springs, New York

One of the most intriguing of the goldsmith/teachers is Earl Pardon, recently retired after a thirty-eight-year career at Skidmore College in upstate New York. In the sense of age and experience, he is the grandfather of craft jewelry teachers: one of his students, Glenda Arentzen, is herself considered a venerable figure among metalsmiths. Yet Pardon continues to produce and experiment in a joyous way that gives no hint whatsoever at his age or position in the craft world.

A strong, easily identifiable element of Pardon's work—actually several of them—leaps out at the viewer. Through the years, he has been using small elements combined in visible ways, contrasting colors, and a multiplicity of materials. But another idea marks his work as singular: each element in a necklace, each section of a bracelet, each brooch is, in fact, a framed painting in metal. His origins as a painter have often been recalled when discussing his use of color and the way he seems to paint his surfaces with various, brightly colored materials. But what sets him apart as a unique artist/jeweler/craftsman is that every single element in any one of his pieces can stand alone, can be pulled out of the piece with no loss of strength.

Finally the debate about whether jewelry making is a craft or an art can be laid to rest. It's all of those things at once, and Pardon sums them up. Like only a few of the best known and most influential teachers, Pardon has continued to develop his own metalsmithing through the years, producing an ever-growing body of wearable jewelry. He is alone in this regard; he defies being discussed in the chapter on teachers because his own production has been considerable. Yet he has been the consistent thread in education since 1951, when he took up his teaching position at Skidmore.

Pardon's techniques are the antithesis of what most goldsmiths/metalsmiths seek: they are, or at least appear to be, all on the surface. You see the rivets that hold things together; you observe how the edges are turned up to frame the elements. It seems as if anyone could do them. But in an era of knockoffs and ripoffs, Pardon's work remains unduplicated except sometimes by his son, Todd. But therein lies the answer: with work that seems so easy to copy, the imitator would in a sense be apprenticing himself to Pardon. There is no possibility of developing a personality, a style of one's own. And, of course, the originality and energy wouldn't be there. Pardon, of course, doesn't copy himself. He changes constantly, within a piece, from one frame to the next. He has said that he rarely draws anymore; his own work inspires him to try the next piece, and the next.

Although there was more recent work available and photographed than what is shown here, this is the work I like the best. It seems to be

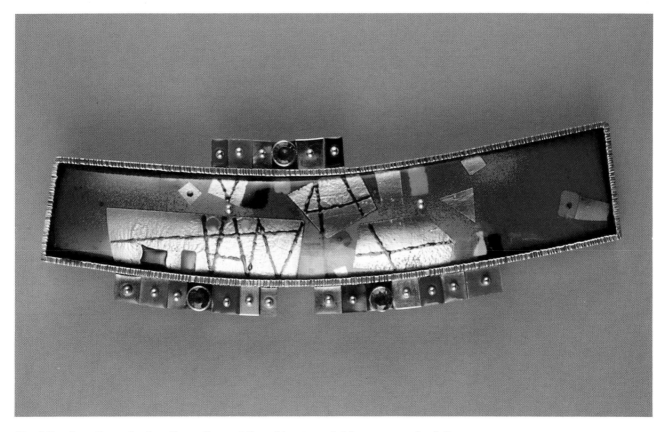

Earl Pardon. Brooch. Sterling silver, 14k gold, enamel, blue topaz, rhodolite, amethyst. (1990)

the absolute perfection of the Pardon style of art and technique. This is the marriage of style and technique. This is studio goldsmithing.

Although Pardon's earlier work, from the 1950s, has the distinctive, quirky look of jewelry from that period, it differs from nearly all the early metalsmithing in that it is finely constructed. This artistic man has always paid the utmost attention to the precision of his constructions. Bezels are perfect, balance is never overlooked. His work has always been playful, but there is nothing childish about it, nothing awkward, nothing incomplete. In a series of segment bracelets from around 1980, Pardon was inlaying tiny circles of metal and coral background materials, always in a painterly way, always carefree in appearance, overcoming the very real and rigid demands of the materials.

He joined the faculty of Skidmore College in Saratoga Springs, New York, in 1951 as a teacher and stayed, with minor absences, through 1989. He was chairman of the art department from 1968 to 1977 and then continued as professor of art until his retirement in 1989. Skidmore's strong art program was well established by the time he arrived there. The school itself, he recalls, seemed to him little more than a finishing school for girls at the time. "They weren't used to seeing someone doing hard work." And indeed, it was an all-girls school until 1971 when it joined the growing move away from single-sex colleges. The change in the nature of the student body for Pardon, however, had come earlier. "Starting about 1962 and continuing for about ten years, there was a renaissance in the whole craft movement, not just jewelry. It was a significant change. I think a lot of artists were turned off the schools of painting and sculpture during the [Vietnam] war years. I think they wanted to work with their hands. That was a

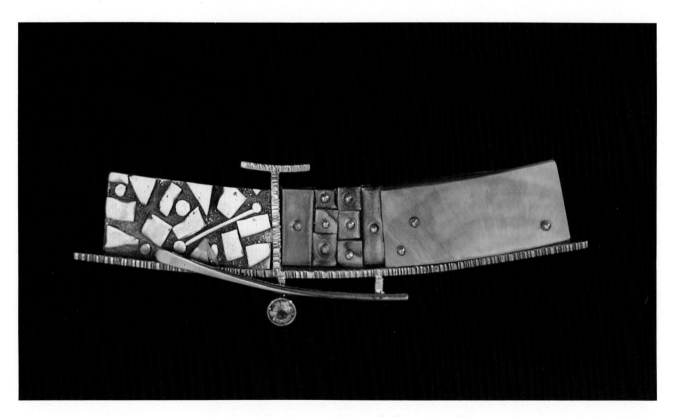

Earl Pardon. Brooch. Sterling silver, 14k gold, enamel, garnet, shell. (1988)

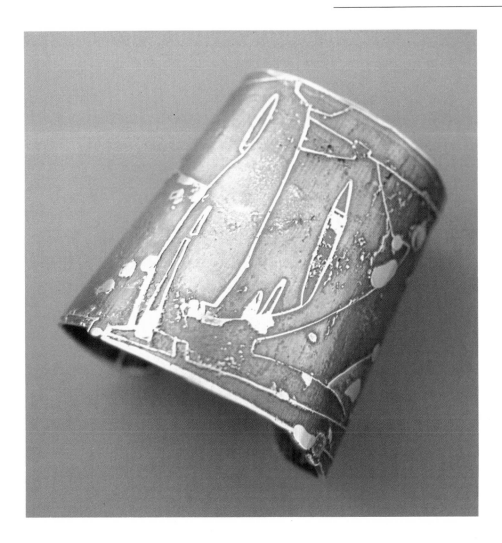

Sharon Church. Cuff bracelet. Sterling silver with overlays of 14k gold. (1978)

significant change." Pardon describes the 1960s and early 1970s as "a glorious time to be teaching. The students were very serious. I don't see that as much now. Art is a difficult field to go into now. Today it's quite different. It's more of a hobby type thing, not a serious art form. A lot of the students take these courses, but they don't look at it as a livelihood." Among his best known students in addition to Glenda Arentzen are Helen Shirk, Sharon Church, and Anne Besse-Shepherd.

In hindsight, Pardon says, teaching only at the undergraduate level deprived him of the challenge that more advanced students would have brought into the classroom. But he says his philosophy of teaching didn't change according to the students or the changing times but rather, more practically, by new technical developments. "My work changed dramatically with the advent of the micro-torch." The whole series of work employing tiny sections of enamels pinned down with gold rivets owes its existence to that piece of equipment. And that carried over into the classroom. Indeed, whatever he was working on at home became part of his classroom work. The students thoroughly enjoyed seeing that work because, they "like to study with someone who is successful."

In his own work, Pardon has always been an architect, building his pieces in a way that is clearly visible. He says that anyone who sees his work could duplicate it, but of course, they would have to bring his eye

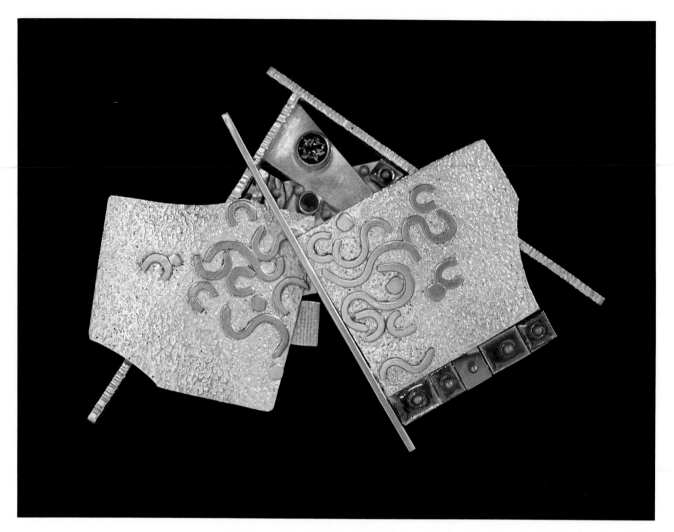

Earl Pardon. Brooch. Sterling silver, 14k gold, enamel, blue topaz, ruby, mother of pearl. (1988) (Photo by Scott Rucker.)

to the mix of colors, his hand to the arrangement, his precision to the technique. As he progressed through the series of ideas over the years, the sense of visible construction could nearly always be seen. He worked out his ideas in piece after piece, reaching the point where each piece acted as sketchbook for the next. Only when he had satisfied himself that he had totally explored an idea did he move on. And when he moved on, it was sometimes to something so different that it seemed to have sprung out of someone else's head. Yet upon examination, there was the Pardon style. It was in the construction, in the seemingly haphazard yet totally balanced arrangement of elements.

Of all the teachers noted here, as well as others well known in the field, Pardon has produced the greatest body of salable work. This may derive in part from his early association with Towle Silversmiths, where he spent a year as assistant director of design. It specifically influenced his series of enamel pieces, an outgrowth of the problem-solving work he did for Towle in the enameling of its classic Revere bowl. And it may be that his longevity at Skidmore can be traced to the balance in his professional life: throughout the years he spent in the classroom, he was also steadily selling his work.

ROBERT EBENDORF
Santa Monica, California

Robert Ebendorf, whose manner of teaching is so low key as to be almost invisible, brought an endless, always new enthusiasm into his classroom at the metal department of the State University of New York in New Paltz. He nourished his students and then sent them out to find their own way. When he left New Paltz in 1989 to move with his wife, Ivy Ross, to California, an era ended.

One former student, Cathy Cohen-Frank, sums up Ebendorf as "someone who truly had an impact on my life as a jewelry artist. He had the unique ability to balance criticism with encouragement. Mostly, though, he gave me permission to explore, purely out of the need to define and develop, a vague yet compelling idea. Bob's gifts as a teacher came so naturally that he appeared unaware of the positive impact he was having on his students."

Robert Ebendorf. "The Group of 9" brooches. Copper, silver, gold. From the collection of Malcolm, Sue, and Abigale Knapp. (1980)

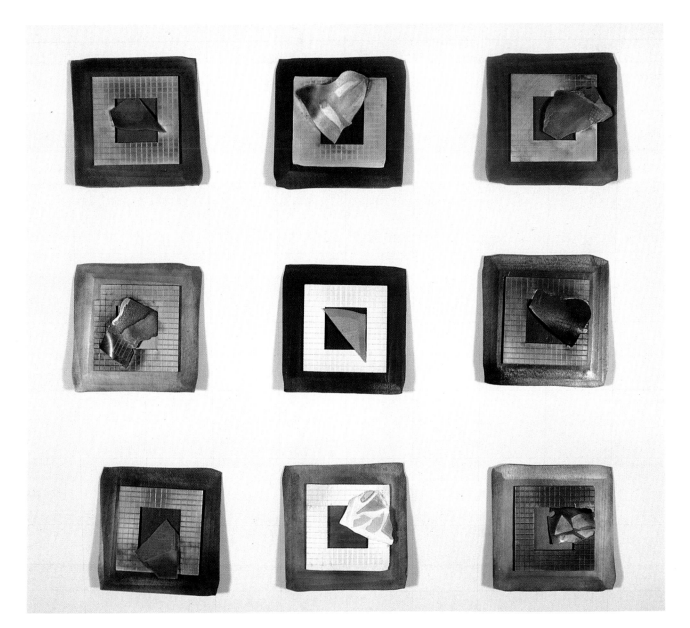

The sharing of information that comes naturally to Ebendorf may have its roots in the ethos of the time in which he grew up—he is very much a product of the 1960s. He speaks always of the openness of those who have contributed their knowledge to the jewelry community, especially the opus that most now use as their basic reference, Oppi Untracht's *Jewelry—Concepts and Technology*.

While his undergraduate students are first groping their way toward proficiency in handling the tools and learning the basic techniques, Ebendorf simply places information in their path. He knows they first must absorb the technical facility and make it a part of their jewelry vocabulary. Then, at a time when they are somewhat more mature, they also come to understand who they are. Only then, with an emerging personality to interpret, can they begin to find a personal voice. He looks for the student to bring a certain passion to the work. In the process, he brings an unending supply of his own passion to them and their efforts. He gives them everything he has, everything he thinks they need to challenge themselves. As they begin to develop that ability, as a certain clarity of thinking emerges, Ebendorf says, "I find myself backing away, because they are on a roll of thinking. I find a strong intellectual grounding in the way the students work today that was not so in the past."

Ebendorf's journey through life and metalsmithing followed a pattern similar to that of other important figures in the world of contemporary jewelry. In 1963, immediately upon receiving his Master of Fine Arts degree from the University of Kansas, he left the Midwest for Scandinavia. A Fulbright grant allowed him to continue his studies in Norway that year. But he went back to Norway, on a Louis Comfort Tiffany grant in 1965–1966, with a very different and specific mission in mind—not an artistic one, this time, but rather a very hard-edged goal—to learn something of commercial methods. He felt a need to bring the very practical aspects of the factory to his classroom. This

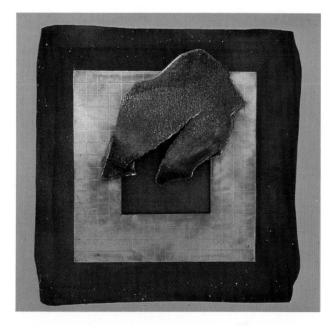

Robert Ebendorf. Brooch from "The Group of 9."
Copper, silver, brass. (1980)

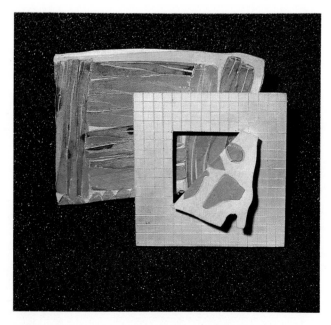

Robert Ebendorf. Brooch from "The Group of 9."
Copper, silver, brass. (1980)

Robert Ebendorf. Brooch.
Silver, copper, brass, 14k
gold. (1980)

was both foresighted and an unusual acknowledgment for an academic. He says, "I wanted to broaden the classroom experience with the practitioner point of view." He took a job in a workshop, putting in a full day sitting at a bench, soldering identical earrings, and seeing the ones that didn't meet quality control standards coming back to be re-done. It gave him a feeling of what some of his students would have to face when they went into the commercial world. And it solidified his thinking about that kind of work experience: "I realized that was something I didn't want to be, I didn't want to have those kinds of restraints. I wanted to be able to be more independent in my thinking."

That is the freedom earned by those who find a niche in the university system, a niche shared by Ebendorf, Pardon, Mary Lee Hu, and Arline Fisch, among others. Each has been set free to develop his or her own jewelry ideas, with results ranging from the most salable to the least, from humble materials to high-karat gold. This group of teacher/jewelers has made the most of both aspects of their work lives —allowing the teaching position and the jewelry making each to benefit and inspire the other. In each case, the relationship with a specific university has been long term. Each has kept that relationship dynamic, being constantly nourished by the new students arriving each year and nourishing the students in turn with the spirit that informs their own work.

MARY LEE HU
Seattle, Washington

Along with their classwork, most of the teachers continue to develop their own jewelry and in some cases, over a period of years, finally achieve success with their jewelry. Such is the case of Mary Lee Hu, the veteran teacher at the University of Washington in Seattle, whose own metalwire-weaving work has recently reached a level of both technical and artistic wizardry far beyond that of her previous work. The number of pieces she can make in a year is small, but each one is a magnificent achievement.

Mary Lee Hu's wirework pieces reflect the maturity and growth of the whole craft jewelry movement. Her earlier pieces have a 1960s hippie ethic to them. They're on a grand scale and speak more of costume than ornament. Hu works almost exclusively with wire of various gauges, employing a vast vocabulary of weaving, braiding, interlacing, and twining techniques, some based on the rich array of basketry techniques, others coming from the fabric world. In the earlier work, there is an airy openness to the pieces, making them at once casual and less refined. The hand of the maker is clearly felt, while the style and motifs reflect Hu's interest in things ethnic. What is remarkable about all the work is the diversity of forms she achieves from this humble material. Using a spool of silver wire the way a knitter uses a hank of yarn, Hu works the wire primarily with her fingers. She is as mobile as a nomad who packs up her portable rug loom when her family migrates to new grazing fields every few months.

Hu's series of work has progressed in great leaps, heading ever so surely toward more elegant forms. The earlier ethnic quality that was so evident grew more subtle as did the dimensions of the spaces between the strands of wire. In every sense, her work has become more precious, culminating in a move to gold wire. This leap, from a material costing about five dollars an ounce to one that costs several hundred dollars an ounce, is a matter of real privation for her. The weaving is denser and requires more metal than an open, airy design. From 14k gold wire she moved on to 18k and 22k, ever more precious, ever more expensive. At the same time, the forms took on hints of antiquity, a closer and closer connection to the roots of all goldsmithing. She has absorbed a great many impressions in her travels and museum going; she feels very connected with ancient gold work, as I learned when we toured the "Gold of Africa" show together at the Metropolitan Museum of Art in New York. (One should always go to a show of ancient jewelry with a goldsmith; it is a revelation to watch and listen as a goldsmith points out the techniques used.) After more than two decades of working at her wire pieces, Hu has truly merged with all the history of goldsmithing that preceded her. While she has achieved a level of perfection that appears complete and therefore unsurpassable, she is an artist who continues to grow. It would seem that there is something beyond perfection.

For Hu's students, perfection is neither a matter of discussion nor a foreseeable goal. She teaches, with pleasure, a beginning metalsmithing course for students in the art program of the university. It is a general introduction to the field, "a broad view of what metals can be. To become literate in talking about other people's work." Along the way, the students learn the basics—sawing, bending the metal, annealing, patinas, soldering, finishing, surface embellishment, forging,

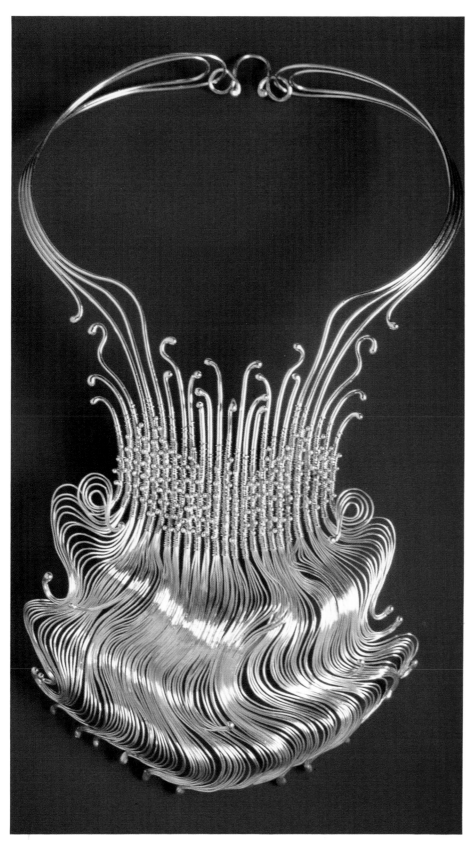

*Mary Lee Hu. Neckpiece #26. Formed of sterling silver wires wrapped with
14k gold. From the collection of Yale University Art Gallery. (1976)*

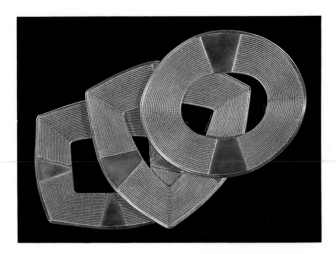

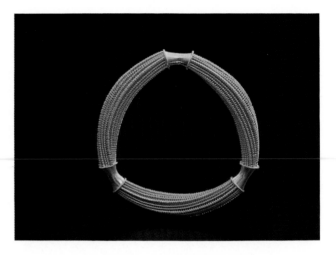

Mary Lee Hu. Bracelets #43, 44, and 45. Flat geometric disks with tightly twined 18k and 22k golds. (1989) (Photo by Richard Nicol.)

Mary Lee Hu. Bracelet #40. 18k and 22k golds; twined. (1988) (Photo by Richard Nicol.)

and forming—after which they move on to the university's other metals teacher, John Marshall, who introduces them to the larger scale of holloware. "Most of them are not going to be jewelers," Hu says, "but they gain a knowledge of themselves, and some discipline." And for some, that class becomes the magic moment when they discover that jewelry is going to be their specialty. "I do have students who are not metal majors when they start but change on the way."

Mary Lee Hu's own technique, more than twenty years in developing and refining, is not part of the regular curriculum and is always the last thing she teaches when she offers her ten-week course in weaving that is independent of the curriculum. She has a horror of turning out wire-weaving clones of herself, though she can't have much concern about being copied—while the technique of weaving from which her work derives is known to cultures throughout the world, and is relatively simple to do on a basic skills level, skillful interpretation is remarkably difficult.

It began for Hu in a graduate-level metals class with Brent Kington at Southern Illinois University in Carbondale. Her assignment was to make two pairs of earrings a week doing wire work. That she stayed with the idea for the next ten months is a reflection both of her unwillingness to let something go until she has perfected it and to the richness she found in the technique. Beyond the earrings, however, she found there were enough ideas to keep her busy indefinitely, working out methods of working with wire that encompass virtually every technique that has been employed by those working with reeds and fiber. Indeed, the section of Untracht's book dealing with wire work is illustrated profusely by photographs of her techniques in progress.

The variety of designs she has achieved and the continual growth of her ideas, along with her technique, may be traced almost month by month because she has numbered her pieces consecutively through the years. The numbers tell another story, too: after more than twenty years, she produced neckpiece number seventy-seven and bracelet number forty-five.

Hu's approach to life stands apart from other jewelry teachers and other jewelry makers. There is a strong element of self-sacrifice in the name of art. One cannot separate the success of the work from the rigors of the life. A couple of years after her marriage to a Chinese mathematician, Hu found herself a widow living in Taiwan with her husband's family. She remained there for a year after his death, taking advantage of the cultural and physical isolation by continuing her exploration of the wire technique. By the time she returned to the states, she had set the course for her life's work. After teaching in Wisconsin and Michigan, she joined the art department at the University of Washington in 1980 and has remained there ever since. She conducts workshops and gives lectures all over the world, which gives her the opportunity to visit museums and absorb the work of other cultures. She is particularly drawn to Asia and has traveled extensively in Tibet, China, South Korea, Australia, and the Asian subcontinent.

Given the Asian preference for high-karat gold, it is fitting that in Hu's most recent work, she has turned to 22k gold. During a show at the Merrin Gallery at the end of 1989, the jewelry took its place most honorably among the ancient works of art this Fifth Avenue gallery is known for. To help visitors understand what they were looking at and appreciate the breathtaking skill on display, one piece was shown under a magnifying glass. Looking at row upon row of endless stitches, one could begin to understand how this work was accomplished. Just the variety of shapes and patterns present in this exhibit revealed the endless possibilities of the work: in the one collection, for which Hu prepared over a three-year period, were round, tubular forms, three-dimensional geometric shapes, and highly stylized flat pieces. Taken together, the pieces comprise a kind of goldsmith's sampler.

The kind of work that Hu produces today can only be undertaken by someone who is subsidized in some way—often, as with Hu, with a full-time teaching position. Others, however, become their own employers by creating a production line that can be made under their supervision, multiplying the number of pieces that can be sold. Various versions of this option are found throughout this book.

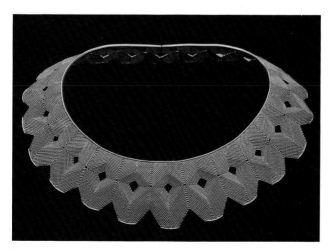

Mary Lee Hu. Choker #70 (collar). 18k and 22k woven golds; diagonal weave in three dimensions. (1985) (Photo by Richard Nicol.)

Mary Lee Hu. Choker #67. Fine and sterling silver wire, 14k gold. (1984) Exhibited in the 1984 Jewelry U.S.A. Show.

ARLINE FISCH
San Diego, California

If it weren't for the fact that Earl Pardon was already ensconced in the metals and painting department at Skidmore, Arline Fisch could well be the name associated with that school. Instead, San Diego State University ultimately became her home, and California living provided the vibrant colors that were a trademark of much of her work during the 1970s and 1980s.

Fisch was not yet a metalsmith during her time at Skidmore but was part of its very strong arts program, graduating in 1952. She came back to the school to teach in 1957 after completing both her graduate work at the University of Illinois in Urbana and the first of three stints in Denmark on Fulbright grants. But the work for which she is best known came about through one of those seemingly random, fateful meetings. "The chairwoman at the time taught weaving and when she retired, she said, 'You take over the department, make it your own.' " She wasn't at all concerned that Fisch was not a weaver. Skidmore sent Fisch to Haystack, in Deer Isle, Maine, where she studied weaving with the renowned Jack Lenor Larsen, and then returned to teach it at Skidmore.

When Fisch accepted the offer to teach at San Diego State University in 1961, she says, "I had never been west of the Mississippi before. I'm a New York girl." Although she would have preferred to stay on the East Coast, she found California to be more receptive to her personal work and had her first exhibition the year after she arrived. Still, she never thought the move would turn out to be permanent. Thirty years later, she continues to teach and to experiment with the weaving-in-metals technique for which she is known around the world.

Although she was never a weaver herself, she taught weaving at

Arline Fisch. "7 Woven Squares" neckpiece. Loom-woven of 18k gold and 22k gold; 18k gold edges and wire. (1987) (Photo by William Gullette, courtesy of Concepts Gallery.)

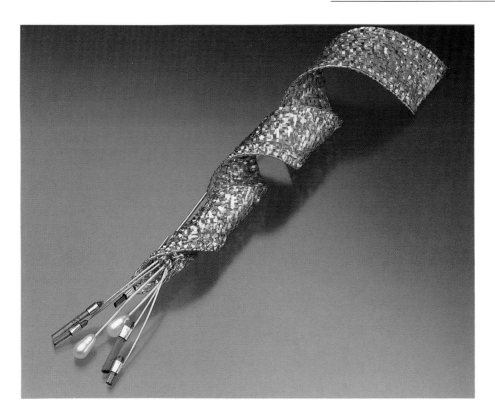

Arline Fisch. "Woven Curl" brooch. Loom-woven of 18k and 22k golds; freshwater pearls and tourmaline needles. (1986) (Photo by William Gullette, courtesy of Concepts Gallery.)

San Diego along with jewelry. Then a trip to South America, notably to Peru, in 1963 set her to thinking about combining the two disciplines. "I saw pre-Columbian things in metal, in fabric, and that made me think about trying it. I thought about what I already knew about the structure and then thought 'what if?'. I started with silver and fabric and then made metal pieces and wove them together with yarn." The idea went on the back burner for years, until she made a 1967 return trip to Denmark. "I went to the Mediterranean on a ship and had five days with nothing to do with my hands. I asked the captain for some wire." In five days, she was able to work out many ideas, but another three years passed before she had a serious span of time, during a sabbatical in London, to work on the techniques of weaving and knitting with wire. Ironically, it wasn't until an editor at Van Nostrand Reinhold asked her to write a book on the subject that she devoted a year to making samples of every kind of weaving work she knew. "I did it first in yarn. Everything I tried worked, every kind of weaving." The book was called *Textile Techniques in Metal*.

At the same time, she was continuing to work in her studio and to teach, resulting in the same kind of cross-fertilization process that Pardon enjoyed. When the book was published in 1975, she was on leave from San Diego State, spending a year as a visiting professor in Boston University's Artisanry program. When no permanent position was offered there, she returned to San Diego State, where she had been a full professor since 1970 and where she continues today.

Fisch's development as a jeweler, which she was able to bring to her classrooms, went hand in hand with her teaching. A design project with the silver maker Reed & Barton brought her directly in touch with the kind of "real life" issues her students would face when they became working jewelers.

Arline Fisch. "Zigzag" braided brooch. 18k gold, sugalite. (1986) (Photo by William Gullette, courtesy of Concepts Gallery.)

But most of her own work had no such restrictions, and she embarked on larger and more dramatic woven pieces that perfectly enhanced her own style in dress—brightly colored, perfectly coordinated, and with the division between clothing and jewelry becoming progressively less definite.

In the 1980s, Fisch began work on a series of high-karat gold pieces, bringing her within the realm of the working goldsmith yet uniquely retaining her signature weaving techniques. Working with specific geometric shapes as her basic building blocks, she interlaces flattened gold wires on a loom or freehand. The variety of weaving patterns are subtly seen in the different reflections given off by the gold. Whereas her brightly colored, large-scale wire work was flamboyant in its use of pattern, the gold pieces are much more subdued. The richness of the metal would be overwhelming were it used with that same kind of flamboyance. Here the gold itself carries the message. As she notes, "The color changes are, for the most part, minimal. The pattern is perceived more as differences in light reflection, and it seems to appear and disappear mysteriously as the plane shifts in space. To focus attention on this unique attribute of woven metal, the forms have been kept very simple."

This metal ultimately seduces most metalsmiths, and in this series, Arline Fisch has demonstrated yet another of gold's most enduring qualities—its ability to be manipulated in any manner that can be devised by the mind of the person working with it. While most goldsmithing techniques are ancient in origin, by adding the equally ancient craft of weaving to the goldsmith's repertoire Fisch has made a unique and permanent place for herself in the literature of the medium.

HAROLD O'CONNOR
Taos, New Mexico

Trying to put a jeweler such as Harold O'Connor in one section of a book is akin to keeping the lid on a Jack-in-the-Box: he always comes out at you in a different way. For years, O'Connor has been known as a teacher and author of a series of books on techniques of goldsmithing. His own jewelry designs were amusing puns, executed in metals, including a noteworthy series of wristwatches that had nothing to do with actually telling time but were instead visual puns on the concepts of time.

Then, suddenly, he presented a bountiful group of wearable and original pieces, heavily influenced by the Orient but unlike the work of anyone else in the field. It was as if he had needed to spend more than twenty-five years of work and study in order to synthesize his thoughts into this collection. It was delightful on its own terms, and doubly so coming as it did from someone who previously had been consumed with process rather than product.

O'Connor's training, both in Mexico and at Pforzheim, was instrumental in guiding the early course of Alan Revere's career, as well. The extreme discipline and attention to perfecting the craft imbued by the school in Pforzheim seems to give those who study there successfully a focus and a strength that is unsurpassed. Add to that a particularly (or one might even say peculiarly) American sensibility, and you get the results shown.

When he emerged from his self-imposed isolation, O'Connor discovered the incredible importance of feedback to a jeweler's work. "I have not been selling in years. When somebody took my work to the Navy Pier show in Chicago, and then when I did the Washington Craft show, I got great feedback; I was working in a closet for years. There's no way to get feedback except from the public. You see hundreds of people passing by your booth, and you see the reaction. Before, with the timeless watches, I was making a statement. Now I am making jewelry."

In order to make the time for his newly successful jewelry line, O'Connor was obliged to drastically cut back the amount of time he had been spending as a teacher. He planned to limit his teaching just to the

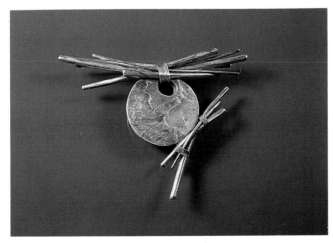

Harold O'Connor. Brooch. Fine gold, sterling silver with mokumé, 18k gold. (1990)

Harold O'Connor. Ring. 18k gold with granulation, sterling silver, Japanese river rock. (1990)

Harold O'Connor. Brooch.
Fine gold, 18k gold,
sterling silver, spectrolite.
(1989)

summer workshops and finally to devote time to producing jewelry. The change in the look of his work reflected changes in his life. When he came into a happier time in his life, he left behind the harsh imagery of cages and things in suspension and moved into work that can be embraced by a much wider market. O'Connor's journey out of the ranks of the teachers into the realm of the jewelry maker is yet another example of how contemporary jewelers continually create their own marketplace.

THE DIVERSITY OF APPROACHES

Here then are some of the various ways of doing it: Mary Lee Hu and Arline Fisch both evolved into high-karat gold collections that consumed much of their time out of the classroom; Earl Pardon steadily created a consistently salable jewelry line through the years along with his classroom work; Harold O'Connor nearly turned his back on teaching as his jewelry work took off; and Robert Ebendorf remained essentially an artist experimenting with ideas that relate somewhat to jewelry but are in no sense competing with the work of his students.

Jamie Bennett, who worked with Ebendorf at New Paltz and continues there, explores the possibilities of enamel techniques and creates his own pieces but is principally a teacher.

Alan Revere, discussed in Chapter 4 of this book, continues to produce his line with a full-time staff while running his school.

Heikki Seppa, whose workshops in anticlastic forming gave rise to Michael Good's line, produces pieces of his own but is known primarily as a teacher.

Mary Ann Scherr, with Parson's School of Design for many years and now teaching at Duke University in Raleigh, North Carolina, has produced unique pieces with a mission over the years: many of her designs incorporate medical monitoring devices for people who have severe medical needs.

Robert Kulicke, discussed in the section on high-karat gold, has been an enabler, creating the possibility for a whole generation of goldsmiths to produce granulation; he has never been a producing goldsmith but is the ultimate teacher—one who nourishes his students and then proudly watches them fly away from the nest.

The legendary Jack Prip, who taught at Rhode Island School of Design in Providence until his retirement, offered students a completely different approach, according to Jan Yager, who studied with him in 1979. "So many jewelry people are into process and teaching techniques, and you come up with ideas that are the result of those techniques. His approach was, think about what you want to do and then figure out how to do it." It makes for a more flexible approach to design and a better problem-solving environment. "The thing that fascinates me about Jack was that he would give you a springboard for a project, and everyone in the class would come up with a completely different approach."

Jan Yager. Necklace. Five pillow forms in oxidized and bright sterling silver, with a rock. Also shown, matching oxidized sterling silver earrings. (1988)

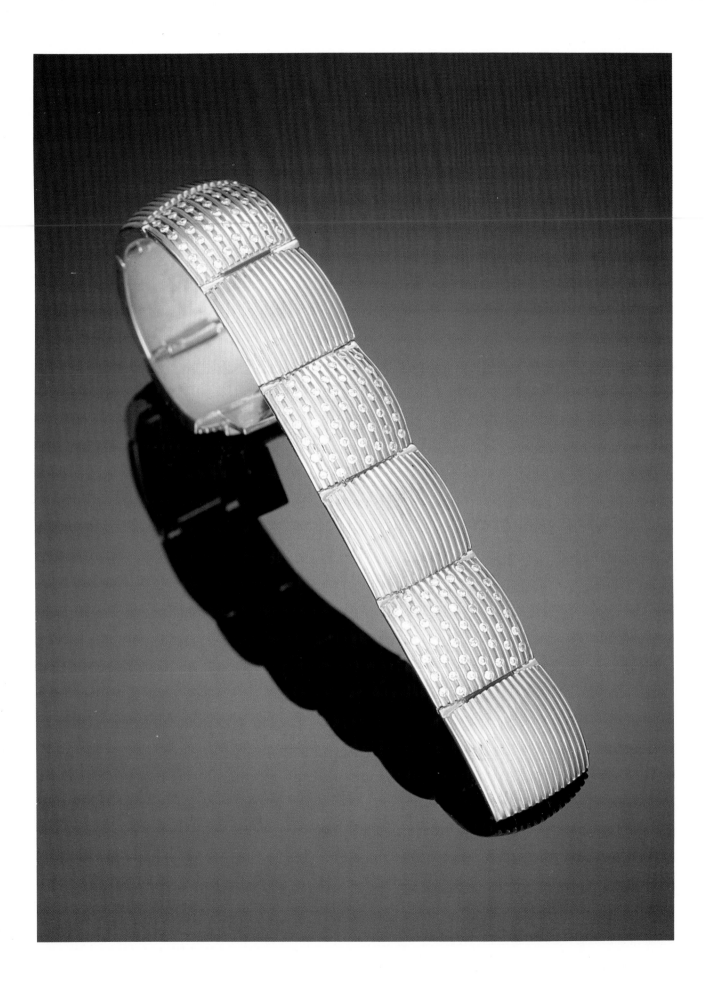

Chapter 4

Craft and Commercial

For a while in the mid-1980s, fine craft jewelry designers successfully bridged the gap between their world and that of the commercial jewelry arena. They exhibited and sold their work at American Craft Enterprises craft shows and also at the Jewelers of America (JA) show, the premiere commercial jewelry event in the United States. The entrance of these jewelers into this most commercial marketplace was seen as an intrusion by some of the older established manufacturers. All they could see was a profligate waste of energy, odd mixes of metals and stones, and jewelry that didn't fit neatly into categories. Unlike the quest for glory implicit in the Olympic motto—"higher, swifter, stronger"—the commercial goal was "thinner, lighter, cheaper," a philosophy not conducive to design for the sake of beauty.

Standing firmly behind their old standards, however, the established manufacturers had a good view of the steady stream of buyers heading for the new exhibits. Granted, in the beginning buyers were more interested in looking than in committing themselves to ordering this new jewelry, but they did respond positively to designers who demonstrated an ability to produce new looks in fine, wearable jewelry. They were innovative and felt few of the constraints of the traditional makers. Perhaps most important, their jewelry was made by hand, and so making a new style was simply a matter of carving the metal in a different direction.

For the traditional maker each new idea, each new style, requires a considerable investment in models. More than 95 percent of the jewelry bought in the United States is made by casting. A model must be developed for each new design to be cast. The guaranteed sale of a certain number of pieces to justify the cost of the model is implicit in

Facing page:
Whitney Boin. Bracelet.
18k gold and diamonds.
(1987) (Photo by Frank
Lindner.)

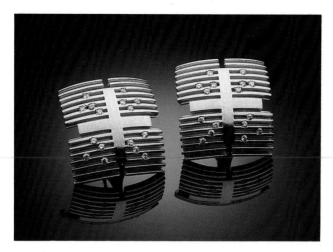

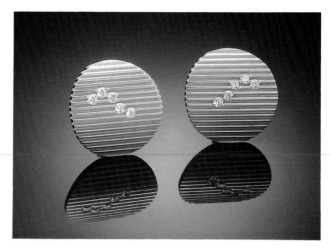

Whitney Boin. "Ridge" earrings. Cast in 18k gold, with diamonds. Two variations shown. (1983) (Photo by J. Valente.)

Paul Morelli. Pins. Stripes of 14k gold and oxidized sterling silver. (1976–1977)

the decision to create a new model. For those who die strike their designs, the start-up costs are even greater. These factors combine to keep innovation at a minimum.

For most fine craft jewelers, who would rather make one-of-a-kind designs anyway, new ideas are more interesting to work out. Where commercial makers see the repetition of units as cost efficient and highly desirable, the craft jeweler sees only the tedium in making the same design over and over again. A gush of new design ideas flooded out into this hitherto hidebound show. The results were predictable, up to a point. The manufacturers started looking for mass-market ways to knock off the handmade designs. Compromises were made so that a fabricated piece could be successfully cast.

But other results were less predictable. The level of many of the manufacturers' designs rose with the challenge, and they began to offer serious competition to the designers. That competition was backed up with a more stable financial base, a wider distribution network, and a greater ability to ride out weak seasons. A few firms absorbed designers who were unable to support the cost of the show on their own or who simply tired of trying to do it all—design, fabricate, market, ship, insure, and promote.

At the same time, the innovative designers began to absorb some of the thinking of the mass manufacturers. As retail store buyers persisted in asking for multiples of their designs, they found their design thinking pushed to embrace quantity production. The pressure to use gemstones in their pieces forced others into design areas that made their work difficult to distinguish from their more commercial brethren. And the rising costs of the show itself inevitably elevated the dollar amount necessary to make their presence both feasible and worthwhile. This in turn led to more and more production work and more and more sameness.

A few designers have made their peace with the jewelry show, each in his or her own way. Whitney Boin and Paul Morelli prove that the traditional casting method may be employed to great effect. Both use it to create original, innovative designs that are exquisitely finished. Alan Revere, however, manages to produce a considerable quantity of jewelry while retaining hand-fabrication techniques.

The West Springfield Craft Show, 1985. Jewelers Donald Friedlich (left) and Paul Morelli talk with author. (Photo by Jason Lauré.)

Paul Morelli. Earrings.
Stripes of 14k yellow,
white, and pink golds.
(1978–1979)

PAUL MORELLI
Philadelphia, Pennsylvania

He is easily the most artistic-looking man at the JA show, standing out from the crowd, standing out as well from the craft jewelers. But he always stood out visually, even when he did the ACE Rhinebeck and Baltimore craft shows. Although Paul Morelli today makes a fine, cast, gold line set with colored gemstones, he brought the marriage of metals technique to mass production in the days when it was totally confined to the craft market. It became a success that was so total he couldn't give it up and move on even when he no longer could bear to look at another piece of striped metal.

The work combined stripes of 14k gold assembled with oxidized or blackened sterling. It was elegant, simple, and original. Although the designs were likewise simple, they took the best possible advantage of the striped pattern. It was 1980, gold had just gone over the 800-dollars-an-ounce mark, and manufacturers were searching for any way possible to reduce the amount of gold in their designs.

Morelli recalls, "I was fiddling around with wire which came to be the stripes, 14k and sterling, blackened, fusing them together. I put a couple of pieces in the collection, out of thirty or forty pieces. Wherever I brought it, people would jump on this striped stuff. I guess it was because gold was so high. People didn't know what the black stuff was, it seemed cheap, they liked the way it looked."

It's difficult to remember now the fear that had struck the jewelry industry in those years after 1974 when the price of gold was allowed to find its own level in the marketplace. After an artificial stability and a price that was a fraction of its actual value, gold began to rise in price. It would reach a peak, then stabilize, then peak again. In painful wrenches it reached $200, then went over $400, spent a tumultuous period at $600, and in January 1980 briefly topped $850. For jewelry manufacturers, it was the end of the world. Morelli's new idea, which I dubbed Metalstripes, seemed like a gift from above. It offered the gleam of gold at a reasonable price, in designs that were both stylish and classic.

The success was especially sweet for Morelli, who had struggled through many lean years. Even when his jewelry was shown at the tiny, short-lived, but prophetic Sculpture to Wear gallery in The Plaza, his income was sparse—the jewelry was on consignment, which meant Morelli didn't get paid until the gallery sold the work. When designer Ivy Ross introduced Morelli to Arthur Cooke, the jewelry buyer for Bergdorf Goodman, his star rose. More important, his income rose as well. After struggling for all the years since he had graduated from college in the early 1960s, Morelli relished the taste of success, and he rode it for a long time.

At the same time as he began exhibiting at JA, he also discovered craft shows, a phenomenon he hadn't known existed. "I didn't know there was a crafts market. I was chasing the New York scene. I never thought about craft markets." The craft world was revealed to Morelli by Rick Snyderman of The Works gallery. He saw the work and, Morelli says, "He went nuts over it and started buying it and buying." Morelli and his wife began pursuing craft galleries all over the United States, and the orders flooded in.

After five or six years at the craft shows, however, he simply stopped attending. The time needed—a week for the Baltimore show—wasn't justified by the orders. And, Morelli adds, "I really lost interest after it left Rhinebeck." Instead, he is now represented at the New Art Forms Show at the Navy Pier in Chicago. Morelli's work is shown as the only jewelry among a group of craftspeople in the block of booths of the Walter Gallery of Santa Monica. Morelli calls it "my graduation from the craft show. That, as far as I can see, is the only direction real true American craft can go. It's the cream of the crop." Unlike other craft shows, where the buying is done by stores and consumers on the spot, Morelli says most of the business generated by the Navy Pier show takes place afterward, through the galleries showing there. He still sells to a handful of galleries "from the craft show days, people who grew with me."

Through the years, he began to add more traditional gold jewelry to his line and in time phased out the stripes. Although the stripes continued to sell, he simply stopped making this line. For Morelli, it was just too boring to continue. Today, his work is made entirely in gold, beautifully finished, and set with unusual, colored gemstones. Ironically, because of his attention to the finish and the overall quality of the work, he still stands out at the jewelry show.

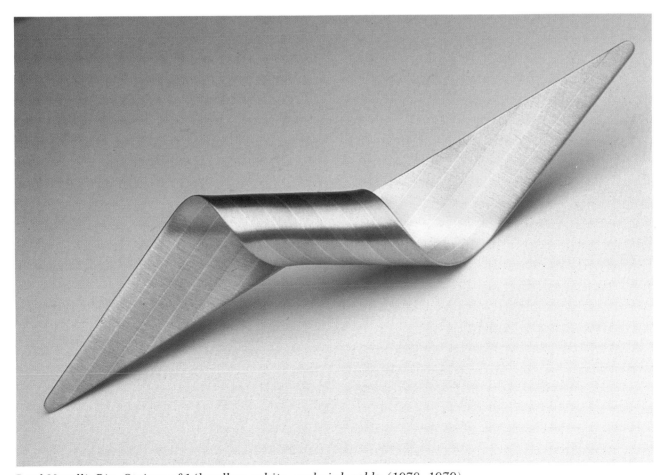

Paul Morelli. Pin. Stripes of 14k yellow, white, and pink golds. (1978–1979)

WHITNEY BOIN
New York City

"Award-winning designer" attaches itself to Whitney Boin's name the way "Oscar winner" always precedes the names of certain actors, and with good reason. He began accumulating awards for his jewelry designs from the icons of the traditional jewelry business when he was twenty-three: Diamonds Today Awards in 1978, 1979, 1981, and 1991; grand prize in the Platinum Design Competition in 1983 and 1985; JA's New Designer of the Year in 1983; first prize in Gold Fashions Trends in 1987.

Boin's unique ability to translate traditional materials and techniques into innovative designs make his work stand out in a world awash in gold and diamond jewelry. Unlike craft jewelers who make their own designs, he is content to put his talent to use in making the model for his designs and letting the casting house do the actual production. Indeed, by carving his model in metal, he makes a unique design but one that can be reproduced precisely from a rubber mold. In this way, he maintains the integrity of his design but at a price he could not approach were he to carve each piece directly in gold. Compare this to designers who use goldsmiths to fabricate their designs by hand. Each has found a way to reproduce design ideas while retaining control of the ideas.

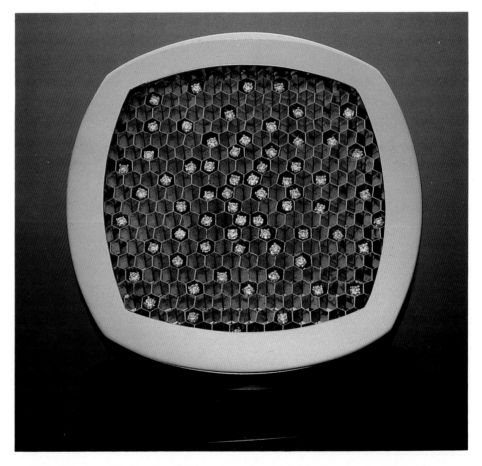

Whitney Boin. "Honeycomb" brooch. 14k gold with diamonds. (1983) (Photo by J. Valente.)

ALAN REVERE
San Francisco, California

Marching cheerfully and precisely to his own drummer, Alan Revere remains one of the few who exhibits at the JA show and continues to vie for and secure booths at juried craft shows. His designs have always straddled the line between craft and traditional jewelry, long before he added the JA show to his marketing efforts. And even now, when his work is marketed to more than 150 retail stores, each piece is made by hand—by a staff of eight skilled goldsmiths. The work leans toward the spare side of goldsmithing, the ideas expressed in impeccably worked but simple shapes.

During the early 1980s, Revere's innovative way with the refractory metals—niobium in particular—reflected perfectly the two elements that have made him the successful jeweler he is. First, he approached the material with his customary precision, the expression of his vigorous training at the goldsmith's school in Pforzheim. Second, he bent the material to his vision, rather than allowing its spectacular visual properties to dictate the look of his jewelry.

He pioneered the use of niobium in its natural, steel-gray color, while using the more familiar rainbow hues in a few well-thought-out designs. Because of his training, as well as his temperament, he has been able to embrace the enormous marketplace the commercial jewelry show affords without becoming overwhelmed by the demands of production. He brought this same clarity to his first craft show exhibits, being one of the first to arrive with a specially designed exhibit to showcase his work. He was also one of the first, and one of the few, to show 14k gold work at a time when most craft jewelers worked only in silver, refractory metals, or even base metals.

Revere's training has been diverse and unique. After receiving an undergraduate degree from the University of Virginia—where, he says, "I wound up taking a lot of art courses, and art history courses, but I majored in psychology"—he discovered the art school in San Miguel de Allende in Mexico. There, on his first day in the jewelry studio, he made a piece of jewelry and discovered his true vocation. He was attracted, he says, by many things: "the preciousness, the universal appeal, the plasticity of the metal, the shininess, the gems, the freedom to design"; "If you don't like it, you can melt it, and you start again"; and finally, "the commerce." It enabled him to follow his bent toward the sculptural but on a scale that was not only quicker but much easier to sell. He sold even his earliest student work, from 1972, meticulously recording each sale in a little notebook. In addition to his regular classwork, Revere took private classes with Harold O'Connor who, he says, "had a tremendous impact on me. I liked the way he worked—precision—nothing was left to chance. Everything was premeditated and controlled." From O'Connor, he learned about Pforzheim as the ultimate goldsmith's training center and as soon as he had earned a Master of Fine Art degree in crafts, he headed off to Germany.

It was a place well suited to Revere's personality, his thoroughness, and his determination. Although he was thrown in with European students, most of whom were master goldsmiths with a decade of experience, and although he didn't speak German when he arrived, Revere found Pforzheim to be everything he had hoped for. He studied with Reinhold Reiling, who exemplified the "Bauhaus kind of logic. Nothing extraneous is permitted. Everything that was there had to have a rea-

The Rhinebeck Craft Show, 1980. Jeweler Alan Revere talks with author. (Photo by Jason Lauré.)

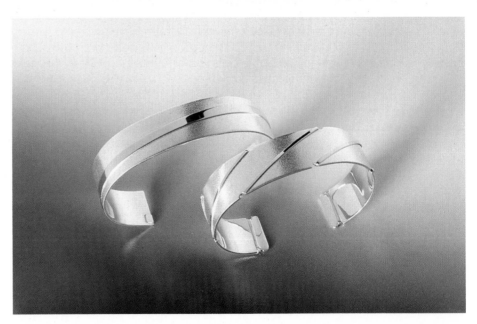

Alan Revere. "Candy Stripe" bracelets. Sterling silver wrapped in 14k gold wire. (1988)

son for being there." For two years, he spent seventy hours a week in the classroom or at the bench. It was intensive, and it was thorough, and in those two years, he says, "I learned how to control metal, how to design, how to engrave, how to set stones, and I learned that I really, really loved it, and that I was good at it."

In 1979, he did his first ACE craft show in San Francisco, and a year later he did Rhinebeck, where I first saw his work. At the same time, he began offering classes in his own school, based on the way he was taught in Pforzheim. More than ten years later, the school has grown to include forty-three different classes, with several hundred people enrolled for varying periods of time each year. While most of the classes offer the basics of jewelry making, he also invites jewelers to conduct one-week workshops on their specialties. Here, advanced students can study anticlastic raising, granulation, or mokumé gane with the best practitioners. Even within the school, he straddles two jewelry worlds: he estimates that 85 percent of the students work in small jewelry shops or have their own businesses and are interested in brushing up their skills or adding a new technique to their knowledge. Within that group are designer craftspeople for whom a short course with a master goldsmith offers both artistry as well as the practical tips that make the method work. Only about 15 percent of the students are at the entry level.

For Revere, the school is not something extra but is ' integral. ' "It feeds something in me. It shares what I do." It also rounds out the complex combination of activities that add up to his business life: designing jewelry and overseeing its production; selling jewelry to wholesale accounts at craft shows and at commercial jewelry shows; and selling his jewelry directly to the consumer during the retail days at the ACE craft fairs.

Even with his larger-than-most production, Revere, like other craft jewelers, has a specific capacity. Like them, he does sometimes get to the point during a year when he cannot accept any more orders for delivery at a crucial time, notably Christmas. His willingness to keep his production at a certain level continues to mark Revere as a craft-oriented jeweler, albeit one who is most in tune with the changes that have occurred at the major craft shows. "ACE is in tune with the aging of the craftsmen," he says. As for his own business, he has no interest in expanding. Instead, he looks forward to upgrading. "I don't want a bigger business, this is enough. To get larger will just be more work for the same amount of money." He is a supremely content man. Goals?, I asked. "I've always felt that I was where I want to be," he answered.

Alan Revere. "Square Coil" earrings. 14k gold. (1988)

Chapter 5

Studio Goldsmithing

THE PIONEERS

A handful of goldsmiths are pioneers in the classic sense: they forged ahead into new territory, unaware of what the hazards might be, inventing themselves as they went. Some of these men and women had formal jewelry training in college, some did not. What sets them apart is a personal vision that each has worked out in a unique way. Each has added to the vocabulary of the jewelry world, both in technique and in artistry. Though their work is strikingly different from one another's, though the paths they traveled were as individual as they are, they are united by a common sense of being artists in metal. They set tasks for themselves out of an innate need to work out whatever particular messages had lodged in their creative minds. Some of the routes they took were perilous and costly; yet, in each instance, they saw no choice. Look at a successful goldsmith and you see a burning intensity caught up in creation, not cash.

Goldsmiths, though their lives are bound up with precious materials, personally live in an atmosphere of simplicity that sets them far apart from their more affluent customers. As these materials—gold, silver, platinum, and gems—pass through their hands, they are transmuted by the goldsmiths' artistry and technical wizardry into something entirely new. Ultimately, what goldsmiths own is the memory of their own creativity.

Facing page:
Carrie Adell. Lariat of 18k gold, shakudo, freshwater pearls; with loose touchstones of 18k and 14k golds, shakudo. (1989)

Although some of the pioneers (as well as the teachers) of the contemporary craft movement are past middle age, and a few have retired, many of these trailblazers are not much past forty.

The working and personal lives of many of the goldsmiths mirror the times in which they live. Many of those who were totally committed to carving out a new kind of lifestyle have indeed been successful in moving away from the often fearful, often narrow examples set by their parents. Those who have succeeded to the greatest degree are those who changed with the decades. Rather than clinging to ways of living that have no place in the 1990s, they have merged their original visions with the natural maturing process to evolve into artists at peace with themselves. This has often meant a considerable shift in the style of their work as well as the materials used to create it.

WHO'S IN, WHO'S NOT

Of necessity, space retrictions are the first editor of any book such as this. But close on the heels of that requirement are my own responses to the jewelry I have seen since the early 1970s. It was my aim here to document a movement and some of the people who were and are part of that movement. I focused on people who have shown a certain staying power; they have continued to develop their themes, their techniques, their materials over a period of years. Some who I would have written about simply faded or exploded out of the scene. I am struck by the number of jewelers who have succeeded in the craft show venue and then decided they didn't want to continue with that success because it had proved to be unsatisfying. Their stories may be found scattered throughout this book. For some, the desire to make one-of-a-kind pieces and find some way to live on that work simply outweighed the security that comes more often with production work. Some manage to straddle the two worlds but find the balancing act to be an unrelenting factor in their lives.

Often, I like someone's work from an earlier period better than the current work. This puzzles me, and I have no answer for it. I am beginning to wonder if there is simply a peak of excellence that some reach sooner than others and that, once passed, is difficult to reclaim. Some, though, just get better all the time; the sense of discovery that I first felt in those early, heady days at Rhinebeck springs up anew when I see their new work.

THE CONTEMPORARY AMERICAN JEWELER

What is an American jeweler? There is a sensibility that transcends artistic style and geographical regions, a fresh and free approach to the materials and a compatibility with the techniques that mark work as "American." Of course, the American jeweler may not have been born here, although all but a few of the jewelers in this book are, in fact, American-born. But whether they come from Maine or Washington, from Florida or California or Ohio, there is very little sense of regionalism about the work.

CHARLES LOLOMA
Third Mesa, Arizona

Charles Loloma, the most successful and best-known Native American goldsmith, preceded nearly all the goldsmiths whose work is included in this book. His work is exquisitely made and beautifully conceived, arising from his personal ancestry. While occupying its own original tradition, it stands firmly in the tradition of contemporary American goldsmithing.

Of all the jewelers included in this book, Charles Loloma is the only one I have not met. This is ironic, because there is no one who better fulfills my basic criteria for inclusion—contemporary; American; jeweler. As a member of the Badger Clan of the Hopi Nation, Loloma could fairly be said to be the most American of all. And he was a contemporary jeweler before most of the others shown here were born.

His distinctive style and purity of line are original, springing from some inexplicable combination of artistry, materials, and imagination. This is Native American jewelry only because a Native American makes it, although his materials are those used by a plethora of Southwestern jewelers merely going through the motions of designing their work. In his hands, turquoise and sterling silver become new. His use of other stones—always opaque—evokes the Hopi mesa where he has spent his life, though it is more colorful than the mesa appears to the casual observer.

In these pieces, notably the sandcast bracelets, one sees the horizontal lines of the mesa. Upon it are upright, irregular arrangements of different sizes of colored stones, nestled together, jostling yet supporting each other by their very closeness. His interpretation of the Hopi village springs to life. For a thousand years, Loloma and his ancestors have lived on this land. His understanding of it is both tactile and imagined; it is his birthright. But the sleek lines of his gold and silver work are entirely his own.

Charles Loloma. Cuff bracelet. 18k gold, channel-set turquoise, coral, and lapis. (1980) (Photo courtesy of Concepts Gallery.)

Charles Loloma. Cuff bracelet. 18k gold, channel-set turquoise, coral, ironwood, and mastodon ivory. (1980) (Photo courtesy of Concepts Gallery.)

Charles Loloma. Pendant. Stylized form of a man in 18k gold, the figure comprising blocks of lapis with turquoise and coral accents. (1981) (Photo courtesy of Concepts Gallery.)

He has spent considerable time away from Arizona, including three years at the School for American Craftsmen at Alfred University in upstate New York, where he studied ceramics and acquired the solid underpinning of a formal craft education. He moved into jewelry making in the 1950s, and for twenty years traveled the world both to teach and to study. Unlike some whose experiences in other cultures are immediately translated into their own work, Loloma has shrugged off these influences, remaining true to his original vision. In a 1979 article in *Americana*, Loloma said "I could appreciate what was done in Egypt, but when I got home, I did my own designs. Nobody can pretend to be anybody else." Of course, many do pretend exactly that, sometimes by trying to emulate another's ideas, sometimes by copying outright.

What they cannot borrow is the essence of the Hopi in Loloma, the closeness with the land, the connection with his tribe and his traditions. That comes across in his sense of the jewelry being an extension of the wearer, not just an ornament. The relationship of the piece to the person wearing it is reflected in the placement of gems on the inside, unseen by the other, cherished privately by the owner. For Loloma, these hidden gems reflect the inner feelings he senses in another person.

Loloma died in 1991 at the age of 70. But his tradition-shattering designs truly are timeless and stand here as a proud and appropriate introduction to the work of this group of contemporary American jewelers.

MICHAEL GOOD
Rockport, Maine

Here is the essence of the contemporary American goldsmith, working out of a white clapboard converted barn in the tiny coastal town of Rockport, Maine, far from the commercial jewelry industry. His philosophy comes before his work yet cannot be separated from it. He makes just as much jewelry as he is able to make with a small staff, while retaining a quality of life that is consistent with his understanding that as beautiful as his jewelry is, it is only a commodity. He sacrifices neither his ethics to it nor his well-being. His philosophy is as understated and as deceptively simple as his jewelry; yet, each was achieved only after a decade of effort.

The elegant spiral forms of Michael Good's jewelry have brought a new vocabulary to an old industry. For once, we may talk about a new kind of goldsmithing, a method not practiced five thousand years ago. This is fabrication at its purest: the jeweler starts with a sheet of 14k or 18k gold, six inches wide and six feet long. There is virtually no machinery between the jeweler and his material. He draws patterns on the sheet with a marker, then cuts each pattern out. The simple cutout is then placed over a wooden form, and the jeweler begins to hammer it with one of a variety of wooden mallets, both the form and the mallets having been made in the workshop as well. As the jeweler works, the metal begins to curve around itself in two directions. The flat form becomes rounded while at the same time the edges begin to curve away from each other.

The piece takes shape before your eyes; the basic shape of a bracelet may be formed in twenty to thirty minutes, blow by blow. The process is the same for an earring or a neckpiece. All that changes is the size and shape of the pattern, the template that like the human gene carries with it its ultimate destiny.

There are no locks, no catches, no earring backs, no hinges, no solder, nothing extraneous, nothing that hasn't evolved organically out of that flat piece of gold. The process, called anticlastic raising, determines the shape of the piece, which derives from the way the sheet is compressed at the center and stretched at the edges, forcing it to curve in two opposing directions.

Michael Good and the method first met through fellow goldsmith Glenda Arentzen, who showed him a draft of a book by Heikki Seppa, a Finnish goldsmith who has taught generations of jewelers at Haystack in Deer Isle, Maine, and at Washington University in St. Louis. The elegance and simplicity of the technique fascinated Good, who had already tried his hand at making jewelry from sheet metal and who immediately grasped the endless possibilities of the technique. A series of workshops with Seppa crystallized all his thinking about jewelry making and by 1979 Good had embarked on the first of his anticlastic pieces. He has never looked back.

He compares the simplicity of the basic technique to someone learning a musical instrument. Though anyone can be taught the notes, only a few rise up to elicit the beauty waiting in the instrument. Each piece, though it may be one of a series built from the same template, is different in subtle ways because it is worked by hand, and those hands grow in experience each time the process begins anew.

The pieces are resilient and flexible; they embody gold's unique ability to be stretched and formed yet to retain its shape. The finished

Michael Good. Triple loop bracelet. 18k gold; diamonds set into seam. (1984)

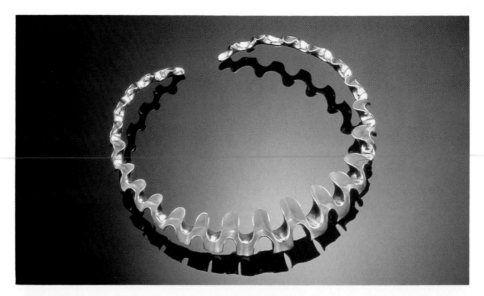

Michael Good. Ruffle neckpiece. 18k gold; interior surface in matte finish. (1983)

Michael Good. Helicoidal neckpiece. 18k gold; formed from one sheet of metal. (1983)

work is thin and lightweight yet strong and voluminous. Because the original metal was milled into sheets and then hammered into shape, it becomes densely compacted, with scarcely any porosity. And it gleams inside and out, the ultimate test of the goldsmith's skill. There is nowhere for a mistake to hide; Good and his goldsmiths must search for a place to hallmark each piece.

The purity and organic nature of his designs evolved not only out

*Michael Good. Bracelet.
18k gold; anticlast formed
from flat sheet of metal.
(1985)*

of the technical knowledge imparted by Heikki Seppa but also from the years Good spent searching for a way to make the world right. At nineteen, rebelling against the materialism he saw among some of his family members, he left college, where, he says, "I didn't believe anything I heard. I went to the slums of New York. I thought, 'I'll go and do good works.' It was part of the times. I was very active politically, I was very idealistic. I thought you could change everything." He discovered after ten hard years on the Lower East Side that it couldn't be done overnight, and with his own health in jeopardy, he and his wife moved as far away in spirit and environment as they could manage—to a piece of land in Maine, twenty miles from the Canadian border.

"Part of running away to the land like that was the only way we could keep our sanity. We had to start from ground one. We brought in electricity, we built other people's houses." The work of Buckminster Fuller was an important part of his thinking, the way architecture could be made more organic, could relate better to people. These designs were elegant, simple, yet totally practical, and they could be built by people for themselves. His awareness of architecture grew naturally from his childhood, during which he was surrounded by an uncle and a grandfather who were architects and a mother who was an artist. Although born in Pittsburgh, his parents were from Belgium, and Good was raised partly in Europe and given a classical European education.

When Good retreated to Maine, he kept much of the idealism that he had struggled to apply to the streets of New York. He created a communal atmosphere rather than a traditional business structure. "The old style, I would hire somebody, I would pay them the minimum wage, I would convince them I was doing them a favor by training them. Over a period of time, you develop the employee and employer struggle. You try to get as much as you can for as little as you can. The other person tries to do as little as they can and get as much as they can. The employee was basically another machine. You tried to keep it oiled enough so it gets its job done, and that developed the capital for you, the big guy, the upper classes.

"We're different from the old people. It's much more communal. There's no hierarchy. If you know something, you're expected to share it with your neighbor." Rather than forcing each person into the next available slot, Good works to bring out the best of their talents and their natural leanings. Within his workshop are some people who are content to fulfill the ideas presented to them and others who bring their own design ideas to the work at hand.

The basic technique lends itself to simple pieces and to very complex ones, too. What matters is the process. "The process is what I like to do; the process itself determines the esthetic of the piece. This technique is a way of looking at shape, looking at form. Look at how simple they are—they're nothing—yet they're extraordinarily exciting. They're extremely organic, they bring all the ideas of nature. I keep working out new versions; my fascination with this grows, it just becomes more organic. You're dealing with the essence of natural formations. I'm much more interested in the process. The object is what I sell, and the object is what communicates." When he teaches at Haystack or at Alan Revere's school, he considers how to communicate the thinking process, which he says is so much more important than the technique.

The sense of natural formations, of the organic world, is part of Good's everyday life. His home is a two-minute drive from the workshop, but his heart is in a cabin about an hour away, on a lake of such purity it seems primeval. Here, alone in his kayak, Good strokes his way up and down the lake, watching the great blue heron that lives on the lake. The icy blue waters are surrounded by dense forest on all sides; the few houses built along the shore are all well hidden by the trees. The facilities are primitive; all that matters is that time out on the lake. It is the essence of the here and now—Good lives totally in the present. "I make less and less references to past and future or present. It's all of a piece. We're all in this game today."

Michael Good kayaking in Maine. (Photo by Jason Lauré.)

CARRIE ADELL
Santa Fe, New Mexico

The path to becoming a goldsmith meanders and branches in many directions. Whether these artists stumbled into metals after years of exploration or knew early on that this would be their chosen field, each created a unique place within the medium by dealing with individual and often complicated circumstances. When the complications include being a wife and mother, the path to a successful career as a goldsmith often turns tortuous.

The women noted here either came to goldsmithing after their children were grown or struggled to fit jewelry making into the clamorous demands of their home life. For many, this has meant a late blossoming. This very lateness, however, brings the benefit of maturity, a very desirable quality for an artist in any medium. And so it is with Carrie Adell, whose work expresses in metals her overriding concern for the environment and her unique statements about that concern.

Her first major pieces evolved from a specific and visually provocative site, Point Lobos Reserve in California, just south of Carmel. Here, the very origins and age of the planet are graphically expressed by the results of the shifting and thrusts of the mountains. Bands of color are twisted and left exposed to the elements. For Adell, "It tells the story of how the Earth was. You can walk those millions of years on the beach. The colors tell when it happened. They're defined like an artist's palette. There's infinite variety of pattern in the stripes and laminates. All the processes are embodied in the rock."

Those visions, which she photographed repeatedly, were in her mind's eye when she created her neckpiece called "Sediments." "I was laminating strips of many different metals on a base of copper." The strips were discards she found on the floor of her metal supplier. She scooped them up, took them home, soldered them to a sheet of copper, and pushed them through a rolling mill. The mill was secondhand, and her experience using it was minimal. Because her laminated metals were irregular in thickness and because she was inexperienced in using the mill, the laminate ripped. But as she says, "It ripped right. As I worked on the piece, it grew from just a choker to a collar, and it spoke sediments. It looked exactly like Point Lobos Reserve."

The finishing touch was a sprinkling of diamonds, to represent the scree, the detritus at the base of a cliff where rocks accumulate as they tumble down. "I made diamonds as the scree because it's all precious, not just the diamonds, but every molecule, because we interact with every molecule on the Earth. The 'Sediments' piece was a consummation of what I needed to say."

There are other statement neckpieces, including "A Rocky Place," "Solar Wind," "Another Box of Rain," and a self-portrait called "Carried Around." This last piece comprises Adell's own hand cast in bronze carrying a globe fraught with symbols of her life and thoughts. Inside is an eye looking out at the world. The poem that accompanies it reads:

We each create a world
From which we see others
Looking back from theirs.

From these large-scale pieces, Adell evolved a totally new kind of work she calls "touchstones." These pieces have occupied her for the

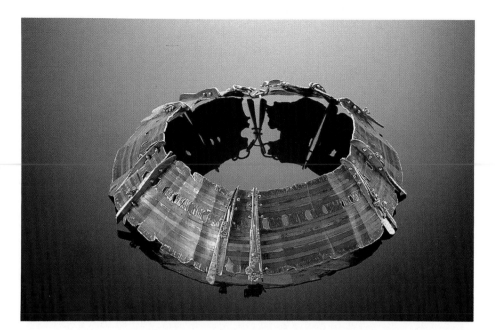

Carrie Adell. "Sediments: No Deposit, No Return" neckpiece. Marriage of metals: sterling silver, copper, brass, nickel, 14k gold, 24k gold electroplate; diamonds. Bottom: detail. (1984)

past five years, and represent a highly successful blending of an artist's personal statement and highly pleasurable, visually pleasing jewelry that, while not mass produced, is nevertheless accessible to a wider audience. The name itself is as complicated as the method used to make them: in metallurgy, a touchstone is used to test the purity of gold and silver; more generally, it means a test or a criterion for determining quality or genuineness. These small pieces carry a great deal of meaning.

Touchstones are individually made elements meant to resemble precious rocks. Each comprises two sheets that are hollow formed. Adell fashions the sheets from a variety of metals using several techniques including shakudo and mokumé gane. Metals are overlaid and soldered into collages, metal patterns with the appearance of wood grains. No two are ever alike, although the seeming randomness of the patterns is quite carefully controlled during the milling process. Many combine 14k or 18k gold.

Each piece is sold as a unit to be slipped onto a simple pin, or worn as an earring or a brooch. They may be combined by the wearer in any manner she chooses; there is no right or wrong way. Ironically, some customers are unable to cope with this choice or with the simple chore of slipping these finely wrought "rocks" onto the gold wire; for them, Adell makes units that are preassembled. But that defeats her original philosophy: the touchstones are meant to be handled by the wearer. The patina she imparts to them is meant to be worn off slowly through the constant touch of the hand.

Adell's touchstones are the most painterly work she has done as a metalsmith and as such combine her painter's eye with fine metalworking techniques in a truly unique fashion. These are not just signature pieces but totally original work, an expression of her concern for the Earth, her desire to touch everyone she meets, and a complete validation of the years she has invested in her jewelry. When she introduced the touchstones at the Jewelers of America (JA) show in 1987, her best customers at first were the other goldsmiths, the ones who could truly appreciate their technical virtuosity. "The two reasons I go to shows, or teach, or appear in public are to answer the questions, 'Am I here?' and 'Am I doing it right?'. I needed to know, How was I doing? Was I barking up the wrong tree?" The spontaneous response of her fellow goldsmiths gave her enormous validation. "I felt wonderful, really wonderful."

Although she was married at seventeen, Adell completed her Bachelor of Fine Arts at Hunter College in New York in 1953. When her husband was drafted into the army during the Korean war call-up, any semblance of a home life had to be put on hold; by 1956, the couple made up for it by settling in New York and producing three children, each two years apart. Although this effectively tethered Adell to her home, she was busily making objects.

Carrie Adell. "Sticks & Stones" brooch. Shakudo, 14k and 18k golds, palladium, sterling silver, stainless steel, copper. (1987)

Carrie Adell. Collection of loose touchstones. (1989)

Carrie Adell. "Inclusions and Rockfall" earrings. 18k gold, 990 (a gold/ titanium alloy), shakudo, fancy color diamonds, freshwater pearls. (1988)

Her life as a traditional housewife always coexisted with both the desire and the need to make things—lots of things, in many media, a profusion of crafting, an explosion of artistic expression—to the point where various advisers implored her to choose just one discipline.

"I picked up metals when the youngest was three [in 1963]. I was working in enamel, I was making furniture and lighting, everything that needed to be made so we could have it, I made. I made it out of necessity. What I saw in the stores was exorbitant and not to my liking in design. I was a hausfrau; I picked up artwork between the diaper times." At some point a friend said "You've done clothing, interior design, exterior design—pick a discipline, and stay with it until you become a professional."

But the discipline picked her. "I was fooling with metals," she says, and they proved to be "resistant to being glib. I couldn't just dash something off. Metals were hard and unfamiliar, so I had to think about what I did. I didn't have my muscle memory developed yet where the tools are an extension of the body." For Adell, whose company name, Carried Away, expresses her unrestrained style of working, resistance was a welcome ingredient.

A seriously inhibiting factor was the expense of the raw materials. She progressed slowly by making a piece, wearing it, selling it off her body, and then making another. These little sales enabled her to slowly buy the most basic equipment for her little home studio. "I only bought tools as the job came up where they were needed. That's how my studio was built. I didn't have to take money from the household." There was no master plan, no graduate studies in metal. "I got hooked on the metal, and I stayed. But even in metals, I didn't know what I wanted to do. I made cold joints because I was afraid of soldering." When she had made enough to buy a torch, it replaced "a little hand tank that blew the solder right off the piece.

"I didn't have a teacher to say, 'Don't do it this way.' It took years of 'hands-on' to find tricks to use." Then, in the fourth year of her exploration in metals, she found an adult education course in a high school near where she lived in northern New Jersey. The teacher was Glenda Arentzen. "I learned about annealing. She set me problems. She taught me about the New Jersey Designer Craftsmen. I sent my work to be juried, and I became a member. Then I had a place to figure out what questions I had to ask and whom to ask them." The class with Glenda Arentzen proved to be a watershed in Adell's progression to professionalism. The year was 1968.

By 1970, she was showing her work at the Bennington Craft Show, staying with the show year after year when it moved to Rhinebeck, through 1978 when she and her family moved to California. She returned in 1982, both as an exhibitor and a juror. But when the show moved to West Springfield, she did not. She took a look at those facilities when the 1984 Society of North American Goldsmiths (SNAG) conference brought her back to the East Coast and sums up succinctly why she chose not to participate: "I did not want those toxic fumes, the heat, the crowding; eight days in that barn would have killed me."

She turned instead in quite a different direction, with the help of a free exhibit space at the JA show in New York in 1986 that she won through a SNAG competition. During the intervening years, she had continued her metalworking studies with Linda Weiss and taken workshops with Michael Good and Patricia Daunis, absorbing their techniques. "I wanted to get the broadest possible palette of expression so when I wanted to say something, I could. Each workshop I did enhanced my vocabulary."

As she was steadily working on her techniques, Adell became disturbed by the destruction of the natural environment, a source of both resources and dilemmas for many metalsmiths. She expressed her feelings in a series of wonderful, unique pieces, made in a melange of metals. Each carried a significant title and often a poem that expressed the genesis of the piece.

When Carl Sagan asked "Who speaks for the Earth?" she replied,

The earth speaks for itself.
We do not listen
Heeding our own greed, as though
We had another place
to be.

But still, every metalsmith is a participant in the destruction of the Earth, a notion that troubles and concerns this group in general and Adell in particular. If you have seen the results of gold mining, or indeed any kind of mining of the Earth's minerals, the resulting residue is not only a blot on the landscape but often an actively tainted polluter. The mining of gold—the basic raw material for much of this work—not only leaves enormous chasms in the ground but is processed at the surface with a cyanide solution. The working conditions for miners, both underground and at alluvial mines, are shocking to these "children of the Earth." Adell anticipates a day when she will leave behind newly mined materials and resort to using only found objects and recycled materials. "Otherwise," she says, "I'm not telling the truth here."

Carrie Adell. "Heartfelt Touchstones" pin/pendant. Sterling silver, copper, 18k gold, shakudo. (1988)

Stuart Golder weaving work in progress. (Photo by Ettagale Blauer.)

STUART GOLDER
Cincinnati, Ohio

In the world of commercial jewelry, the goal is to keep manufacturing costs low, especially as material and labor costs go up. In the world of contemporary goldsmithing, the goal is to constantly improve the quality of the work while continuing to develop as an artist. Although it is true that some goldsmiths, like artists in many fields, seem to delight in taking the hardest possible road even when equally fine but more reasonable alternatives are available, most willingly embrace whatever technological advantages present themselves, while continuing to pour as much creativity and energy into their work as they possess.

Stuart Golder, a goldsmith living in Cincinnati, devised a method for weaving gold wire into jewelry designs—not as a result of taking a class in the technique but from watching his first wife, a weaver, at her loom. He decided to try to adapt her techniques to his materials. When I first saw his work, it was the most refined of its type I had ever come across. The gold wire used was so fine that it was already difficult for the eye to distinguish at a glance the technique that he was using. But in the years since, he has evolved his technique, raising it to a completely new level of sophistication and quality. At the same time, he has improved his jewelry-making abilities and his sense of design so that his pieces are much more refined, more elegant, more *jewelry*. This evolution is a rare direction for a goldsmith; while a precious few continue in this way, all too many are content to simply repeat their past successes.

How can a jeweler raise the level of his or her work while at the same time continue to satisfy some kind of production schedule? This jeweler didn't. He simply took a year out to make the changes and to produce a body of work that could be shown coherently. In one respect, he managed to take this year off by living, as most of the goldsmiths in this book do, very, very simply, away from the cities that are both costly and unappealing.

His *tour de force* is jewelry made with wire so fine it creates a mesh of one hundred threads to the inch. Working on a loom similar to the ones on which Native Americans do their traditional bead work, Golder added his own refinements, developing modifications to the loom that allowed him to work with fine gold wire. After investing untold hours in the weaving of each section of wire, he fixes the piece with solder. It is, as he says in his understated way, a "tricky" process. Once again, experimentation was required to understand how much solder powder to use. The powder is heated to make it flow; the amount used is determined entirely by eye and by costly and heartbreaking trial and error. If there is too much solder, the piece changes color, growing muddy looking. If there isn't enough, the ends of the wires, the parts that are ultimately fitted into the overall frame of the piece, may come apart. At the moment the piece is soldered, if there is one false step, the work is melted and the hours of labor lost. There's no possible way to repair it. That is the peril when Golder is working with gold of one color. Working with white and yellow gold is trickier. Even if they are of the same karat purity, they require two different kinds of solder, each reacting differently to the different alloys in the gold. White gold, for example, is alloyed principally with nickel, while yellow gold is alloyed with silver and copper.

Each year, Golder takes a workshop with another jeweler, adding to his store of technical wizardry, though not immediately or directly to his production. He has taken a yearly workshop in Seattle with Steve Dixon because he likes the mokumé gane technique that Dixon has mastered so beautifully, but none of it has ever been applied to his own work. It's a classic busman's holiday. He's taken workshops in other Oriental metal techniques as well as in reticulation, a skill that he later shared with Dixon. This is the goldsmith's equivalent of challenge dancing or of two soloists pushing each other to greater heights in jazz. Sometimes it is the subtleties of the designs that are created by these other processes that he can feel working their way into his woven pieces.

Occasionally, the lessons learned are applied to his work in a more direct way. In the case of a workshop on forming that he took with Heikki Seppa, Golder created a pendant based on the double helix form of the DNA molecule. The new technique he learned from Seppa made the shape possible and probably nurtured the idea of the shape as well. A visit to fellow goldsmith Patricia Daunis led him to goldsmith Michael Good, the ultimate proponent of Seppa's anticlastic forming.

"I had heard Good's name from Seppa. When I was in Maine, somebody said, 'You have to see Michael Good.' I just called him up, and he was really friendly. And the first thing he does, he gets out his little tool, and he says, 'Here's how to do what I do.' This is incredible. He has no misgivings about sharing all this information."

While some jewelers are also excellent salespeople, outgoing and able to deal enthusiastically with customers at shows, Golder is one who finds that doing the work, preparing for a show, getting to a show, and setting up the show are more than enough to drain all the energy out of him. At the moment when the retail customers appear, he has been least able to project the energy required to take the jewelry that final step. And because of the labor-intensive quality of his work, his prices are relatively high, and so the jewelry requires greater explanation to the customer who feels, totally without justification, that she can get something "just like it" for much less. In our mass-produced world, even people who frequent craft shows and are dedicated craft buyers are unaccustomed to the extraordinary number of hours and the high degree of skill required to do this unique work successfully and beautifully.

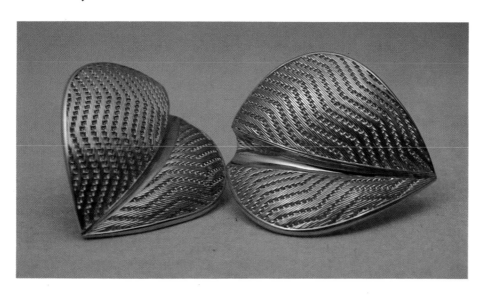

Stuart Golder. "Leaf" earrings. Finely woven 18k gold in undulating pattern. (1987)

Stuart Golder. "Burst" brooch. 18k gold; variety of woven patterns borrowed from cloth-weaving techniques. (1989) (Photo by Ralph Gabriner.)

At the New York Armory Show, one of the most sophisticated environments for the display and sale of American craft, Golder finds that few people understand at a glance what he is offering. It's vital that they be stopped long enough to be told that the work is woven, a concept that women in particular grasp immediately once they hear the word. But in order to be told, they must first pause, and in this Golder has been helped immeasurably by his good friend and fellow craftsman Michael Dorsa, who has traveled with him to shows as his spokesman. Animated where Golder is reticent, Dorsa enthusiastically puts the jewelry in front of potential buyers and immediately announces that the work is woven. This sets the stage for the conversation. At some point in the conversation, the listener asks if he is the artist, at which point

Golder comes forward and describes how he does the work. The stage is set for the sale. Now, the more usual factors of cost and personal taste assume their rightful place.

Today, there is no wholesale aspect to Golder's work. Everything he makes he sells directly to the retail customer, either at a craft show or through special commissions from the customer. This doesn't prevent store owners from trying to order a dozen pairs of earrings at wholesale. In this instance, Golder has to explain that the price he is charging is the minimum price he can charge and still afford to do the work. There is no room for a retail markup.

Golder's road to jewelry making was circuitous to a fault. He was sidetracked into pre-med courses for three years because his father and brother were doctors; then he wandered into industrial design, which excited his interest in materials and design. And then, by chance, he discovered metal casting. But even after the casting course, he still had no drive to dedicate himself to life as a jeweler. It was, after all, the 1960s, and so he turned next to making and selling leather sandals in his own shop in the "Bohemian section" of Cincinnati, staying resolutely out of the mainstream of commercial America.

Following his sandal period, Golder made rings out of twisted wires and then took a jaunt across country to California. He sold his rings at street fairs, where his display materials consisted of a card table with a cloth over it. Eventually, a bit homesick, he found his way back to Ohio, always looking for a way to make a living without compromising the way he wanted to live. In 1974, Golder and his first wife were living in the woods, raising sheep and Angora rabbits, with his wife spinning the hair from the rabbits. "For ten years, I was a closet jeweler. I stayed out in the middle of nowhere. We had no plumbing, we had wood heat, a huge garden. We were vegetarians and grew our own food." He was making elegant little boxes that he sometimes sold, for a fraction of their value. And then he decided to try weaving wire, emulating his wife who was weaving rabbit hair.

Stuart Golder. Woven bracelets. 18k gold and sterling silver. (1989) (Photo by Ralph Gabriner.)

Stuart Golder. Detail of "Surf & Turf" bracelet. 18k gold and sterling silver. (1989)

Two grants from the Ohio Arts council enabled him to buy gold wire to pursue the weaving. And then a major grant from the National Endowment for the Arts carried him through until he applied for, and was accepted at, his first Philadelphia Craft Show. It was a singular moment. But a rejection the next year so crushed him that he didn't even try again for another five years. His work wasn't shown again until the 1982 Philadelphia show. The rejection, significantly, was not of his work, which was of the same type and quality as the year before. He was rejected essentially on the basis of his slides. "I had no sense about it. My slides were horrendous, and that was probably it."

At this time, he was selling some work at wholesale, which he readily admits was the same as giving it away, perhaps just covering the cost of materials. There was no profit being made, but there was valuable exposure. That exposure, and a chance to see what other craftspeople were doing, the types of techniques they were using, and the prices they were charging, brought Golder to some realizations he might never have reached had he remained at home in Ohio.

"I could do simpler pieces and crank out more of them, and wind up at the end of my life wondering, 'Why did I do that?' " Luckily, he says, he realized it would be more satisfying to use his talents to create fewer, more noteworthy pieces. At heart, he will always want to go back into the closet. "I'd like to come out and do a few shows a year and spend my time in my studio."

In a very meaningful way, Golder is the quintessential example of what the craft shows, and indeed, the craft movement, used to be about. At an ACE show, the artist must be present. But in so many cases, the artist is merely the figurehead. It is at the retail-only shows —Washington, Philadelphia, and the Armory in New York—that people come as much to meet the artist who made the work as to buy the work. And finally, Golder says, he's learned to enjoy coming to the front of the booth and talking to people. But only for a few days a year. Then it's back to the studio in Cincinnati, happily, to disappear once more into the quiet world of the goldsmith.

LUNA FELIX
Santa Fe, New Mexico

One important aspect of American jewelry that places it ahead of most contemporary work coming out of Europe is its quality of maturity and refinement combined with technical expertise. American jewelers are well past the experimental stage; they have worked their way through the technical minefields and, during the years of their own personal development, have established an esthetic that is at once mature yet iconoclastic. The question of what is art and what is craft no longer pertains because this work is both. It embraces the craft of physically making objects of precious, hard materials and the art of design, arranging those materials in ways that are specific to goldsmithing but also discrete from piece to piece.

One essential expression of these criteria is the work of Luna Felix, a jeweler who was born in Morocco when that North African country was still a colony of France but who enthusiastically embraced the Arab culture she came into contact with every day. By the age of sixteen, she had escaped what would have been a very confining existence for a modern, independent-minded girl, and made her way to the United States. But the rich images of the dynamic cultures she grew up with remained with her, available to tap when the need and the opportunity arose.

In 1972, through one of the many acts of fate that seem to rule her life and which she embraces with verve and enthusiasm, Felix was introduced to Bob Kulicke and the Kulicke–Stark Academy he and Jean Stark ran on upper Broadway in Manhattan. That school is responsible for bringing granulation into the vocabulary of the American goldsmith and changing the face of high-karat gold jewelry. In this workshop anyone could come and learn this ancient technique, which had been lost to goldsmiths for most of the centuries since the Etruscans practiced it more than two thousand years ago.

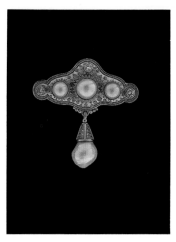

Luna Felix. Brooch. 22k gold with granulation, natural American freshwater pearls, diamonds. (1985)

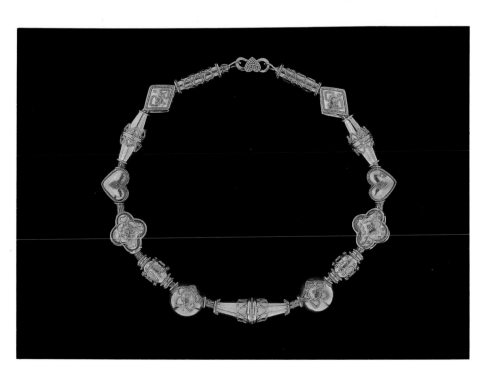

Luna Felix. Heart motif neckpiece. 22k gold with granulation. (1982–1984)

For Felix, seeing granulation was like encountering an old friend from home, a visual experience that she could immediately relate to. Working with the metal proved to be her true metier. Although she had developed her sense of style and artistry before this, having created clothing and accessory lines built on others' work, this was the first time she was able to use her ideas in a form wholly her own. The techniques she learned at the school made it possible for her to express herself in the most satisfying way.

"Your finished product is the sum total of not only what you have learned," she believes, "but thousands of years of what you are, your environment, your education, your sensitivities." For Felix, those thousands of years crisscross a variety of cultures and histories that were not distant, dusty images, but vividly accessible.

Certainly the time was right for Felix and for granulation. For while many other jewelers came out of that same school and a number of them have gone on to establish their own distinct lines of jewelry employing granulation, Felix has flourished in the jewelry world by taking the techniques and meshing them perfectly with her heartfelt enthusiasm for the United States.

After successfully establishing herself as a goldsmith in New York with a studio in Soho, Felix next traveled throughout the American West, searching out native American gemstones and artifacts, and found her vision expanded by the sheer physical expanse of the country. At first she was content to create exceptional work inspired by her travels in New Mexico, but that soon proved to be less than satisfying. A person of intense needs and expectations, she was driven to embrace totally the life she had experienced, and she moved herself, her studio, and her companion, Curtis Woods, to Santa Fe.

The style of living there is remarkably similar to that of Morocco. Significantly, by settling in Santa Fe, where every house must, by local ordinance, be made to look like authentic adobe, she has also captured the essence of Arab life, where houses are all blank and whitewashed on the outside, giving no hint at the level of opulence within. The houses are plain, even spartan on the outside. Your wealth, your treasures, your family life, all find expression internally, privately, within a chosen circle. No one displays wealth or opulence or even design on the exterior, where it might be seen by any passing stranger. And so it is in Santa Fe. Their house is, outwardly, a simple and classic adobe structure, very old. But inside it is the *Arabian Nights*, it is *Scheherazade*. Carpets are layered one on the other, chests studded with metal nails are everywhere, pillows are strewn about on the beds and couch. The sense of Luna Felix style is implicit and pervasive. Her world is one of color, design, ornamentation.

While still studying jewelry making in 1975, she received her first order, a major one, to do all the jewelry for a huge wedding. There were sixteen rings in all for the whole wedding party. At once, Felix was in business. "With each piece," she recalls dramatically, "it was as if my life was at stake." And indeed it was. Both her artistic and commercial worlds took off at that moment. By word of mouth, and by being brought to the attention of people within the jewelry industry, she quickly established a thriving clientele.

With the explosion of interest in granulation and the look of Byzantine jewelry in New York in the late 1970s, a wonderful little store opened called Byzantium. Susan Reinstein and Stephen Paul Adler, along with business partner Bud Hart, created a tiny, plush shop on a

Luna Felix. "Pueblo Shards." 22k gold with granulation; amethyst clasp. Executed in collaboration with Curtis Woods. (1987) (Photo courtesy of Aaron Faber Gallery.)

scruffy, off-the-beaten-path street in Soho. It was truly in the middle of nowhere, but to those doors came a steady procession of fashion editors, and the store's reputation soon became national, out of all proportion to its size or production. There, Luna met Curtis Woods, a kind of "ghost" goldsmith, making jewelry anonymously. Although Byzantium only survived for a few years, it had a widespread impact and also launched Felix, as well as Susan Reinstein, into their own businesses.

Felix was now selling to about two dozen galleries around the country and also producing a silver line that, while successful, proved not to be worth the effort needed to keep it going under her own supervision. It is relatively easy to sell a great deal of silver production work, but the profit on each piece is tiny. The gold work takes much more effort and time, both to make and to sell, but the profit is much greater and the satisfaction is immeasurably greater.

"When the silver became big," she says, "suddenly I was hiring people to make it, to send it out, to invoice. It's the same kind of energy you have to spend to do gold or to sell gold. To make money in silver, you have to have a factory, you have to have forty people working. That is contrary to my philosophy. I like handmade things." The silver line still exists, but it's completely in the hands of a man in Texas who reproduces it and is responsible for everything but the design. "It does not interfere with my concentration on my true love, which is to work the gold.

"I anticipate, as the years pass, I will do fewer pieces, but more intricate, more precious things that will take me maybe six months or a year to do. There will be the constants, the rings, the earrings, to supply the galleries with a certain amount of quality things. I think the ultimate legacy will be to work on things which challenge me in every way possible. Every piece will be like a major motion picture." It's a pretty, and accurate, metaphor for Felix, whose personality and appearance strike one as larger than life and always intensely felt.

One would think that it would be difficult for Felix to let a piece of jewelry go, having invested so much of herself in it, but for Felix just the opposite is true. People become very attracted to her work, and she says "Once they own it, they feel it is totally theirs; my ego departs. I think the success of a jeweler is to treat yourself as the productive servant, making something magical for someone. Jewelry is very talismanic. People wear jewelry because it is meaningful to them. The people who come to see my jewelry, and to people like me, they feel it calls their name, it was made for them."

For all the artistic expression, goldsmithing, especially granulating, is very hard physical work, work whose continued existence is fraught with danger. There is a perfect moment, after the tiny gold granules have been applied one at a time, and the piece is in the kiln, and the jeweler is working with an acetylene torch. Felix says "You feather, feather it, and then you see the metal starts to get a glow. At one moment you will see the granules take the same glow as the surface, there is an even heat, and it cements. One moment more, and you have a total collapse. When that happens, you lose all the work. You have to start all over again."

It's fitting that Felix has chosen, or perhaps been chosen by, a form of goldsmithing that is all or nothing. She has in her own life chosen to start all over again, and she lives a kind of all-or-nothing life. The middle of the road does not appear on her map.

Yet with all that, Felix says, at this point, "I like to think granulation is the icing on the cake. It's not all that I do. Sometimes I will indulge. I will put granulation where it is not all that visible or necessary—a little secret." It's another reminder that the interior Moroccan way of living is a crucial part of her artistic and cultural sensibility.

Luna Felix. Neckpiece. 22k gold-winged pendant with freshwater pearls and rubies; handmade 22k chain. (1988) (Photo courtesy of Aaron Faber Gallery.)

RICHARD KIMBALL
Denver, Colorado

Take an essentially Eastern sophistication and transplant it to the expansive West, add a lifetime of exquisite attention to fine craftmanship and an innate artistry, and you might, in a thousand years, create Richard Kimball. Kimball, who has lived in Denver and its environs for all of his adult life, save for a few years at college in Virginia, expresses the raw, open spaces of the West in his work in the most subtle and refined ways.

Unlike some artists who take images of the West and render them literally into their work—sawtooth coyotes, cacti, cowboys, and jackrabbits all confronting the viewer—Kimball allows these ever-present Western scenes to influence and form his jewelry with elegance and suggestion. He absorbs the landscape, he transforms and interprets it, and only when it is wholly within his grasp does he work out his ideas in the metal. And he does work directly in the metal.

"I am not a paper designer. The pieces take on their own life at the bench—right in the materials the piece is being made of." Which is not to say that he doesn't draw designs in preparation for his metalwork. His notebooks, small in scale, are filled with pages of sketches, clouds everywhere, and thoughts, quotes copied out of books he's reading, and recipes, too. They're diaries as much as sketchbooks. His keen and thoughtful intelligence soaks up impressions, visual ideas, verbal thoughts, emotions, and more and then it all simmers on the back burner.

When he sits down at his bench, he's ready to turn it all into jewelry. "The methods used are anything to get it done. I like to work quickly," he says, although adding that this isn't always possible. "I am constantly reading, constantly trying new techniques so I don't have to think about how to make a piece. If I'm satisfied with my drawing on paper, it's a matter of taking a sheet of gold and cutting it out and going from there."

He rejects the easy, romantic view of the West, the "noble cowboy" image, aware of the toughness that the land more honestly evokes. The first pieces of his that I saw some fifteen years ago intrigued me with their expression of specific forms that I couldn't quite identify. But when I traveled out to his boyhood home, an hour's drive from downtown Denver, and saw the ravines he had worked into those pieces, I marveled both at the view and at his interpretation of it.

With that view in sight, standing where he has stood for so many hours over the years, I understood the inspiration. I have seen it translated in his work in a series of brooches. I have seen it used as gracefully as a cloud in a two-inch brooch that encapsulates a vista stretching to the horizon. He works on these ideas in series, each design different but related to the last, until he has explored the theme to his own satisfaction. Then the series is complete, and once it is he finds it very difficult to go back over the same ground. He did so once as a special request. He recalls that an architect friend of his and his wife, Julie, "fell in love with a steel and gold piece I had given to Julie." This was from a very successful but older series. "It's taken me two years to do the commission, which is hardly admirable, but it's hard going back. I felt like I was singing the same old songs. You see, I work in series. Once a series is done, it's done. To have to redo a piece so it looked fresh was hard. It took a long time."

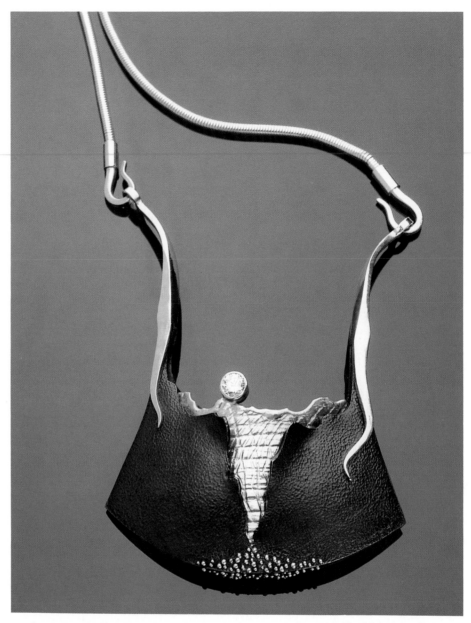

Richard Kimball. "Horizon" series neckpiece. 14k and 18k golds, steel, diamond. (1980–1984)

There are ravines and rainstorms in many of these pieces, darker areas that represent the water flowing beneath the ground that makes the foliage greener there, and yet each of the pieces stands entirely on its own. Knowledge of the specific meaning of the pieces is not necessary to enjoy their excellence, but knowing how they were inspired does give the viewer a sense of sharing the artist's vision more completely. Where some use small diamonds merely to increase the value of a piece, he uses them to evoke tracks in the fields. The areas of reticulation that most precisely emulate the landscape speak through a beauty of their own. The inspiration has been totally absorbed and processed through Kimball's esthetic, and the result is what it ought to be: refined, elegant, and beautiful goldsmithing.

The thoughtfulness, as it is expressed in the metalsmithing, can stand up to the most intense scrutiny. Americans rarely linger long enough to consider a piece of jewelry, or most any object, for very long. But on a trip to Japan, Kimball had the pleasure of having three of his steel and gold pieces intently examined by a Japanese art dealer and historian. "The expectation was that every mark on them, every gesture of the hand, was conscious, that I had meant it to be there, whether I had or not. One of them was one of the best pieces from the series, and I was totally conscious of doing that. It was wonderful and frightening at the same time to have pieces looked at in that way. This man had seen sunsets, mountain scenes, in ink and brush paintings, he had seen them rendered in lacquer, he had seen them expressed one way or another." Now he was seeing them interpreted in metals and recognizing the inspiration; the artistic connections were evident, the hand was sure. The sense of there being exactly enough work on each

Richard Kimball.
"Horizon" series earrings.
14k and 18k golds, steel,
diamonds, granules.
(1980–1984)

Richard Kimball on the family ranch. (Photo by Ettagale Blauer.)

piece was the key to their success. "One of them had only a few chisel marks, and a few pieces of gold on steel, and if there had been more, they would have been too many. Somewhere along the line, I learned that. It was a great thing to learn."

Both the landscape and the resulting jewelry have grown organically. Kimball finds he makes jewelry the way a writer of fiction creates his characters; the pieces change and grow and develop in the process of being made. Though he may draw a piece, it invariably changes in the metalworking as the hand interprets what the mind dictates. The artist and the metalsmith are intrinsically connected, but each speaks a slightly different language. It is what separates a designer from a goldsmith, and why the hands-on process is an integral part of what every goldsmith in this book does, no matter the technique or style.

Unlike many of the goldsmiths profiled here who came to metalsmithing by chance, Kimball grew up with it. He worked actively on his family's ranch from the time he was a child, learning to repair farm machinery, and he was making jewelry in some form or another with a hobbyist's kit when he was eight. With a six-thousand acre backyard to roam, the lean and lanky Kimball became intimately familiar with and comfortable in the truly wide open spaces. Though the landscape is spotted with the occasional house, most of the terrain he knows best remains remarkably undeveloped, giving his creative imagination the greatest scope. The topography of his work reveals his vision; this is the eye of someone accustomed to looking far off to the distance, not hemmed in by buildings and sight lines that extend only across the street. When he glances out over the land, he sees a diverse topography, with changes in elevation, creek bottoms, and evidence of the civilizations that preceded ours.

For all this rusticity and expansiveness, Kimball's work is also representative of a truly refined sensibility. In part, this comes from his emphasis on fabrication, of actually building a piece by fusing metal to metal, adding sections of technically quite different materials as needed, with little concern for what is considered possible or even economical. He never tires of trying new ways to express his ideas in metal. Even some totally failed experiments left him satisfied that he had pushed the metal—in one memorable case, palladium, a member of the platinum group—beyond the point it could organically go. Having gone that far, he could retreat to the realm of possibility and use that knowledge in future pieces. And with no misgivings, he could continue to work the unsuccessful piece and try out all kinds of processes before sending the whole mess back to the refiner to be reclaimed.

None of this experimentation is gratuitous. He sometimes tries to merge two metals that may not be mutually compatible because he likes the colors or the surface possibilities. In the process, he adds to his tactile sense of what a metal will let him do. He has incorporated palladium into a number of pieces (though only after those unsuccessful attempts to make it perform as if it were platinum). Like a good cook who will suddenly find something completely new to do with eggs and flour, Kimball found palladium responsive to his touch—and he just happened to have a few pieces of it around that he had been using for bezels.

Although Kimball sells through a few jewelry galleries, he also has his own shop in Denver—a place where a customer may select a string of pearls or a diamond for an engagement ring. The shop functions as a laboratory in itself, a place where Kimball can see the pleasure a customer derives from a finished piece. Many goldsmiths have this contact at craft shows and derive enormous pleasure from seeing how their work is received. For Kimball, who doesn't sell at craft fairs, the reaction from local customers is all the more important. The fact that it is coming from members of his own community intensifies both the pleasure and the need to create solutions to problems posed by them. By virtue of having this continuing presence in Denver, he is more intimately connected to his customers than many jewelers. The piece a client asks for often spins off into a new direction for his own work;

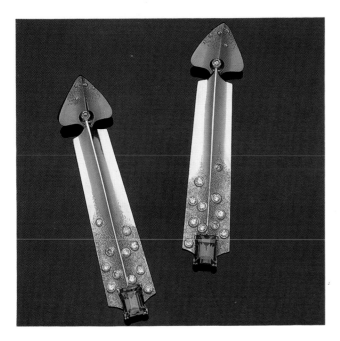

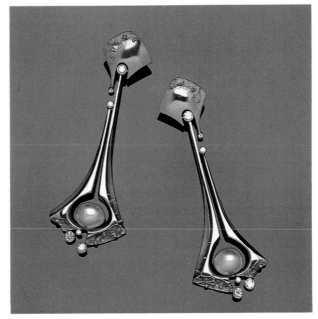

Richard Kimball. Earrings. 14k gold, tourmalines, diamonds, granules. (1988)

Richard Kimball. Earrings. 14k yellow gold, South Seas pearls, keshi pearls, diamonds; varied textures. (1989)

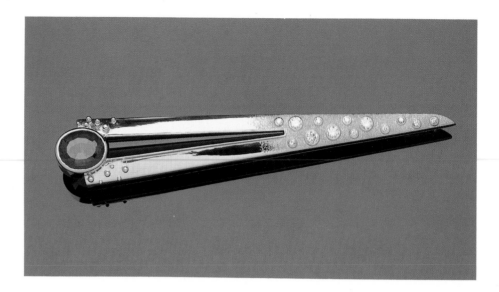

Richard Kimball. Brooch.
14k gold, rubellite, diamonds,
black onyx inlay. (1988)

he enjoys this unwitting collaboration.

The windows of his shop are also a window to his clients; pieces they see in the windows draw them inside, where Kimball often becomes engaged in conversations leading to personal commissions. It is essentially the old patron relationship brought up to date. Once, a king would have commissioned a scepter from a goldsmith. Today, a woman commissions a necklace for a ball. Just as the goldsmith's techniques are timeless, so too is this relationship, with a twentieth-century flavor. In Kimball's case, there are collectors who own as many as ten pieces of his work and whose children are now coming to him for their wedding rings.

He relishes the patron–artist relationship, noting "Most of the things we admire and look at were commissioned pieces; Michelangelo painted on commission." And the great works of Fabergé were all commissions for the czar and his family. Why should there be less quality in a work because the ultimate consumer is known in advance? It is precisely because of the work on view that the customer asks for the commissioned work; if it were to be totally different, there would be little point in approaching a jeweler whose artistry and technical skills you admire. Kimball puts so much into his pieces, so much refinement, the details don't all reveal themselves at once. "People who buy pieces sometimes realize later what they got. They will note that the diamond ring has bead work; they will notice the details. If you make a good piece, that's what happens."

He is keenly aware of his place in the jewelry world, and the place he would like to occupy in it in historical terms. He wants the customer to consciously choose his piece over a commercial piece because there is more artistry in it. "I don't want to be producing the same work ten years or two years from now that I'm producing now. There's too much to do, too many ideas, to simply repeat. The older that I get, I realize that I do have a limited vocabulary. Most people do—they do have these words."

He speaks of the momentary loss of artistic vision, comparing it to writer's block. To resolve it, he says, "You go back to repeating yourself. I don't always trust my own voice. If you are really open to your muse, you will make some things that will astonish you."

GLENDA ARENTZEN
New York City

When I first visited Glenda Arentzen in her Greenwich Village studio at Westbeth, an urban artists' colony, in the 1970s, it was with the hope of understanding a new kind of work just emerging in the marketplace: marriage of metals. This charming term masks one of the most technically demanding areas of metalsmithing. Marriage of metals, like other advanced metal-making techniques, requires the jeweler to be freely creative yet precisely mechanical at the same time. The pattern of different metals that comprise the design consists of separate pieces that do not stop at the surface but actually go all the way through to the back of the piece. Each section is cut out precisely, according to the goldsmith's design, fitted together, and then soldered in place. There is no room for error and little scope for repair if something doesn't work out the first time around.

The finished piece is impressive, but the unfinished work holds more of a key to understanding. Picture a beautifully seamed dress from the inside, with the construction details visible. Here was such a piece of metalsmithing, with the raw edges of the different metals protruding every which way, blackened from the torch, the ultimate design barely emerging from the process.

Arentzen first saw the technique at a workshop given by Robert Ebendorf in the late 1960s, but she remembers the idea being planted by some samples glimpsed in a metal supplier's office on 47th Street. Little plates of striped and plaid metals, samples the refiner picked up from a refinery in Japan, intrigued her for they answered her desire to find a controlled method of achieving discrete colors of metal. Another

Glenda Arentzen. Four-section kite-shaped brooch. 14k yellow gold; marriage of metals with sterling silver, nickel, ebony; two triangle-shaped cubic zirconias. (1980s) (Photo courtesy of Aaron Faber Gallery.)

five years passed before she began working out the technique and even longer before she achieved a level of quality that satisfied her. "It wasn't easy," she recalls. But, "the more I got involved in metal, the more my eyes craved color. That got me all involved with alloys."

The *tour-de-force* of marriage of metals is a combination of tones that are so subtle that one is not quite sure if the colors are perhaps simply shadows created by the curves and hollows of the metals. Using nickel silver against sterling, for example, results in a gray-on-gray or white-on-white pattern that requires a most sophisticated eye to appreciate. For Arentzen, the technique evolved from constant exploration and studying. "I wanted something very controlled, to be able to see clear colors of metal. That's what I was aiming for."

Such glorious crafting is the hallmark of contemporary jewelry, and Arentzen's work marks her as one of its principal pioneering exponents. Setting herself the task of doing a marriage of metals piece marks the natural culmination of thinking and drawing and taking in ideas. The stimuli pile up in the mind of someone visually adept, someone used to making objects with her hands. At that point, the artistic mind explodes and must find expression—not on a canvas but in metal. This reality makes the ongoing debate about art and craft utterly pointless. Why should sculptors, who develop their ideas through physical processes into hard, three-dimensional forms, merit the title "artist," when jewelers, who follow the same process but on a smaller scale, do not?

Arentzen feels that people who are confused by the diversity of her work are "looking at it from only a technical point of view . . . that craft work is essentially about techniques and materials and the physical. I think that's true, and I hope people like to touch my work, but what unifies my work is a mental set. You see the same design system throughout, and I don't think that varies a great deal. There's always an asymmetrical ring. There's always elements that are trying to escape. There's always a conflict of disparate elements, not totally unified. Subconsciously, I try to keep it on the edge. There's something that says, 'What if?' 'Have you considered?' It's not a set piece. I think that's what gives it its liveliness. That's the way I view life anyway."

While Arentzen finds the physical act of making marriage of metals especially satisfying, it fits well into her consistent, artistic interpretation, whatever the method she uses. Her series of box bracelets, each comprising anywhere from seven to nine individually designed, constructed, and framed elements, has continued to grow and metamorphose since 1971, when she made the first one, through today. Each

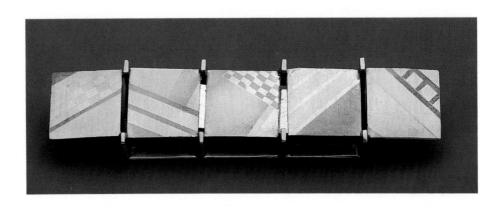

Glenda Arentzen. Five-section bar pin. Marriage of metals: stripes and checkerboard patterns of sterling silver, brass, nickel, copper. (1987–1988) (Photo courtesy of Aaron Faber Gallery.)

Glenda Arentzen. Seven-section box bracelet. Marriage of metals with stripes, overlays, and windowpane patterns of sterling silver, nickel, and 14k gold; sliding pin hinge. (Mid 1980s) (Photo courtesy of Aaron Faber Gallery.)

framed section could stand on its own as a small pin or an earring; the succession of designs within the bracelets complement one another while displaying individual strength as well. Arentzen finds advantages in moving from one technique to another. "One feeds the other and juices up the energy. It's very refreshing. It's a lot of fun for me, and it usually confuses reviewers who think I haven't decided what to do with my life."

Another rich field of study for Arentzen is patination, the coloring of metals. This is the subject that absorbed her, at least part of the time, during the ten years she worked toward a doctorate. She was searching for a palette of colors that would result in new alloys or in alloys with patinas, and as she says in a humorous but quite serious aside, "It should be something that isn't lethal." Many jewelrymaking processes do involve extremely caustic materials; the small workshop is particularly prone to the hazards of breathing in fumes and vapors that are not properly vented.

Her love of color almost kept her out of the jewelry world entirely. "Right from the beginning, I was interested in color. Before the jewelry, I was 'that close' to going into textiles. The painting courses I took were among my more successful courses. I've always been drawn to that." Ultimately she found that all her interests—in color, in texture, in patterns—could be worked out in jewelry.

Arentzen's first job after college was in the New York jewelry shop of Adda Husted Andersen, a Danish jeweler working in the sleek Scandinavian style typical of 1950s design. There, at the bench, she was first introduced to colored gemstones. Errands that took her to stone dealers on 47th Street opened up a world of color that most craft jewelers never experience. In time, she brought this to her work, using the stones not for their intrinsic value but for their colors. Though budget constraints have always dictated the types of stones she could use, commission work enables her to work with the most exciting gemstones, including the remarkable range of colored diamonds.

Even when she works in wax, sculpting with total freedom in a more three-dimensional medium and then having the wax cast in gold or sterling, her design sensibility supercedes the technique and the materials. "I remain dedicated to work that is person-specific. I think that jewelry, as a category of object, lends itself to that specificity because so frequently, the gift of it marks a personal event for a particular person. Also, attachment to the body gives an intimacy potential."

She's come a long way since 1962 when she graduated from the art program at Skidmore College. Up to that point, she had never entertained the idea of earning a living, no matter how modest, exclusively by selling handmade jewelry. There was precious little precedent to support such a dubious proposition. The obvious route to earning your keep lay in teaching. She could look around her and see that the best of the teachers were unable to sell enough work to call it a living. Even those who had advanced goldsmithing techniques and jewelry making to the highest levels of the day continued to need their regular teaching salary. The structure of craft fairs and galleries was not as yet in place. In order to teach professionally, however, Arentzen knew she needed an advanced degree. The academic world of metalsmithing at that time responded to credentials; a Bachelor of Arts was just the beginning. And her skills at that point were barely developed.

Years of further study financed by a Fulbright and other grants, teaching, and selling work by word of mouth sustained her on a minimal level. A year and a half studying in Denmark (plus a few months off to "see all the metal in all the museums possible") inspired and instructed her in the best historical work known. By the time she had acquired her Master's degree at Columbia University in 1970, the structure that would enable craftspeople to become full-time jewelers rather than teachers was beginning to fall into place. But it wasn't until she was well into the advanced work required for a doctorate that Arentzen felt ready to launch herself into a full-time jewelry-making career. Teaching, for her, became a way to stay in touch with the next generation of jewelers and to enjoy the pleasure of sharing her knowledge.

After so many years of subsisting, Arentzen abandoned her doctoral work with just the dissertation between her and that degree. It was time to plunge into the fledgling marketplace. What set Arentzen apart from many of her peers was her ability to find her market without compromising her artistic vision. But entering that market, leaving academia, this is what separates the "art" jeweler from the selling craft jeweler. Flights of fancy must be brought sufficiently down to earth to become wearable work, priced in competition with other jewelry. It is the rare goldsmith who maintains a high level of originality along with the ability to make jewelry for a living audience, not just for a showcase.

For Arentzen, the process of learning techniques began when she was an undergraduate at Skidmore studying with Earl Pardon and with Arline Fisch. She attended Fisch's first weaving class. Arentzen says, "She was a first-rate teacher." But the process has been ongoing. "I took classes on marriage of metals with Heikki in the late 1960s or early 1970s; he gives a great workshop." Still, she says, "I wouldn't put workshops high on my list of influences. You learn something every time you talk to somebody. There are mini-workshops at conferences where you listen for an hour or two." Working in metal is itself the great teacher; the hands try to make what the mind envisions, and that process never ends.

*Glenda Arentzen.
"Breaking Patterns"
drawing, with removable
openwork wire brooch of
sterling silver and 14k
yellow gold with cubic
zirconias. (1989) (Photo
courtesy of Aaron Faber
Gallery.)*

"Two of the best courses I've ever taken in my life," she says, "were in art education, at teacher's college. Their methods course was fantastic. The real issue was creativity and facilitating ideas that are inside someone, to be presented in a visual way. The facilitator has to stir this up and get it out. A lot of it is technical, and a lot of it isn't. A lot of it has to do with issues, and thinking about issues and about life, and about creativity and forms."

Arentzen's understanding of her customer comes from her experience at the craft fairs. She began in the informal days when the craft fair was in the cafeteria of the Bennington, Vermont, high school. "There were about twenty craftpeople there, another five or ten outside, some people who needed bigger spaces were in the gym. There were so few people coming to that fair, we amused ourselves by turning on music and doing a polka around the booths. Can you imagine leaving a jewelry booth? I had jewelry hung on an old diaper stand with little pieces of string."

When the show moved to Rhinebeck, Arentzen dropped out, returning a few years later, around 1974. She did the show continuously then for eight or nine years. When it moved again, this time to West Springfield, she left it permanently. The handwriting was clearly on the wall. "I intuitively felt my retail customers wouldn't go to Springfield, and I was right."

ERIC RUSSELL AND CAROLINE STRIEB
Philadelphia, Pennsylvania

Only the assumption of an innate artistic soul could explain how Eric Russell, one of the most innovative, productive, creative, and thoughtful goldsmiths practicing today, could have weathered the years since he began hanging around craft shows when he was sixteen years old in 1970, until 1982, when he finally felt his work offered him and his partner, Caroline Strieb, a secure and stable base. Though their work shares a commonality of artistry and materials, Russell and Strieb have arrived at their present stage of development from two quite different worlds.

There is a family resemblance between their lines, but they, and often their customers, view them as totally different. Perhaps what they are seeing is, in fact, not the surface but what is underneath. Strieb says, "We always analyzed each other's work, so it's collaborative in a certain way, a kind of editing process. We are in the same room, working there." And, Russell adds, "Some can see it, and just respond to them as two totally different things. Some like one but not the other at all." But as for hands-on efforts, Strieb says, "We share some technology. He does some catches and findings for me." Russell sees this as problem solving of a sort he particularly enjoys. He says, "I like mechanical things you don't see."

The visual differences are easier to see than the technique used to create them. Russell's work generally has some kind of frame around the elements, narrow strips of gold that contain the textured surfaces. Strieb's pieces appear to be bursting out of their spaces; there are usually elements that extend beyond the confines of the underlying shape.

It is clear even to the casual observer that this work is made by hand; no machine exists that could work surfaces in this way, along with the combinations of metals, shapes, and techniques. Through the

Eric Russell. Brooch. Sterling silver, 18k and 22k golds, mother of pearl, aquamarine. (1986)

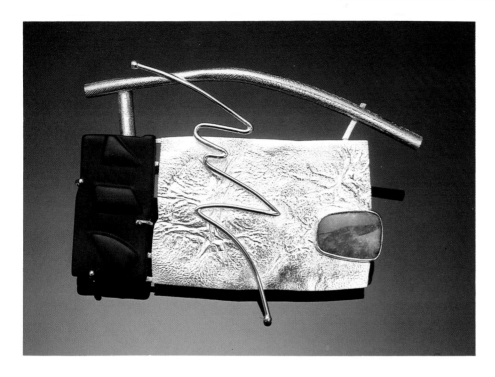

Caroline Strieb. Brooch.
Sterling silver, 18k gold,
opals, carved onyx. (1987)

years, Russell and Strieb's work has retained the sense of controlled chaos—there are many elements in each piece, but they always coexist harmoniously. The work is complicated in appearance, yet approachable. This, too, is a considerable achievement since much work that combines many elements or ideas often comes across as merely chaotic or unedited.

Strieb typically will reticulate the sterling portion of her work, while Russell has evolved very elaborate ways to create textures. He enjoys the physical effort of creating these new processes and uses his greater strength in a way that Strieb could not. He often fuses gold filings onto the surface of the work, melting the metals together just to the point of joining. Complete control is vital or the piece will bubble and have to be scrapped.

Strieb and Russell met by chance in the Philadelphia studio of Jonathan Stember in 1979. Strieb was working there following completion of her course at Philadelphia College of Art. Russell had returned to work there in order to bankroll enough work to fulfill his acceptance at the Rhinebeck Craft Show.

Russell was on the youngest end of the Woodstock generation, a free spirit who was taking classes at the Philadelphia College of Art and hanging out at the Bennington Craft Show while he was still in high school. (He had begun making jewelry at the age of fourteen.) He camped in the fields at Bennington and Rhinebeck because he didn't know most people had places to stay. His equally casual family cheerfully sent him on his way; his father actually drove him to the side of the road in Philadelphia to get a lift to Bennington.

No one in his family was concerned that he was playing hookey from high school to camp out in a field in Vermont. As he says, "My mother's side of the family was creative" and thought this was all perfectly normal. He fixed an eager and observing eye on the jewelry exhibitors at Bennington for three years and then followed the show for another two years when it moved to Rhinebeck.

Eric Russell. Earrings.
Sterling silver, 18k gold,
pearls, rose quartz. (1987)

What Russell saw in those rough-and-ready early years of the craft movement was, for the most part, very simple work, the spirit of the counter-culture making up for the lack of sophisticated techniques. But along with all the twisted wire work, Russell found spiritual brothers in those fields at Bennington—Bob Natalini and John Heller. "This was the kind I was looking for."

Following those early art classes, Russell's real education was gained by apprenticing himself to Natalini, a Philadelphia jeweler who was in turn a self-taught jeweler. From Natalini, Russell learned not only his metalsmithing but also, perhaps subconsciously, the drive to do one-of-a-kind work. "I always assumed that I was going to do well with one-of-a-kind; a blind, a naive assumption. I didn't ever consider giving it up. There is a debate I have between how much production do I want to do, and how much one-of-a-kind can I do." It's a debate that is destined to remain unresolved. The production line offers a measure of financial security; the one-of-a-kind satisfies the artist. "When I got together with Caroline in 1979, we both reinforced each other and supported each other; this is the creative side of the jewelry that emotionally is satisfying."

Russell's work grew more complicated in technique as the years went by, and his skills grew along with his artistic vision. Elements and materials were worked and layered, ideas and techniques soaring upward to a different level, finding a market that was developing along with his work. Natalini's designs remain linked to the 1960s.

At the same time as he was skipping school to go to Bennington, Russell was also taking classes at the Philadelphia College of Art. This hands-on approach, as opposed to a more formal kind of education, and especially his work with Natalini enabled him to make a considerable body of work, enough to begin exhibiting on his own at craft shows.

And exhibit he did. By 1976, he was showing his own work every weekend throughout the summer at an open-air market craft show in Philadelphia. This was followed by a series of retail shows in Maryland,

Caroline Strieb. Earrings.
Sterling silver, 18k and
22k golds, opals, rubies.
(1986)

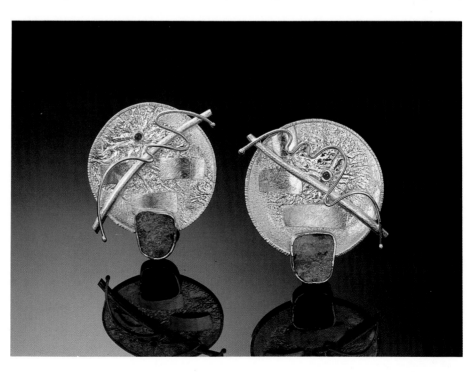

Eric Russell. Earrings. 18k gold, fancy color diamonds. (1990)

twenty in one year alone, that he describes as rather amateurish. In 1978, he was accepted for his first ACE show, in Baltimore. It was a total loss financially, but Russell says, "I saw what I had to do. The next year, I was actually broke, and I got into Rhinebeck!" There's the irony. The talent was now recognized, but he couldn't afford to buy the materials to produce the work for the upcoming Rhinebeck show. The need to make money brought him to a job with Jonathan Stember that winter and to his fateful meeting with Strieb. Within a year, they were sharing booths at the shows, and except for one occasion in 1980 when she was accepted at the Philadelphia Craft Show and he was not, they have exhibited their work together ever since.

Caroline Strieb chafed at most of the art instruction she had in high school and was so discouraged by the rigid teaching of the head of the department that she wound up studying anthropology and archaeology at Temple University. That led her quite literally to "other worlds and other realms." With her first husband, she spent summers in Ireland on digs. From that experience, she says, "I knew I was not going to make a living digging in the dirt." In time, the marriage ended as well.

When she started studying at the Philadelphia College of Art, it was as a clay major. "I thought because I loved to collect ceramics that I would love to make them. But I could see I had no facility for clay; it happens too fast for me. I couldn't get the fluid clay forms I wanted. I could get those forms when I chased in metals. One of my teachers, Olaf Skoogfors, saw me as a metal person because I needed something to fight against." Strieb had fallen under the guiding hand of one of the giants of the metals world. She became a protégé of Skoogfors, who showered her with attention and guided her growth as a metalsmith. For three years, she absorbed all he had to teach. Upon completion of the program, she stayed on at the art college to supervise his metals program; within six months, Skoogfors had died, at the age of forty-three. Shortly thereafter, Strieb left the school and took a job managing Jonathan Stember's studio on Rittenhouse Square. And then Russell walked in out of the cold that winter.

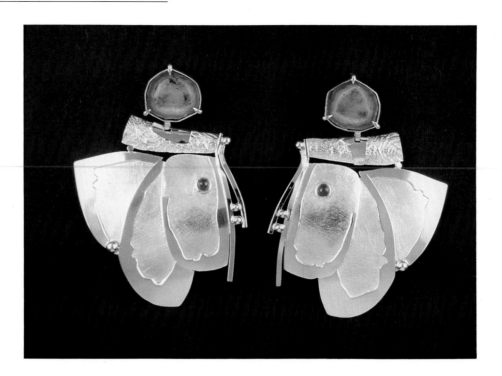

Caroline Strieb. "Chrysanthemum" earrings. Sterling silver, 14k and 22k golds, watermelon tourmaline. (1984)

"It's hard for me to edit out what is not essential," she says. "Without Olaf, I was beginning to flounder artistically. My output dropped." That was when she began to work for others. Within a year of meeting Russell, she had given up doing benchwork for other designers and was working entirely on her own line. She and Russell were kindred spirits. Today they agree that each could pick up the sketchbook of the other and feel completely comfortable. They produce entirely discrete lines that are soulmates in artistic expression although markedly different in construction and techniques. Strieb took to heart Skoogfors's admonition that students find their own language.

From 1981 through 1985, Russell and Strieb did only the Rhinebeck and Springfield ACE shows, with the year's production also being sold at gallery shows. The creative level and the atmosphere at the ACE shows in those years was at its height and their hands-on approach, their multilayered, mixed-metal pieces of sterling and gold epitomized the best of the craft jewelry being seen there.

But as Russell notes, doing only one major craft show a year made for lean winters, and in 1985 they applied for the February Baltimore Show and were accepted. "We thought Baltimore might be a good way to tide us through the winter; it was the right move." Ultimately, they found the Craft at the Armory show in New York their ideal venue.

He says, "The Armory show has been very good for us. It's exactly our clientele—New York, urban, sophisticated; the gemstones are not intimidating to them." It's an upscale audience that brings an experienced eye to the work; craft-show wise, they're ready to write checks for big-ticket items. Russell is as pure a product of the craft world as exists today, and he is one who has done it his way, holding on to, and believing in, his one-of-a-kind work. That he has sustained himself with his production work is even more to his credit for it has all the integrity of his unique pieces. This need, and ability, to be one's own patron is one of the ways in which goldsmiths keep themselves going when there are few clients around to support their unique work.

Russell also has considerable experience with the pleasures and perils of commission work, that peculiar collaboration of client, goldsmith, and gallery working together to create a piece. How does an artist deal with creative input from the client?

The best experience, he says, is when the client says, "I like your work, I have this much money to spend, I want pearls and gold, please make something for me. I can come back to the person with a couple of ideas. With two or three sittings, we have it." The process has included making a paper model and then a copper model of a neckpiece that had to be fitted precisely to the neck of the client.

"More often, people want to work with you, but they want to limit it." What may complicate the process, or ease it, is the involvement of the gallery owner or director, whose ongoing relationship with the client usually involves more than one jeweler. Information is filtered and interpreted through these various personalities and somehow, a unique piece of jewelry results. "Some clients can look at a two-dimensional-tissue drawing and understand it; I have to learn how good their perceptional skills are.

"Sometimes the client wants a piece from you which is just not something you would make. For a designer to keep a client, you design a piece that the client is satisfied with. It fills a couple of needs for everybody involved, and you accept that." For Russell, there may be pleasure in solving the technical requirements of a commission, whatever its artistic merits. "I've made pieces that were just an incredible lot of fun, technically."

"I learned, when I was about twenty," Russell adds, "that the work I make is purchased for people to wear. There is a difference between the work I made for myself [to be sold exactly as he makes it] and the work I made for people [by commission]. It's a different attitude. With the proper attitude you can do anything as long as you understand what you are doing."

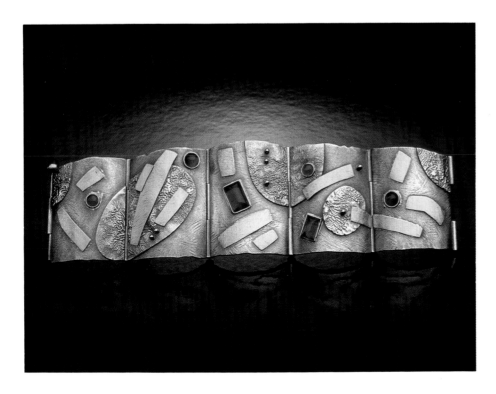

Caroline Strieb. "Pods and Crystals #2" hinged bracelet. Sterling silver, 18k gold, colored gemstones. (1987)

DONALD FRIEDLICH
Providence, Rhode Island

If you page through this book, you will find one element uniting virtually all of the jewelry: it is not striving to be anything but jewelry. For some young goldsmiths, that is not enough. Through their jewelry designs, they hope to deliver a message, or they strive to stretch the medium, or they want to protest against excess. There may be as many statements as there are jewelers; for me, the first statement must be beauty, and that is the criterion by which I have selected this work. In a sense, it selected me because it evokes a response from me that other work does not.

In the process, I have gravitated toward work that is not on the cutting edge. It is not in any sense extreme or even experimental, though it does look that way when viewed from the perspective of the traditional, mass producer of jewelry. But, when viewed from the outer edges of the innovative jewelry world, it is quite conventional. The single exception here is the work of Donald Friedlich. In his work, and in his own words, Friedlich captures as well as anyone the sense of what it means to be an artist working in the medium of jewelry.

Born in 1954, Donald Friedlich is among the youngest of the pioneering jewelers in this book, but in terms of his approach to his work he is at the same time one of the most mature and thoughtful of the group. He sees his jewelry as an expression of ideas and is totally committed to the form, but he resolutely rejects conventional approaches, conventional materials, conventional themes. He has managed to sustain himself against rather high odds within the mainstream of the craft movement; he is one of the most experimental of the craft jewelers who competes in the more lively aspects of the craft marketplace. He creates pieces that in every aspect, except their size and the fact that they are meant to be worn, reveal the sculptor at work.

Friedlich works in series, exploring an idea in one-of-a-kind pieces until he has satisfied himself that there is nothing left to say. The names of these series—"Erosion," "Balance," "Interference"—hint strongly at the seriousness of his ideas, while a glance at the results reveals his devotion to the abstract. In each group, he deals with visual expressions of tension, an unusual task to place on the fragile shoulders of a piece of jewelry. His work is extremely difficult and demanding. He asks a great deal of his customers, as much as any abstract expressionist.

It is striking, in considering contemporary jewelry, how much impact Japanese metals have had. In Friedlich's case, it is the Japanese esthetic that most clearly underlies his work, both in the specifics of the work of the sculptor Noguchi as well as in the spare qualities of Japanese gardens and the elegance and simplicity of traditional Japanese packaging. He strives to incorporate these graceful and understated elements in his pieces, and he succeeds to a remarkable degree.

Friedlich works in such non-traditional materials as slate, and lets his ideas evolve over time in what he calls a "soaking period. It's a process of clarifying what I want to do and getting around to it." The time frame is usually a year, sometimes longer. He keeps coming back to the concept in his sketchpad, drawing and refining, working out the ideas until it all falls into place. There will be a moment of clarity, and then suddenly he can see a whole series of pieces to be done. Only then does he actually start the fabrication.

Donald Friedlich. "Balance" series brooch. Slate, bronze, sterling silver. (1982) (Photo by James Beards.)

Donald Friedlich. "Interference" series brooch. Slate, 18k gold, titanium. (1986) (Photo by James Beards.)

His goal in these small pieces, roughly two inches square, is to create a powerful impression, a powerful image, "to create a sense of tension, make something dynamic and interesting and sensual and also beautiful." Unlike artists who favor concept over esthetics, he says "I want to make something beautiful and unique and powerful. If you look at Picasso compared to Matisse, Picasso so tortured, Matisse so elegant, I would still go for the Matisse every time."

While his earlier brooches were all made of slate, a dark and forbidding material, the next group was made of slices of pastel-colored stones, and that was followed by translucent, textured glass.

The glass series, called "Patterns," he describes as "more delicate, more peaceful, and softer." He feels he is now working "more by intuition, not as rational. It's exciting; I feel less structure." The pieces are "more feminine in character." His work has become lighter in color and in spirit. Not coincidentally, during this period he met the young woman whom he married in 1990. The glass pieces most clearly show his evolution as an artist. Technically, he has set himself another formidable challenge. Through careful sandblasting, the glass is textured and patterned into an undulating grid. One section is masked off during the process and remains clear. Behind the whole piece is a layer of niobium. With the various surface facets, the ups and downs, the impression is of frosted and tinted glass set with a gemstone; yet it is all an optical illusion.

Given the nature both of the materials and of the concepts of this kind of work, as well as the limited number of pieces an artist can produce, most metalsmiths of this sort actually produce most of their income through teaching. Friedlich, however, has evolved two production lines that provide his basic support; he is, in effect, his own patron.

When Friedlich began studying jewelry, first at the University of Vermont and later intensively at the Rhode Island School of Design (RISD), he found, he says, "this whole new side of my head that I didn't know existed."

A chance encounter with the jeweler Timothy Grannis led to a job offer that was a kind of paid apprenticeship. More important even than the development of his jewelry-making skills was the inspiration provided by Grannis, the first working studio goldsmith he had ever en-

Donald Friedlich. "Erosion" series brooch. 18k gold and red jasper. (1985) (Photo by James Beards.)

Donald Friedlich. "Clothes Pins." Brass, gold plated, or silver plated; etched and assembled. (1983) (Photo by James Beards.)

countered. Friedlich began to understand how to market handmade work. During this period, he enrolled in a workshop at Haystack given by Arline Fisch. During a three-week period, Fisch set the students three design problems, including work in her specialty, fabric techniques in metal. For Friedlich, the workshop offered a number of avenues of inspiration: being exposed to "a teacher with broader experience, a well-equipped studio, and a lot of people excited about what they were doing in craft." He speaks of Haystack as "a magical and beautiful place."

From there he made the decision to enroll at RISD; he liked the idea of being fully immersed in a school wholly devoted to art rather than in a school with an art department. He was twenty-five years old when he entered RISD as a sophomore and sees what an enormous advantage it was not to have gone there straight out of high school. He was ready to make the fullest use of everything that was presented to him; he says he "worked very hard" while he was there, although in fact he works very hard at everything he turns his hand to. While at RISD, he was presented with a design problem that led ultimately to his very successful production line. The goal: to create something using twelve cold connections. The workshop with Arline Fisch, the fabric techniques, flashed into his mind. Although he used quite different techniques, the image he chose was clothing—specifically, items of metal clothing hanging from hangers, on a clothes rack of the sort one sees all over Seventh Avenue, the clothing manufacturing district in New York. The solution to a classroom design project proved to be the start of a considerable source of financial support. He went on to set up a manufacturing process for the pins that he calls absolutely foolproof. The patterns are photo etched, a process he learned in a workshop given by Ivy Ross.

He had created a product combining the strength of his design talents and the production capabilities for which Providence is famous. Thanks to the amount of design time devoted to them initially, the pieces are very easy to put together; he says a "semi-skilled gorilla could do them." Called "Clothes Pins," these cute little items continue to provide a very serious percentage of his yearly income. It's a well-conceived, well-made production line that he is comfortable with. It has its own personality and character, one that doesn't borrow or distract from the series of abstract brooches that he considers his main work.

Another healthy percentage of Friedlich's income comes from his second production line, a series of earrings made from a laminate he devised and had made by another commercial firm. This material was Friedlich's response to another problem—one of manufacturing origin. He had developed a collection of roller-printed earrings of sterling with gold plating. After the earrings were plated, he would have selective areas stripped to reveal the sterling below. But ongoing problems in achieving the desired result led him to develop a laminate of 18k gold on sterling. His success with this material gave him greater control over the end product and a line he could depend on. Like his "Clothes Pins," it provides a comfortable percentage of his income each year. Both lines are well priced, attractive, and wearable; for Friedlich, they serve the purpose of leaving him free to devote time to his one-of-a-kind work.

At this moment, the tension that was the original theme of Friedlich's brooches seems to have gone out of the work. Although he remains committed to alternative materials, the esthetics have come more and more to the forefront of his design. But with the use of niobium and its visual reference to a colored gemstone, he has perhaps given a hint at the work yet to come, the work that may just at this moment be entering the soaking process.

The idea of using gemstones he sees as a real possibility, but not merely as pretty highlights. He would like to find a way to replace the entire piece of glass with a slice of colored gemstone that he could work with the sandblaster. Given his command of the jewelry vocabulary, the shape of his statement may be whatever he envisions. Working out the technical details is simply a process, a means toward a goal.

Donald Friedlich. "Pattern" series earrings. 18k and sterling silver laminate. (1985) (Photo by James Beards.)

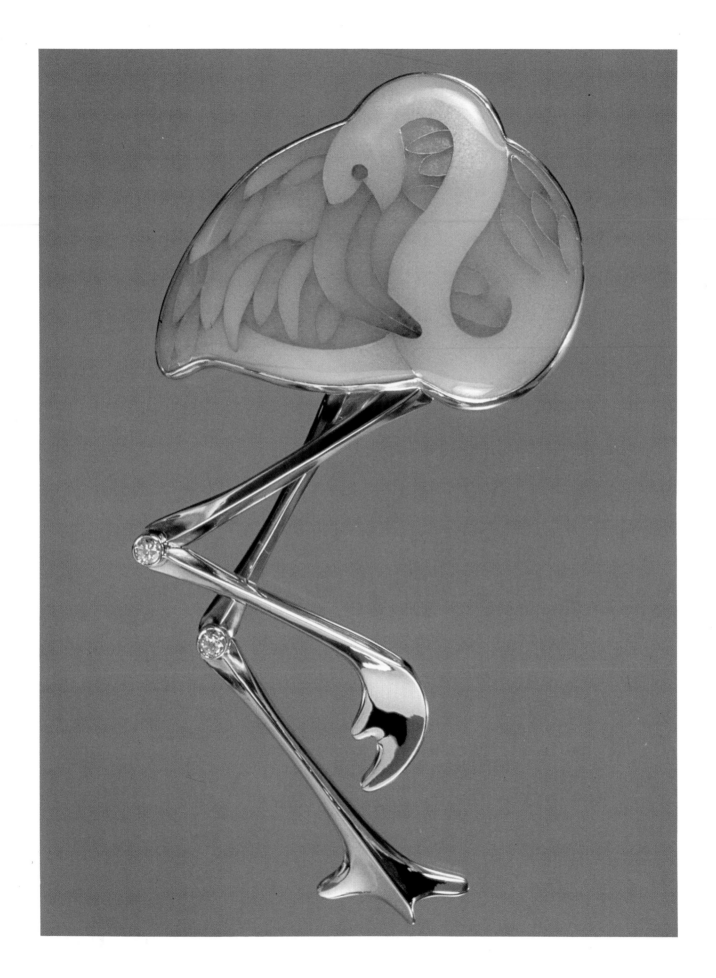

Chapter 6

Cloisonné

Painting Pictures with Enamel

The successful goldsmith must bring two contradictory qualities to the work: to be highly emotional in expressing artistry and yet coolly precise in execution. And while goldsmithing, as a medium, demands this difficult juxtaposition for any kind of work, the jeweler working in the enameling technique called cloisonné requires it to an extreme degree. Like granulation, enameling is a demanding taskmaster that offers no scope for error. If the work stays the slightest bit too long in the kiln, or the heat is set slightly too high, or just a bit too much pressure is applied when smoothing each layer, the work is destroyed. Yet, to stand apart from the ordinary, an enamelist must be a free spirit when it comes to design. And finally, the enamel itself must be set into a piece of jewelry that is both pleasing to the eye and wearable. This latter demand is a challenge simply from the standpoint of weight, enamel being a form of glass.

The term *cloisonné* is derived from the French word, "cloison," meaning "cell." The jeweler starts with a backplate of pure gold or fine silver and upon it creates a design of gold wires. These wires, standing on edge, are affixed to the plate and form a group of little cells into which the powdered enamel glass is placed. Layer by layer, the enamel is built up. After each layer is applied, the piece is fired in the kiln. The more intricate the design, the more detailed the wire pattern. All the forms of enameling in use or on view today take their names from the French: *guilloché, champlevé, plique à jour, grisaille, basse taille.* Only cloisonné is widely used today. Although enameling was known and used by the ancient goldsmiths, it is the French terms that have become common coin; there are no English equivalents to describe these techniques. Like *bas relief, collage,* and *papier mâché,* they come to us intact, transcending the boundaries of language.

Facing page:
Connie Brauer.
"Flamingo" pin/pendant.
Opalescent cloisonné
enamel on fine silver;
24k gold wires; 20k, 18k,
and 14k golds; diamonds.
(1984)

Cloisonné is executed on plaques of pure gold or silver. Alloys such as 14k or 18k gold or sterling silver are combinations of metals, all of which react differently to heat. When an enamel piece is fired, these differences are stressful enough to cause the piece to crack. With pure metals, that additional stress, at least, is alleviated.

CONNIE BRAUER
Denver, Colorado

The consummate jeweler is one who not only can do many goldsmithing techniques well but actually does them all in the course of creating the work. In the world of the goldsmith, the cloisonné artist ranks among the highest. Enamelist Connie Brauer does do it all well and has devised a unique surface look.

Brauer, like many of the goldsmiths, starts with 24k gold plaques from a local bank. Weighing one ounce, and measuring about one-by-two inches, these plaques may be alloyed to create high-karat alloys or used in their pure state, as in this case. To make the gold wires, Brauer works the plaque through a rolling mill. As the mill compresses and stretches the metal, the plaque grows to six feet in length and becomes thin enough to bend with a fingernail. This process alone takes up to two hours. The thin sheet is then sliced into 1/16"-wide strips that are used to form the cells. Although such mechanical processes may evoke images of compulsive personalities, there is little option. Commercially available materials are too thick and not high enough to meet Brauer's specifications for the cell wires. As a by-product of this time-consuming process, the enamelist achieves control over one of the basic components of the work and eliminates one variable that could adversely affect the work.

In her notebook, Brauer sketches the shapes and ideas for her work. These casual drawings scarcely hint at the perfection and precision of the designs she will make, but they do show the overall direction of those pieces and her preference for gentle curves. When she is satisfied with a design, she moves to the hard materials from which it will be executed. She works directly in the metal; there are no molds or models, no waxes or castings. Every piece of metal is worked by hand, with a minimal amount of equipment.

The overall shape of the design is inscribed on a thick sheet of gold or silver to form the basis for the work. This shape is then cut out to become the canvas upon which the wire work and the enamel are placed.

The first layer of every design is a clear enamel applied all over the plate, both back and front, and then fired. The amount of enamel used on the front must be counter-enameled to the same degree on the back of the piece. This prevents the piece from bending or warping when it is fired, since the enamel and the metal contract and expand at different rates in the heat of the kiln. If the piece were not counter-enameled, it would be too fragile and the enamel would tend to separate from the metal. Since the counter-enamel doubles the weight, however, it acts as a governor on the design, placing an automatic limit on the size of earrings and pins.

Working from her own sketches, Brauer begins to place the delicate wires on the backplate to form the design. The process is, to this observer, excruciating just to watch. It requires intense concentration, total absorption, and patience beyond one's imagination. Yet those who practice the art do it with pleasure.

When she is satisfied with the placement of the wire, she tacks it lightly in place with a special glue. This will dissolve in the heat of the kiln when the first layer of enamel is fired. The wires are thus welded in place by the enamel itself.

To achieve the gradations of color that form the final design, Brauer applies thin layers of enamel, one after the other, firing the piece and cooling it down time after time. A design will take anywhere from thirteen to thirty layers before it is complete, and at any time during the process it is subject to cracking, either in the kiln or simply during the process of being handled. In between each firing, the enamel surface is stoned, a method of smoothing the surface and preparing it for the next layer. The pressure here must be just enough to do the job without cracking the enamel. A careless move, a momentary distraction, and the work can be destroyed.

Her opalescent enamels set Brauer's work apart. The translucency of her colors, the particular quality of the enamels, resulted from a simple accident years after she began working in the medium. At a certain point in her work one day, she unwittingly unplugged her kiln. The resulting look, called opalescent, was the product of this unexpectedly lower temperature (1150° instead of 1500° for regular enamels). Not knowing what had caused the enamels to set in this particular way left Brauer with a mystery that she spent three years solving. The process she uses today involves repeatedly taking the enamel in and out of the kiln for short periods of time, a technique she says "adds insult to injury. It's more time consuming than regular enamel."

Her production depends not only on this special trick but also on the particular enamel powders she uses, made by just one firm, Thompson Enamels of Kentucky. When the firm altered the original formula, Brauer's jewelry-making life began to take on the aura of an O. Henry story. She was, quite simply, running out of enamel. The company even tried to make special, tiny batches for her, but like a cook who has left out some crucial element from her recipe, they were unable to replicate the original material. As Brauer discussed this dilemma within the crafts community, people began to look out for little caches of enamel,

Connie Brauer. Earrings and pin/pendant. Opalescent cloisonné on fine gold; 24k, 20k, 18k, and 14k golds; pearls. (1989)

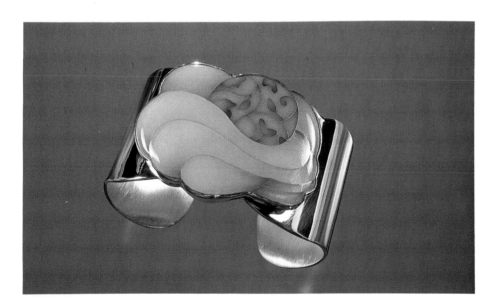

Connie Brauer. Sterling silver cuff bracelet. Opalescent cloisonné on fine gold; 24k, 20k, 18k, and 14k golds (1989) .

and she started to receive small packets from all over the country. Because the network functioned so well and because the amount she uses is so small, Brauer's supply of enamel powder is now secure. She has enough to last for as long as she chooses to work in this medium.

When the enamel work is complete, the traditional goldsmithing takes over. Each enamel is set within a gold or silver bezel and then finished for its intended use—set with a pinback, with earring posts or clips, into a cuff bracelet of her own design, or affixed to a bail for use as a neckpiece. If gems are to be set into the enamel itself, provision has already been made for them with those sections of the design left free of color. Again, handling the work is fraught with potential for disaster, but experience has taught her just how much the enamels can take.

This is remarkably difficult work—physically, mentally, technically, and graphically. Brauer might work on a particularly intricate design for weeks. She estimates her production to be eight to ten major pieces a month. What with the backup work required—billing, ordering supplies, selecting gems, and the like —and time off to refresh her mind and re-energize her body, she makes no more than one hundred pieces a year. There are no assistants in this workshop, no one milling the gold or firing the kiln or even sweeping up after the artist. Somewhere, somehow, sketching new designs goes on as well, for Brauer likes to introduce a whole new series twice a year. Her remarkable bird series —based on many trips to zoos and research in books on animals—was retired a few years ago in favor of less representational designs.

Brauer's color palette—a vigorous selection of pastels—is her stock in trade, as is the unique quality of her enamels. These are further enhanced by her choice of opals and pearls as accents, each gem chosen specifically by Brauer to highlight the enamel tones. As her work has become more jewelry-store-oriented, she has added fine strands of pearls and lengths of colored stone beads as companions to her enamel pieces.

When Brauer works on her enamels, she is totally absorbed. When she walks away from the bench, though, the enamels simply disappear. The total concentration and intensity are counterbalanced by time off that is the antithesis of the work, and in this Brauer is as well organized and dedicated as she is in her business. Every other year, she leaves behind the work and her home, everything that is familiar and comfortable, for two months. Her destinations are always exotic, usually Third World, where she finds untouched environments and a life that can be lived on minimal funds. The trips—to Japan, India, New Zealand, Bali—are taken entirely for their own sake, not as artistic inspiration.

She has lived in the northern reaches of Pakistan near the Afghanistan border; she gets as close to the people as possible. She has traveled to Bali, soaking up the beauty and getting to know the local people. Usually, she lives with friends immersed in those cultures. The trips are doorways into other cultures, a chance to live something of that life in an attempt to understand why a culture produces a certain type of person. She explores the archaeology of the country, the jungles and wildlife, whatever makes it unique.

Thus refreshed, whether by the beauty of the culture or the extremity of living on the edge of existence, she returns home to Denver, picks up her brushes, and resumes creating modern works in the magical art of this ancient technique.

MERRY LEE RAE
Aptos, California

The enameled jewels of Merry Lee Rae are dramatically different and completely delightful, a personal expression of this warm and enthusiastic artist. Her vibrant and lively pieces have so much energy and such elaborate stories to tell that they often stretch across several panels of a necklace, in the manner of a medieval triptych.

Rae, like the other enamelists shown here, has such complete mastery over her material that it belies the perils inherent in this medium. It begins with the very ingredients of the enamel itself; according to Rae, the problem is not limited to the supply dilemma that Brauer encountered. "The problem with the colors," Rae says, "is that every batch is different. I have to figure out what makes each batch work, every time. The fusing temperature can vary by as much as one hundred degrees. The opalescent [she uses the white along with the regular, deep tones in her designs] works differently; if the temperature is off, the enamels won't fuse to maturity. I mix the enamels with a lower-temperature flux; you can trick a bath to fire correctly."

The problem, according to Rae, is that most of the people who purchase enamels for jewelry making are hobbyists. They are like amateur photographers who, when their photos come back from the lab looking purple, blame themselves for the errors, never dreaming it's the fault of the supplier. And for a professional jeweler like Rae, who says, "I probably use two hundred dollars worth of enamels a year," there isn't much she can do to pressure the manufacturer into providing a more consistent product—other than to go elsewhere.

Rae's neckpieces are distinguished not only by the intricate cloisonné work but by the undulating lines of the settings that echo the imagery they contain. Each panel is shaped to fit the cloisonné; then the panels are linked up to form a flowing picture. They are reminiscent

Merry Lee Rae.
"Landscape with Puffins"
neckpiece. Cloisonné
enamel on sterling silver.
(1987)

of the illustrations in children's books in which animals lurk behind trees or slither on vines or seem ready to pounce from one part of the design to the other. A flower piece turns out to be the setting for a frog who sits, plumply, on his own lily pad. In another multi-panel floral neckpiece, the eye travels across to take in the lovely garden scene and then discovers that in a central drop, suspended from the neckpiece, an enamel panel contains the roots of the flowers, deep in the earth.

To achieve the gradations and depth of color, Rae will apply as many as twenty layers of color, firing after each layer. The jeweler working in this medium employs virtually all of the qualities of the artist and the craftsperson at the same time, along with the skills of a chemist and the logic of a mathematician.

Rae was a skilled metalsmith before she became an enamelist. She had an early start: her father was "a hobbyist silversmith" and from the time she was about thirteen she began taking craft classes. She says, "I always did as much jewelry as I could, but I never expected to do it for a living. I was a math major." The math training stood her in good stead when she did come to cloisonné, which she calls "a technically scientific medium. There's a scientific approach to controlling the variables instead of leaving it to the kiln gods."

In the early 1970s, Rae traveled to Sweden as a foreign exchange student, studying there for sixteen months. She lived far in the north in the small town of Ostersund, "almost to the Arctic Circle." To circumvent the language problems she majored in math, but took art classes as well. "Math and science and art; you don't have to speak the language well to excel in those areas." The training in Sweden, she feels, has a lot to do with the quality of her work today. "They are real serious about training their metalsmiths."

Enameling came later, and not in school. "I learned it from a book, *The Art of Enamelling* by Margaret Seeler. That is still the best book."

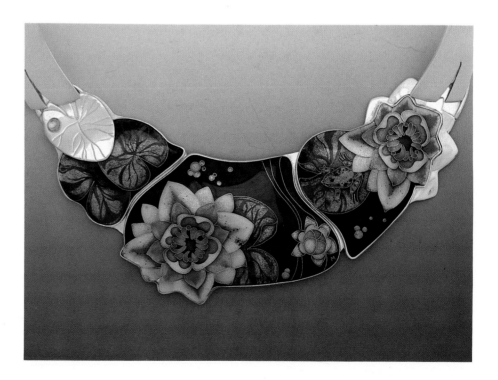

Merry Lee Rae. "Lily Pad" neckpiece. Cloisonné enamel on sterling silver. (1981)

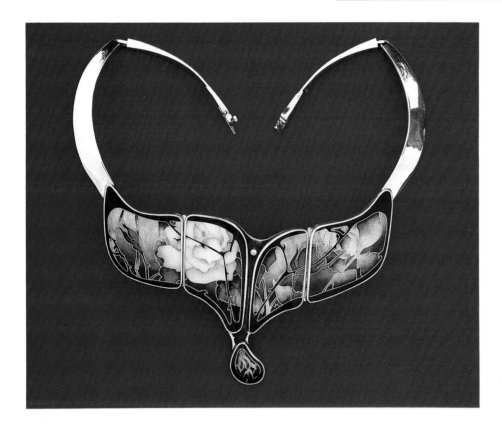

Merry Lee Rae. "Flowers from the Earth" neckpiece. Cloisonné enamel on sterling silver. (1981)

As she was learning her skills, so was John Howell, then her husband. "John was a hobbyist of everything, including gem cutting, when I started doing enamel. His parents bought me the first kiln. We would do the enamels at night and work till two in the morning, then get up at six to go to work. We were together ten years, and we basically started the enameling together. I was a little ahead, but not much." Both of them studied with Elsi Stucki, a Swiss-trained metalsmith, and, Rae says, "I attribute a lot to her. For years we would go back, John and I. My enamelist skills would improve to the point where my metalsmithing skills looked crude by comparison. I would go back to catch up, and kept going back. It allowed me to do some big, impressive pieces in a classroom setting. It forced me to do spectacular stuff; that was my play time, and I didn't have to be concerned about it being cost effective." Those dazzling show-stoppers drew me into their booth at the Rhinebeck Craft Fair, where they first appeared in 1979. After John and Merry Lee split up, each found a separate path to doing the enamel work on their own.

To fund the elaborate pieces, which are spectacular but can be supported only by a very limited clientele, Rae developed an extensive line of moderately priced earrings. The success of that line proved to be its own undoing. "I had two hundred accounts that carried the earrings; I was doing too many different things. I wanted to do bigger pieces." Rae solved the problem by selling the earring business to one of her former enamelists. "A year ago, I had four people working for me, and now I have none. It feels good to be just running my own business. It makes sense to do the things that are really important and be happy with that every day, rather than to be in the fast lane and not be able to find the exit ramp."

KATHRYN REGIER GOUGH
Huntington, New York

Kathryn Gough's training as a painter is evident in the look of her cloisonné enamel work. Both her abstract designs and her floral pieces reveal the painter's eye. Gough takes advantage of her superb color sense in the original combinations of colored stone beads with which she pairs her enamels.

In some pieces, the design of the cloisonné is echoed in a piece of carved gem material; in others, the shapes and colors are so perfectly matched, puzzling out which is which becomes a rather pleasant chore for the eye. Gough employs a variety of styles not only in her subject matter but also in the manner of her settings. Some are simple geometrics; others have the same organic lines as the objects portrayed in the enamels.

Her color palette continually changes. She has worked in the palest of pastels, aiming for a white-on-white look; she has created a series in vibrant earth tones, and then followed up that work with a series of rich florals. Then she pushes on to a dramatic and abstract group of red, white, and black pieces. Her work falls into artistic periods, similar to that of painters who work on canvas.

In some pieces, she uses gold foil within the layers of enamel, which lends a golden glow to the piece; it appears to be lit from within,

Kathryn Gough. Cloisonné enamel neckpiece with beads. (1986) (Photo by Tommy Elder.)

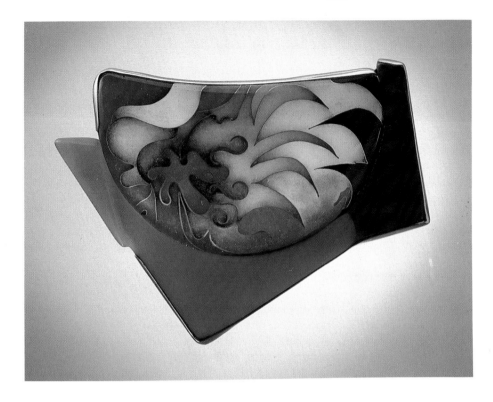

Kathryn Gough. Cloisonné
enamel brooch with onyx.
(1987) (Photo by Tommy
Elder.)

and in fact, it is. The foil may be applied somewhere around the third
or fourth layer of enamel of the twelve or fourteen layers used in each
piece.

Gough arrived at her enamel work through a circuitous path, one
that rarely saw much support from her family. Born in Kansas and
raised in Virginia, she was discouraged from following her artistic bent
and wound up instead studying home economics in college. Not until
she was already supporting herself as a teacher was she free to take
her first painting class.

Then she just plunged in to art and crafts courses. Although her
husband's work, flying for the Navy, saw the couple and their growing
family move fourteen times in twelve years, Gough signed up for adult
education courses, "snatching it wherever I could get it." She spent a
number of years on the West Coast before coming east to Long Island,
where she now lives. There, in the mid-1970s, she took her first jewelry
class from a high school teacher. Subsequently, she says, "I took weaving, pottery, every type of craft. I studied graphic arts, engraving, I just
studied everything, wherever I could find a class. There wasn't much
on Long Island. Then I went to the Craft Students' League in New
York. As a young mother, I would dash in one afternoon a week; I took
metalsmithing, I studied silversmithing and raising and making con-
tainers. Then I took lapidary and then an enameling class." She even
managed to travel to Haystack to take a forming class with Heikki
Seppa.

But her enameling technique is essentially self-taught, worked out
at the bench. It is quite different than that of other enamelists, even
those who work in floral motifs. The painterly quality comes through, a
feeling of looking at a rounded, three-dimensional piece, rather than a
flat design. "I do things with shading that is nontraditional in enameling. I think there are five or six people in the United States like myself."

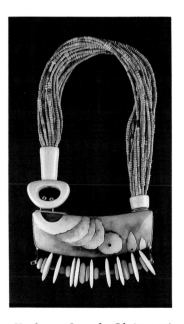

Kathryn Gough. Cloisonné
enamel neckpiece with
clay beads and bone disks
from Africa. (1986) (Photo
by Tommy Elder.)

SYDNEY JO SCHERR
Raleigh, North Carolina

The most personal work of the group of enamelists shown here is that of Sydney Jo Scherr; if you know how to look at her work, you can share a part of the artist's soul. Like a novelist who starts with autobiography and then embroiders heavily on the underlying fabric of fact, Scherr makes jewelry from her dreams, from her frustrations, from sources both happy and sad. Some pieces she feels are too personal to be sold or worn outside of her family. Although I have sometimes wished other jewelers felt that way and kept some of their most bizarre works to themselves, in Scherr's case the original thoughts have been interpreted in such a decorative way that all the pieces may be worn by anyone with an appreciation for their artistry. But knowing why she chose some of her images brings you closer to the soul of the artist, and these pieces prove beyond doubt that enamelists are artists.

An examination of her "Window Pin" series reveals much of what she expresses in her work. Each of these charming pieces combines an enamel picture of a real building, or part of one, fitted into a frame with an openwork grill cover on a hinge. The picture may be glimpsed through the grill just as you view a scene through a window; when the grill is unlatched, the picture comes into full view. And what an eclectic group of buildings these are: here is the Taj Mahal, there is the Wailing Wall in Jerusalem, and here is the Chrysler building. Each image is absolutely faithful to the original, so that if you have seen the particular work in question you recognize it from the jewel; yet, each has a feeling of whimsey about it, the way Red Grooms approaches his New York constructions. The grills on some of these pieces are quite forbidding, yet underneath is that cartoon-like image.

All of this delight emerged from abject misery. Scherr, a native of Ohio who earned her Bachelor of Fine Arts at Kent State University and her Master of Fine Arts at Southern Illinois University, had recently come to New York. Both the city in general and the place she lived in were distressing. Her bedroom had windows that had been permanently covered with immovable Contact paper. To compensate for the loss of any kind of view she made her first Picture Window pin, of the family house in Ohio: a young girl with long hair—the artist herself—is looking out the window.

From such personal images, Scherr was able to move on to do commissions for pins in this series. These are just as personal in subject matter, but the images come from clients. A husband commissioned her to do one as a gift for his wife. Scherr visited the couple's home, "even looking in the closets to see the colors of his wife's clothes." She met the family pet, saw the kind of furniture they had, and left with photos of his wife. The resulting pin grew out of all those images.

For a family of eleven grandchildren who commissioned her to do a picture of the Wailing Wall for their grandmother, Scherr found herself researching the image in the library. The Taj Mahal pin, on the other hand, is her own personal fantasy, the castle she knows she will never live in.

Although she still does these pieces from time to time, Scherr has since moved on to other series. In early 1983, she devised necklaces of beads made with cloisonné enamel and appliqué as well as some with inlaid metal. These posed formidable technical challenges. "In order to

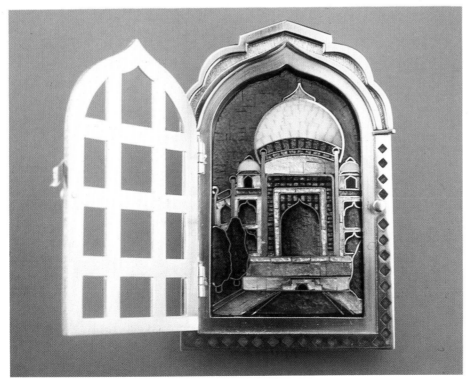

*Sydney Jo Scherr. "Taj Mahal" picture window pin, closed and open.
Sterling silver hinged frame with 14k gold; cloisonné enamel. (1986)*

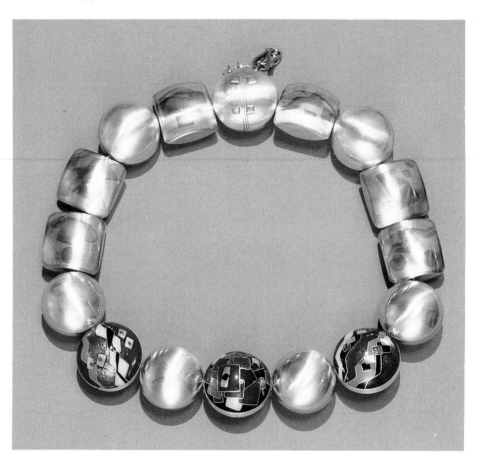

Sydney Jo Scherr. Necklace. Cloisonné and appliqué enamel. Marriage of metals: 18k yellow and 10k pink gold, nickel. (1985)

keep the lines of the inlay crisp and clean, I had to do the inlay on the formed hemisphere instead of flat sheet metal.''

During that same period, she set herself the task of making folded pieces. "There were about twelve pieces in this series. I wanted to see how distorted I could make the metal and still be able to enamel it.'' Each time she overcame the technical obstacles, she moved on to other, self-imposed challenges. What is unusual about this process is the attractiveness of the work, and the wearability of it. Jewelers experimenting with techniques and ideas are much rarer these days than they were in the 1970s, but what is rarer still is for the work to be so accessible. The person buying one of these pieces may marvel at the intricacies of the images or the infinite variety of the surfaces and yet be unaware of the extraordinary complexity of the work that made it possible. And that is exactly what sets the successful contemporary goldsmith apart from the art jeweler.

In her graduate thesis, Scherr set herself to "reassess the traditional boundaries of vitreous enamels. By nature," she writes, "enamels are a challenging medium—reacting to the atmosphere, temperature change and to the expansion and contraction of the underlying metal. Central to the technical questions was the use of applied patterning. The problems I hoped to solve involved elimination of the bezel as container and protective wall of the enamel and soldering in combination with enamel.

"Solder and enamel melt at the same temperature and cool at different rates. It became apparent that in order to develop the patterning, most surface tension would have to be eliminated. This was achieved by severely undercutting each pattern element so that the solder joint was much smaller than the surface image. Understanding this encouraged further investigation, which eventually evolved to mitred joints, angles, spheres, and undulating surfaces—moving far beyond what I thought were the limitations of an enameled surface."

Scherr has long since left that window behind her. She moved out of New York to a building in Raleigh that houses artists' studios. This subsidized commune, called Artspace, made her part of an instant community. Here, one of the requirements is that each studio be open to the public for fifteen hours a week. Scherr fulfills her required time by leaving her door open for two whole days and then working behind closed doors the rest of the time. But any time she needs company, she can call on one of the other thirty-five or forty artists, in all media, who have their studios there as well.

What goes around, comes around. Scherr's mother, the renowned jewelry teacher and designer Mary Ann Scherr, now lives in Raleigh as well, where she teaches at Duke University. And Sydney, who taught at Parson's School of Design in New York, now can often be found giving workshops on enameling at Penland School in North Carolina.

In her latest work, which she calls her "moody dark series," Scherr moves totally away from the imagery of her earlier pieces into totally abstract designs. She feels the pieces are menacing and moody, but adds, "I think these are my strongest pieces, since they are not about design or technical experimentation or ability. These come straight from the heart."

Sydney Jo Scherr. "Dark Brooch #2." Cloisonné enamel on fine silver with inlays. (1988)

THOMAS FARRELL
Philadelphia, Pennsylvania

The very nature of cloisonné, based on the pooling of color within wire cells, lends it ready recognition. That is, until you look at the work of Thomas Farrell. Although most of his work shown here employs the cloisonné technique (some uses champlevé), Farrell complicates the technique and blurs its identity through his own brand of alchemy. He evolved the technique over time, experimenting freely and generating a fair share of mistakes, until he created the look he was searching for. In the process, he says, "I probably have a twenty-pound scrap bin of enamel".

He begins with a base layer of black enamel, establishing a background for everything that will come after. He then adds a layer of fine gold or fine silver foil and fires that right on top of the base. Only then does he create a pattern of wire cells that will remain visible when the enamel work is complete. Layer after layer of enamels are then added on. "There are many layers on top of each other. I have a range of two hundred to three hundred enamels of varying opacity and translucency, which I use in a variety of ways." Farrell calls his technique "collaging." As he works, the look of the surface changes with each firing, and when he likes the combination, the piece is done. He doesn't work with drawings or sketches but aims instead for a certain color palette. "I have a general idea if I want a pale or vivid color range, but I never know where it will go until it's done. Even when I do it in a production format, every single one can be different."

Farrell came to jewelry in general, and enameling in particular, by chance. When he first went to college, he had in mind to be an anthropologist, but he saw that ten years of fieldwork would have to follow before he had achieved anything. Jewelry, an unlikely second choice, was a likely option simply because he was attending the State Univer-

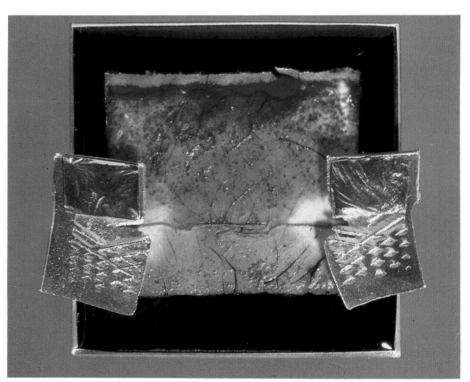

Thomas Farrell. Brooch. Enamel on copper with 24k gold foil; constructed setting of sterling silver, 14k gold. (1988)

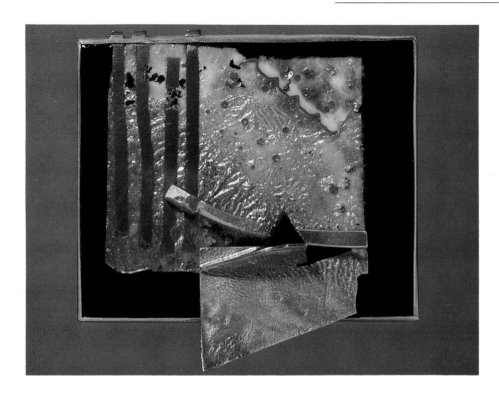

Thomas Farrell. Brooch. Enamel on copper with 24k gold foil, fine silver and copper; constructed sterling silver setting with copper and onyx. (1988)

sity at New Paltz with its strong metalsmithing and jewelry department, then under Kurt Matzdorf and Robert Ebendorf. By the time Farrell had given up on anthropology, he had already taken a couple of their courses and discovered he liked the medium. Barbara Mail, a classmate of his at New Paltz, was tremendously encouraging to him and often helped him work through some of the questions she had about his experiments. "I would say, 'what would happen if I did this?' and she would say, 'Do it'." A great deal of it was thrown away, but in the process he learned a great deal about what would and could work. He followed up his work at New Paltz with a workshop under Jamie Bennett at the Penland School of Crafts in North Carolina. (Bennett now teaches at New Paltz.)

He tried and rejected both painting and ceramics. "In school, painting meant canvases that were five feet by five feet; ceramics was too big and bulky." Instead, he was able to create the look he wanted in jewelry and specifically in enameling. "I started out doing marriage of metals because I wanted as much color as I could get. I found that was very limiting for me; it didn't give me the colors I wanted. You could get a wide variety of patinas, but it's hard to get something that is brilliant." He considered gemstones but found the cost prohibitive. In enamel, he was able to get the look and the color and control the price all at the same time. "It's nice to be able to create my own composition with color, line, form, and texture and not have to look for a stone to fulfill it."

Farrell fashions his enamels on silver rather than gold. While he says he likes the idea of creating something that is precious, he believes that his pieces, made on silver, will outlast those made of gold. "It won't be melted. People buy it not because of the value but because they want it. A lot of jewelry is being bought today because it has a certain value to it—diamonds and gold. I think gold is a justification for people to pay for something. The silver is not worth melting down."

Chapter 7

Granulation

The use of gold in its purest form—24 karat—is rare, even in those Eastern cultures whose jewelry is of a greater purity than is typical of the West. But the dilution that has taken place in the gold standard used for jewelry in the United States is considerable. We stand alone in the world in our acceptance of 14 karat as the norm for gold jewelry. For most of Europe, the standard is 18k gold. Not only is jewelry made of this more precious alloy more truly gold, it has a richness of color the American consumer rarely experiences. As a result, what the commercial jewelry marketplace has taught us to call "gold" is a pale, insipid version of gold's alluring warmth and vital color.

Eighteen karat gold is more nearly the standard in handcrafted jewelry. The additional cost of the higher-karat gold alloy is minimal when compared with the cost of the labor that is devoted to the creation of the piece. Whereas in commercial jewelry the raw materials are a major portion of the retail price, in crafted jewelry they often take a backseat to the artistry involved.

Goldsmiths love to work with gold because it responds to the touch. The greater the percentage of other metals added to the gold, the further one retreats from the qualities that make gold what it is.

If 18 karat is good, then 20 karat is better, and 22 better still. And this is the area where a growing number of goldsmiths have made their mark. Gold of this purity has a look of antiquity; it whispers of ancient Egypt, of Byzantium, of the Etruscans who flourished and perfected the art of the goldsmith in the area we know as Italy. Many contemporary goldsmiths who work in high-karat gold were trained in a common esthetic tradition. Their work is singular in its embrace of granulation, though they are much more than simply devotees of this one astonishing technique that connects this jewelry with the work of a millenium ago. They wrap their gold designs around gems of soft hues—not the jewel tones we associate with ruby, blue sapphire, and emerald, but the pastels of citrine, tourmaline, and the softer palette of fancy color sapphires—pinks and creamy yellows and muted greens.

Facing page:
Susan Reinstein. Amulet necklace #2. 22k gold pendant covered with granulation; set with 45-carat blue sapphire and small fancy color sapphires; suspended from handmade woven 22k white and yellow gold chain. (1986)

ROBERT KULICKE
New York City

Although few techniques or themes are the work of any one person, the very existence of granulation in contemporary goldsmithing may fairly be attributed to the interest and obsessive efforts of one man—Robert Kulicke.

The technique of granulation was known to the goldsmiths of antiquity some five thousand years ago and practiced until the eleventh century, but was lost to those who followed. Not until the mid nineteenth century, when a goldsmith named Castellani evolved his own technique (one that remains not totally understood) was granulation used on jewelry again. In those days, the goldsmith first had to form the tiny granules to be used as surface decoration, itself a time-consuming, labor-intensive process. Castellani, along with Guiliano, the jeweler most closely associated with him, used their technique to create superb works in the manner of the ancient goldsmiths. But Castellani guarded the secret of his discovery, and the specific recipe he used died with him.

In the twentieth century, various attempts were made to find a way of achieving the same look, and a British patent was applied for by H.A.P. Littledale in 1933 based on his rediscovery of the technique. In Germany, Hans Michael Wilm worked out a method that would prove crucial to Kulicke's effort. On our side of the Atlantic, teacher and

Bessie Jamieson. Neckpiece. 22k gold with granulation; emeralds; wire work. (1986) (Photo by Justin Kerr, courtesy of David & Langdale.)

Susan Reinstein. Earrings. 22k gold covered with granulation; aquamarines. (1985)

metalsmith John Paul Miller evidently was successful in devising a way to do granulation but always kept one crucial piece of information secret, making it impossible for anyone to actually learn it from him, a point raised by several of those who are familiar with his teaching. In this instance, the old saying, "Those who can, do, those who can't, teach," has been turned on its head. Here was someone who could "do," but wouldn't teach.

But Kulicke, an open man, generous beyond reason, had been studying the techniques of the ancient goldsmiths for years. His interest stemmed from a desire to understand how the great pieces of antiquity were made. He had no intent, at the time, of using his knowledge for any commercial purpose or even as potential instruction. His quest was the pure love of learning. In his struggle to understand the secret of granulation, he called on the knowledge of Patricia Davidson of the Brooklyn Museum, who had had some success with the process but was not able to produce with any constancy. By the end of 1968, Kulicke had evolved a method of granulating on a flat surface and immediately began sharing it with his students at the Scarsdale Studio Workshop School, and soon after at his own school, the Kulicke Cloisonné Workshop on upper Broadway in New York City. This marked a breakthrough in the teaching of this process in the United States. But the outstanding problem that remained unsolved was a formidable one: Kulicke still didn't know how to prevent the granules from rolling off a curved surface when the piece was being fused.

Since Kulicke's teaching method centered on sharing everything he knew about the process with his apprentices, who in turn shared it with their students, a growing group of goldsmiths was emerging who could do granulation. The key to the problem of the curved surface was solved outside the studio when, in 1972, Cornelia Roethel, a master goldsmith who had been taught in Germany by the son of Wilm, shared a crucial piece of information. This resolved the last remaining problem, and all that remained for Kulicke was to find a way to teach the technique. He and the apprentices worked additional years until they had developed the method used today, and I can personally attest to its brilliant simplicity. In one evening, Bob Kulicke taught me the basics of how to granulate on silver, and I walked out of the class with samples I had made.

Not only does the student learn how to granulate, she (almost all the students are female) also makes her own granules, as I learned to do. Kulicke feels that commercial granules—made by a supplier to the electronics industry—are boring in their very perfection, in their uniformity. The jewelers who make a living from high-karat gold jewelry, however, rely on the availability of the readymade version—making their own granules would be carrying the authenticity of the technique to a point of compulsion even these self-described obsessives find unnecessary. The consistent quality of the commercial granules enables them to line up row upon row of these tiny balls of gold—some so small they bring to mind fairy dust.

There is undoubtedly a thrill in making your own granules; the process evokes images of alchemy and magic. The metalsmith first slices up a sheet of metal into strips, then runs the strips through a rolling mill until they are thin enough to be bent with a fingernail. Each strip is then cut into tiny squares, all the same size. The squares are arranged on a charcoal block, and then, working with a finely tipped torch, heat is applied until the metal begins to glow. The heat is withdrawn a moment before the little square suddenly rolls itself up into a ball, and it's done. It's over in a matter of seconds. Do that a few hundred times and you have enough granules to begin making jewelry. Each student at the school does make her own granules.

With Kulicke himself instructing me, I mixed up a bit of hide glue, and arranged the granules on a metal plate in a pattern that he sketched onto my notebook. One of the crucial elements of the teaching process at the school differs entirely from the methods used in more conventional jewelry classes. The sequence of teaching is totally structured and, says Kulicke, "The student cannot fail. Only the teacher can fail." The teachers tell the student exactly what to make; everyone makes the same pieces according to samples they have in their hands, and in making those identical pieces, they learn the technique. This is not a school for design but one in which to master techniques. And in the work of some of its best-known graduates may be seen the wisdom and success of the method.

What my little lesson proved to me was what I had been told ten years earlier when I first visited the school: this exquisite technique could be taught to virtually anyone with reasonable dexterity and infinite patience.

The school has changed names twice since it opened, first becoming the Kulicke–Stark Academy when Bob Kulicke married his second wife, Jean Stark, and taught her jewelry making. More recently, after he and Jean Stark dissolved both their business and personal relationships, Kulicke turned the school over to Bessie Jamieson. It's now called The Jewelry Arts Institute. Today, without question, The Jewelry Arts Institute can fairly be called the mecca of granulation and cloisonné, and among its faithful are the "designer" names who inhabit this high-karat world. The paths they have taken are diverse, as will be seen in the profiles that follow.

JOSEPH ENGLISH
Newton, New Jersey

Joseph English was introduced to granulation in a manner typical of the Kulicke school—he was dating Bob Kulicke's daughter from his first marriage, Frederica, known as Freddie. They married, and English became one of Bob Kulicke's first apprentices, contributing a great deal to evolving methods for teaching chain making, another of the school's specialties. English also helped to devise methods for teaching classical setting and the techniques of granulation.

English recalls some of the experiments that went on during the process of coming up with a teachable granulation method. "Originally when I started working with Bob, we both came to the conclusion that silver granulation was a fusing process entirely. There was a surface flow, and no copper solution was used. It's done in a kiln. With the kiln, you can control the heat. If it's fifty degrees too high, it's a puddle." Actually, as I learned by my own hand, the granules melt blob-like onto the surface rather than standing up crisply and distinctly. "Fifty degrees too low, and it doesn't flow at all. With silver, unlike soldering, once you have it in your mind it always happens the same way. Granulation always occurs at the same temperature. It's just the skill of learning, melting a few pieces [in error].

"The technique I use is very teachable [and is the technique the school continues to use]. You mix an alloy of one-half pennyweight copper, one-and-a-half pennyweights silver, and twenty-two pennyweights of gold. I use a solution of glue, soldering flux, and water—ten

Joseph and Smadar English. Necklace. 22k gold with granulation; green and pink tourmalines and fancy sapphires. (Photo courtesy of Aaron Faber Gallery.) (1990)

to fifteen parts water. I leave it in the kiln for five minutes until it oxidizes. The copper in the gold oxidizes and turns black. This was an easy technique to show students. When you heat with the torch, the oxide burns off." At this moment, the granulation occurs, as I observed when working with silver. And as English concludes, "Most of the secret of granulation is skill." That is certainly the only secret remaining, since the technical and chemical secrets are available to anyone who wants to enroll in class. Kulicke says it took him and his associates twenty years to evolve a method that they now teach in a year.

English taught at Kulicke–Stark until 1976, when he moved to Soho to open his own school, the Jewelry Workshop on Spring Street. Among his students at Kulicke–Stark was Susan Reinstein, who went on to open her own jewelry shops. Among the teachers working for Bob Kulicke was Luna Felix, who taught the chain-making class. She followed English to the school on Spring Street before setting out in her own business. English ran the Jewelry Workshop from 1976 to 1981, then reopened it in 1984 and ran it for another three years until the triple threat of making his own jewelry, operating the school, and spending time with his wife, Smadar, and his young children, forced him to close it again. In the 1970s, one of the students was Stephen Paul Adler, a controversial figure in this little jewelry world, whose professional training is in psychology. He would figure largely in a wonderful little gallery called Byzantium that was born, flared brightly, and then died all within a short space of time.

The marketing of contemporary goldsmithing at the high end of the price range offers a narrow slice of an already narrow market, but it has evolved into a very special part of the studio jeweler's world. This is a group that embraces the physicalness of jewelry making. They immerse themselves in the metal as a form of meditation. Most sell their work through a limited number of galleries and also work extensively with private clients. Their production is so small, in terms of sheer numbers of pieces, that they only need one or two successful outlets.

CECILIA BAUER
New York City

Cecilia Bauer emerged from the apprentice program at Kulicke–Stark, where she continues to teach on a part-time basis as a needed respite from the intense concentration necessary to make her own jewelry. Her granulation method is a refinement of the basic skill she was taught and now teaches. The line between chemist and goldsmith blurs when one talks to a granulator; for the goldsmiths, it's a practical application of the high school chemistry we have all long since forgotten.

Bauer describes the physical process she follows: "I copperplate the granules. This raises the melting temperature of the granule itself because the copper has a higher melting point than the gold. The backsheet [the plate of metal onto which the granules are arranged] I keep reticulating—I heat it up and the copper oxidizes and comes to the surface. Then, nitric acid eats off the copper." As a result, the surface of the backsheet actually contains a very thin layer of 24k gold that melts at a slightly lower temperature than the rest of the sheet, which is 22k gold. Bauer finds this creates more of a balance between the melting temperature of the sheet and the granules. "When you fire with

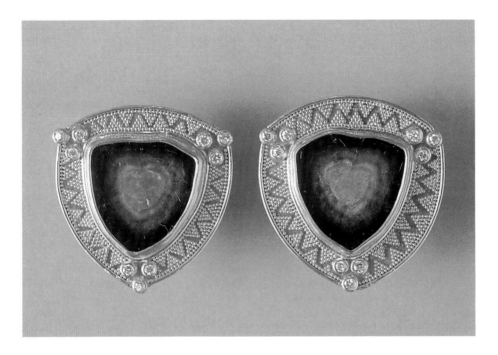

Cecilia Bauer. Earrings. 22k gold; zigzag granulation patterns; watermelon tourmaline, diamonds. Two views. (1988) (Photo courtesy of Artium.)

the torch, the skin of copper pulls off the granules and deposits itself at the point of contact. It creates its own alloy to fuse it to the gold. The bond that it creates melts at a lower temperature than any of the materials you are using. It is, therefore, a solderless solder."

The basic method involves the use of hide glue to lightly tack the granules to the backplate before they're fired. The glue is mixed with water and flux. When the piece is fired, the glue burns off completely without leaving an ash to get in the way of the bond. For different karatages of gold, slight variations of this technique are employed.

Beyond the chemistry, the skill involved focuses on the placement of the granules. Bauer says, "I get lost when I do it; it becomes very compulsive. It's very meditative. Your concentration has to be total. It's obsessive; when I do a pattern, I don't want to leave it until it gets to a point [of completion]." That point may be reached in the wee hours of the morning, but no matter. Considering that a pair of earrings with very fine granulation may require more than fifty hours to place the granules, it's not possible to do all of them in one sitting. For this reason, Bauer must find a place to stop that feels comfortable—perhaps a section of a pattern that is complete in itself. Asking how many granules are on an earring is like asking how many angels can dance on the head of a pin—the surface isn't much bigger, and the task infinitely more difficult. But the granulators don't think in such terms. They are devoted to the pattern and will do whatever it takes to achieve it. Most, like Bauer, learned all they know about jewelry making under the tutelage of Kulicke. "I learned all the ancient techniques, chain making, making granulation. I have no other jewelry experience at all. I think most of the people who work in this tradition and go there find the same experience. This is the only way I'm interested in jewelry. I've tried casting. I don't like it for myself."

While Bauer was getting her career going, however, she did benchwork at home for various 47th Street jewelers, and she appreciates what they did for her own work: "I worked like crazy doing production, all of which was very valuable and taught me a lot of things. It made

Cecilia Bauer. Long earrings. 22k gold; rows of granulation separated by wire work; patterns of granulation on round drops. (1989) (Photo courtesy of Artium.)

me fast, it made me clean and accurate. If I was going to make money at it, I had to be able to do it. I couldn't take two hours to put a post on an earring; I had to get fifty posts on in an hour, or I wouldn't make any money."

Now, working entirely on her own, Bauer can indulge her own ideas. "This absorbed me in the way I like to work. I came from graphic design and switched into this. I guess graphic design was a lot the same, too. I worked in etchings and engravings. Little picky, precise kind of things."

Bauer and the handful of goldsmiths who feature granulation in their work are able to produce so few pieces a year that finding a market is no longer the issue. She estimates her annual production to be no more than one hundred pieces of jewelry. Bauer is one of the few who works entirely on her own, without assistants or employees of any kind. She works almost entirely on private commissions.

At the other end of the high-karat area of goldsmithing is Susan Reinstein, herself an alumnus of Kulicke–Stark, who has turned her talent for design into a business employing a half-dozen goldsmiths, two shops in New York, and outlets in Japan.

At one point, Bauer was one of those people working for Reinstein, doing both chainwork and granulation. As Bauer says, "We're all a little group that came out of the same place and end up traveling in the same circles."

SUSAN REINSTEIN
New York City

Spiraling out from that circle were an unlikely twosome—Susan Reinstein and Stephen Paul Adler. Adler, a student at the Jewelry Workshop during the period when Reinstein was running the little gallery there, was drawn to the idea of a jewelry business. A genius at self-promotion, he was by profession a therapist and had taken jewelry-making courses as a pleasant respite. In short order he gathered together a group of jewelers who shared a common aesthetic vision and offered their work in an extraordinary venue, the shop called Byzantium.

Like Camelot, for one brief, shining moment, Byzantium glistened on the contemporary jewelry scene, and then it simply disappeared. Byzantium was the creation of Adler, Reinstein, and Bud Hart, a business partner. Determining who actually was responsible for the shop and its output is like counting the grains of sand in a shifting dune; it's never quite within your grasp. But no matter, the jewelry designs that emanated from the shop well suited the name and exemplified the classical look of high-karat gold in the Kulicke mode. The designs were showcased in a miniscule shop that may have seemed smaller than it was because it was always full of visitors. The unlikely location made its success seem as if the owners were laughing at the gods. While New York is known for its shifting neighborhoods, down-and-out one day, trendy the next, Byzantium's location in an old Italian section of lower Manhattan was truly quixotic. The shop, a precious fortress filled with exquisite jewelry, was housed in a tenement.

When it opened in 1980, Byzantium was an overnight success; it blazed briefly and beautifully and then, within three years, it was history. Adler went on to other ventures, opening up in the basement of a

Susan Reinstein. "Magic Carpet" bracelet. 22k gold with granulation; aquamarines; six hinged panels. (1984)

shop on Madison Avenue for some months, then selling by appointment only. Reinstein sold privately for two years out of her Soho loft.

When Susan Reinstein left Byzantium, she had established a clientele with a desire for her jewelry but no longer had a place to showcase it. Equally important, she had established a relationship with Brian Ross, a gemstone dealer, whom she met during the Byzantium era. He offered her the pick of his stones, enabling her to unleash her artistic ideas without the pressure of economics.

As the two of them formed a bond, both professionally and personally, her collection of finished pieces grew, both in quantity and in importance. She continued to present her work at trunk shows on the road. These gave her an outlet for her work but created their own problems: for Reinstein, being on the road was a nerve-wracking experience because of the pressure to sell in such a brief space of time and the ever present potential security risk.

She and Ross needed a permanent home for the work. Their dream was to have a shop similar to that opened by Robert Lee Morris, the designer who pioneered the showing of craft jewelry in Soho. Indeed, it was while walking home from a visit to his shop that they found their own site: a virtual shell of a space, one that probably hadn't been improved since the day it was built many decades before. In this seemingly unpromising site on Prince Street, a block that retains the old flavor of the area, Reinstein/Ross opened for business on May l, 1985, two years after Byzantium closed.

The shop gave them total control over every aspect of the work—

*Susan Reinstein.
Earrings. 22k gold covered
with granulation; rubies
and chrysoprase drops.
(1987)*

the jewelry was designed, made, displayed, and sold within the same space. The workshop was set up downstairs, out of sight but within easy reach. The main floor was devoted to displaying and selling Reinstein's designs.

The relationship between goldsmith and client is extremely strong here. Both sides enjoy nourishing that closeness. Unlike the road trips, where decisions had to be made on the spot, relationships in the shop could develop over time through repeated visits.

Still, there was no guarantee that this trendy neighborhood, with its lively mix of art galleries and restaurants and the booming weekend crowd they draw, would attract the particular audience this work needs. The Soho customers were on the cutting edge of art and design. Would they respond to the subtleties of Reinstein's interpretation of the classical, high-karat gold look? It requires the customer to make a serious commitment to a quiet statement of style. Although Reinstein was prepared to put in the time to educate customers, the shop on Prince Street was a success from the first day. An independent goldsmith put herself on the map, selling only her own designs. It is an achievement that may be singular in the business. I know of no other store in the field of handmade, high-karat gold jewelry. The few craft jewelry stores that do exist feature the work of a number of jewelers, perhaps ten or twenty, or even more. The variety of styles widens the appeal to the public. A shop featuring just one jeweler's work is inherently limiting.

This success was followed by a second store uptown on Madison Avenue. Although Reinstein and Ross saw themselves as downtown people, an analysis of their customer list revealed that the clients for the higher-priced items were from the Madison Avenue area. Once again, they chose a side street rather than the main avenue. Downtown, they preferred quiet Prince Street to throbbing West Broadway; uptown, it was a store front just off Madison Avenue.

In addition to bringing the work closer to the customer, the new store provided two important bonuses: it was deep enough to provide workshop space on the same level as the gallery itself, and it had a garden in the back. The customer who enters the shop can see the work being made just behind the display area; and looking straight through, he or she can also see the outdoor sitting area. This openness is refreshing and virtually unique in the jewelry world. It has the feeling of a custom tailor, one who fits the work to the body. In this very personal end of the jewelry world, it provides the ultimate connection between maker and wearer. Here, the goldsmiths can be seen alloying gold, pulling strips of gold through a rolling mill, bending over the benches, making jewelry.

Unlike most high-karat gold craft jewelers, Reinstein has control over the colored stones she uses. For two months of every year, she and Ross travel to Asia on a buying trip. Much of that time is spent patiently sitting in the heat and dust of Thailand and India looking at parcel after parcel of rough-colored gems. From the sea of colors they select stones that will eventually find their way into Reinstein's designs. Because they are always explaining the jewelry to customers, they find it easier to work almost exclusively with sapphires, a stone that comes in an enormous range of colors. Although sapphire is associated primarily with the color blue, this fairly hard gemstone occurs in a broad spectrum of colors, from buttery yellows to forest greens. Since they are all

Susan Reinstein. Neckpiece. 22k gold clasp with granulation; fancy color sapphires; attached to strands of pearls and gemstone beads. (1984) (Photo by Cora Duback.)

the same mineral, they have the same degree of hardness. This eases the difficulty of setting since they respond similarly to the heat and pressure of the various goldsmithing techniques.

The palette of sapphires allows Reinstein freedom to use what she considers her principal talent as a colorist, combining color and shape into pleasing arrangements. Describing her method of designing, Reinstein says "I don't sketch. It's more spontaneous to work directly in the metal rather than working from a drawing." She likens the process to architecture. Each piece is built step by step, wire by wire. But it begins with the gemstones.

"It's always the colors and the shapes of the stones that determines the color of the gold I use." In alloying the gold, Ross has worked out a particular formula that gives the metal a tone they call apricot. He brings his degree in metallurgy to this task and cheerfully pores over formulas looking for the ideal combination of color and strength. The unusual warmth of the apricot gold complements the cognac and champagne color range of many of the sapphires. After selecting and arranging the stones for each piece of jewelry, Reinstein directs the bezeling of the stones in 22k gold wire.

A backplate is cut out from a sheet of gold that was alloyed and milled in the shop. The stones, each in its protective and decorative gold bezel, are soldered to it. If the piece is to be enhanced with granulation, the backplate is always 22k yellow gold because, Reinstein says, "I was taught to granulate 22k gold at Kulicke–Stark." Granulation offers a texture in harmony with the soft look of high-karat gold wire and the pastels of the sapphires.

Along the way, decisions are made as to the type of hinge or clasp the piece needs, and that is made in a matching gold alloy. Even the solder used to join elements together is made in the shop. And all of this is within view of not only the customers but also the salespeople. It is a rare experience in the jewelry world, where the making of jewelry and its consumption are usually as far removed as the growing of an orange from the glass of juice at the breakfast table.

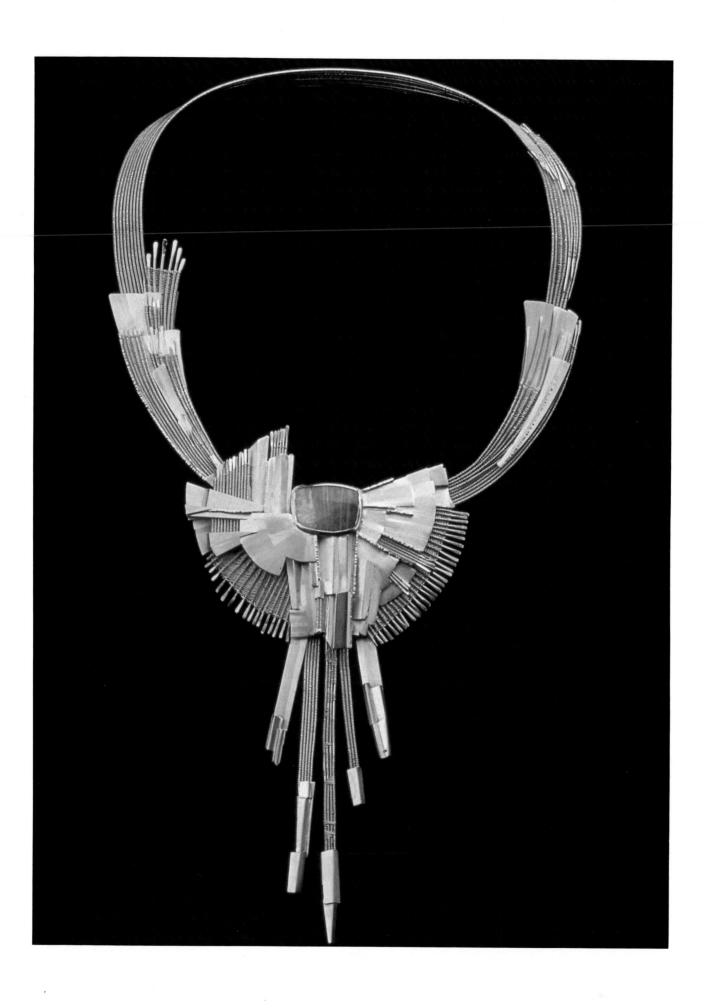

Chapter 8

High-Karat Gold

For commercial jewelers, gold is a commodity. For contemporary goldsmiths, gold is a magical metal that lets them fly higher, faster, more beautifully. The intrinsic value of gold, the market price that is a function of the world's faith or lack of it, in itself may not be divorced from gold's real qualities. It is priced high because it is desirable, and it is desirable because it allows artists to do things that no other metal can do nearly so well. Gold is not merely beautiful, although it is undeniably beautiful. It is also ductile, the most malleable of metals. It may be stretched and pounded and drawn into the finest, thinnest, narrowest of forms, yet it retains its essential qualities. It may be cast, or die struck, or forged, or hammered; yet, with a flick of a cloth, its luster returns. It is impervious to all acids, save sulfuric acid, guaranteeing that it will survive the hazards of time. It tells us the story of our own history through objects that have escaped its only enemy: being melted down and transformed into something else.

VICKI EISENFELD
Avon, Connecticut

The marriage of metals work of the 1970s has evolved into a sophisticated integration of technique with artistic vision and the use of high-karat gold. Nowhere is this more apparent than in the upscale designs of Vicki Eisenfeld, who maintains a studio in the Farmington Valley Arts Center in Avon, Connecticut.

Trying to place Eisenfeld within a single area of goldsmithing presents an interesting challenge: Should she be grouped with those who weave wire? Or with the high-karat makers? Or the marriage of metals practitioners? The work variously combines all these elements, and proves that the overriding factor in contemporary jewelry is not tech-

Facing page:
Vicki Eisenfeld. Neckpiece. 14k, 18k, and 22k golds; marriage of metals, interlacing wire work; boulder opal. (1989) (Photo by Tim Nighwander.)

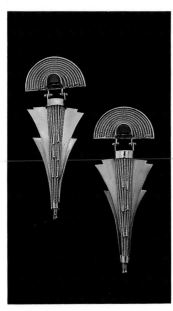

Vicki Eisenfeld. Earrings. 14k, 18k, and 22k pink, yellow, and white golds; marriage of metals and wire work; garnets. (1989) (Photo by Tim Nighwander.)

nique or material but the goldsmith's individuality. Technical skill is at the service of the idea, not the other way around. Those who lose sight of this fact are doomed to become mere mechanical manipulators of metal.

Eisenfeld has never concerned herself with the terms that apply to the wire work she employs in her dramatic designs. "I don't use a loom, so I'm not sure if it should be called woven," she says. "I do work the wires over and under, and that's weaving, isn't it?" Leaving the question of language for others to decide, Eisenfeld is content to work out her ideas in a variety of techniques and a rich array of golds. She combines 14k, 18k, and 22k golds, in pink, yellow, and white gold alloys. Although this tricolor gold palette is the mainstay of some of the most banal commercial jewelry, Eisenfeld makes of it something wholly new. In some pieces, she incorporates the additional subtleties of sterling silver and fine silver, increasing the range of whites beyond that of white gold. These fine differences in tone and the shadings that they make possible are an outgrowth of her wire work. In the late 1980s, before she began to use marriage of metals, Eisenfeld was exploring the possibilities of metal colors exclusively with wire work.

With the addition of marriage of metals, she was able to extend the sweep of her pieces and at the same time add the richer look of color she was seeking. The scope of her design vision broadened as pieces incorporated sections of marriage of metals with wire work, each seeming to grow naturally out of the other. The various techniques in combination make these pieces extremely complex in design and execution; yet, there is no sense of the work becoming overburdened or of being worked simply to display her ability.

Vicki Eisenfeld. Brooch. 14k and 22k golds, sterling silver, fine silver; marriage of metals and wire work. (1988) (Photo by Tim Nighwander.)

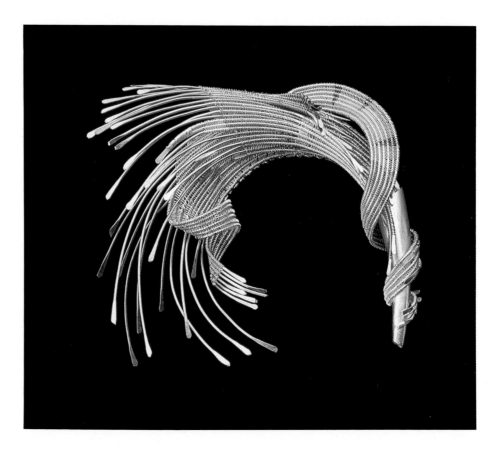

*Vicki Eisenfeld.
Neckpiece. 14k, 18k, and
22k golds; sterling silver,
fine silver; marriage of
metals, interlacing wire
work; citrine. (1989)
(Photo by Tim
Nighwander.)*

Eisenfeld feels her use of marriage of metals has been evolution-
ary, a process the basics of which she learned years before she incorporated it into her work. Similarly, her wire work, the basics of which
she learned more than ten years ago at a workshop given by Arline
Fisch. She didn't apply the technique to her designs for many years.
Then, one day, she simply found herself with the wires in hand and the
weaving, or twining, began. Putting it all together—the marriage of

metals and the wire work—was a conscious decision to bring more color into the work. The pleasure of working in high-karat gold—the greater flexibility of the higher-karat gold wire—was essentially for the color, but the higher value of the metal was not overlooked. It's difficult for an artist who puts so much labor into a piece of jewelry to recoup that effort at the point of sale. For Eisenfeld, the value added by the 22k gold helped in the realm of sheer economics.

The maturity of Eisenfeld's work has been hard won; like other female goldsmiths, she has had to juggle the diverse and intense demands of home and family. In her case, there was the added disruption of frequent moves as her husband, a doctor specializing in the cases of sick infants, went through medical school, an internship, and the Army, and finally set up a practice. For Eisenfeld, who graduated from Carnegie Mellon University with a Bachelor of Fine Arts, the challenge was to continue her jewelry education whenever and wherever she found it.

She managed to attend the course with Fisch at Penland, a metals class with Michael Croft, and a stone-setting workshop with Deborah Aguado. All of them were important; all of them added to her jewelry vocabulary. Over time, she absorbed, experimented, and translated their various teachings into her own rich and varied style. But they were important to her for more than the actual techniques they taught. "When we were living in Huntsville, Alabama, I took a course with William Harper. He wondered if that kind of teaching helped anyone really," she recounts. "That's what kept me alive!" For jewelers so far away from centers of metalsmithing, from museums, from the lively interchange that artists need to imbibe regularly, such contacts are nothing less than a lifeline.

The ability of jewelers to take the same materials, in this case various colors of 18k and 14k gold, and to express wholly different thoughts offers a sense of discovery to the viewer. Our expectations of goldsmiths are more limited than they ought to be, a reflection of the visual and technical narrowness of commercial jewelry. Yet painters all use the same raw materials and still come up with totally individual expressions. Why should we expect anything less of the contemporary goldsmith?

ROSS COPPELMAN
Yarmouth Port, Massachusetts

Two other practitioners of high-karat gold are Ross Coppelman and Lilly Fitzgerald, both of Massachusetts. Through the years that I have watched their work evolving, they have sometimes seemed very close in concept and in execution. Now, they have moved into decidedly different visual treatments, while still using the same materials. Both work in 22k gold and make bold use of gemstones in their designs, but Coppelman's pieces have moved into a look I call progressive antiquity —back to the future, if you will. He works the gold surface intensively through heating. In response, the surface takes on a rough-hewn look; it appears to have traveled through millenia to reach today's marketplace.

The outline of each piece is more rugged looking, as well. There is a sense of spontaneity, albeit well controlled, adding to the feeling of

Ross Coppelman. Brooch. 22k gold, watermelon tourmaline, cabochon tourmaline drop, pearls, bezel-and prong-set diamonds. (1987)

the piece as an artifact, a feeling Coppelman particularly likes. When fabricating his 22k gold work, he says, he joins elements by heating. High-karat gold becomes almost a living entity when heat is applied skillfully. "Things fuse together at that karat. The whole surface of the metal bubbles. It gives my work a soft yellow finish that reminds me of artifacts. It's the same principal as reticulation. Reticulation is more complicated because you have to prepare the surface of 18k. You don't with 22k. All you do is heat." While Coppelman uses some 14k and 18k gold to give added strength to what he calls the "underpinnings," everything you see on the surface is 22k gold.

The work is a far cry from his beginning pieces, circle rings of sterling silver wire, typical hippie jewelry. "I moved slowly into gold, 14k gold, and it was very commercial looking. The first real departure came when I tried to fit an onyx disc into a bezel and it shattered. The pieces that it broke into were raw and so much more interesting, and I started hitting discs with hammers. It was the first time my work took on a real different look. I became emotionally involved. It was the first time I did not do the predictable. This was the first departure. The work has become a real expression of the best parts of me."

It took Coppelman years to find the feelings he wanted to express as well as a medium in which to express them. He originally expected to express them more literally, in writing. "I majored in English and psychology; I thought I wanted to write but had nothing to write about. After college, I was really lost." He had, he notes wryly, a "Harvard degree and no prospects."

But he had seen the vision of what his work would some day be-

Ross Coppelman. Brooch. Bezel-set rose quartz, pearls, prong-set diamonds, 22k gold. (1985)

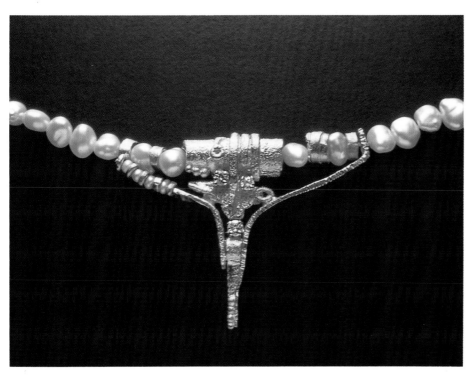

Ross Coppelman. Neckpiece. Textured 22k gold pendant integrated into strand of Biwa pearls. (1981)

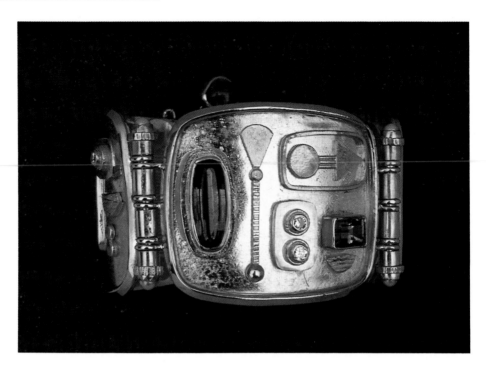

Ross Coppelman. Hinged cuff bracelet. 22k gold, tourmalines, pearls, diamonds; motifs fused to surface. (1989)

come in the showcases of a jeweler named Miye Matsukata. "She had a small jewelry studio in Boston. She was a respected goldsmith in high-karat gold, organic, handwrought pieces."

For Coppelman, the work was a revelation. "I never saw anything like that, the color of the gold and texture of the gold which she achieved not through heating, like I do, but I think through hammering." He never approached her to find out. "I was much too shy to go upstairs to talk to her." (When she died in 1981, her studio and her design ideas were continued by two goldsmiths, Alexandra Watkins and Nancy Michel, under her studio name, Atelier Janiye.)

By the time I saw Coppelman's work at Rhinebeck in the early 1970s, he had found his own voice. The way he incorporates gemstones into his jewelry is a textbook example of the difference between contemporary goldsmithing and commercial work. The stones are highlighted, enveloped, embraced within his original mountings, but they never seem to be used simply in order to add value. There is a sense of harmony among the various materials that sets the work apart from and above more traditional work. The design and the technique are part of the equation, but I believe it is in the approach that the inherent difference between the contemporary goldsmiths and traditional jewelers is most evident.

If there is a mystery to how this happens, perhaps it is answered in the places where goldsmiths choose to live. Coppelman, who was born in Brookline, Massachusetts, makes his home in the town of Yarmouth Port. It is a summer resort, totally tied to the seasons. As he says, "There is no market here. The work I love to make I have to go to New York to sell. And that's fine." But as for living, he's always happy to go back home. "It's so calm here."

LILLY FITZGERALD
Spencer, Massachusetts

The gems in Lilly Fitzgerald's pieces are more dominant; the high-karat gold is used as a framework. "I use the stones for color because I don't paint any more. The stones are the main attraction for me." That could also be said of the most traditional, high-end jewelry coming from such makers as Harry Winston or Bulgari. But Fitzgerald is using the stones for their color, not simply to create pieces with monetary value. She seeks out the color of turquoise, tourmaline, lapis, pale moonstone, and vivid opal. Fitzgerald, who studied fine art in college, developed such a lively business making jewelry for friends that she left school in her third year to become a full-time jeweler. She is essentially self-taught, and although she has taken some jewelry courses, says, "I work it out at the bench."

In the 1980s, she created a series of pieces with little cities rising up in perfect miniature from the borders. Of those pieces, she says, "People in New York think it's New York, people in Chicago think it's Chicago." Fitzgerald, who lives and works in the small town of Spencer, Massachusetts, about forty miles west of Boston and what she calls "a cultural void," didn't have a real city in mind when she created the pieces. Interestingly, these generic constructions allow the clients to personalize the images.

Lilly Fitzgerald. Brooch. 22k gold, black opal, diamonds. (1987) (Photo by Jonathan Kannair.)

Lilly Fitzgerald. Brooch.
22k gold with granulation;
Mabe pearl, diamonds.
(1986) (Photo by Jonathan
Kannair.)

Fitzgerald sells nearly all of her work directly to the customer, either at the Philadelphia Craft Show, "when I get in," or at a show she arranges for herself. She takes a room in a fine hotel in New York, sends out invitations to her list of clients, and works directly with the clients. "It's better than waiting to hear if I've gotten into the Armory show. I can set my own schedule. When I do shows, I don't get time to talk to anybody."

For the future, Fitzgerald's goal is "to make make fewer and fewer pieces, more important pieces. I make probably fifty to sixty pieces a year; I would like to do about ten."

JUDITH KAUFMAN
Avon, Connecticut

The restraint and cool precision of Fitzgerald's pieces are a world apart from the work of Judith Kaufman, who also features colored stones in her work. Kaufman's bold designs, with their rugged shapes and craggy surfaces, reflect a completely different artistic vision. Unlike Fitzgerald, who began working in 18k gold and moved up to 22k, Kaufman started working in silver some fifteen years ago and then began to combine silver and brass to express her design ideas and get the mix of colors she wanted.

"I wanted to work more creatively; I couldn't afford to make mistakes in gold. I was using silver and brass and got a feeling for the combination of metals. Finally, I came to gold. It's still very difficult just to hack into a piece of gold. I don't sketch. I start out with sheet and wire." For Kaufman, who says she is "a frustrated painter," working directly in the metal is like drawing in gold. The resulting designs bear a family resemblance to one another, but Kaufman cannot explain where the elements originate. What do the flames represent? She doesn't know—"It just happened." Perhaps from things she's seen, places she's been—among them, Spain, Greece, and Israel. "I like ancient and futuristic."

There is a sense of artifact here, as in Coppelman's work; yet, again, the style is completely different and identifiable as being Kauf-

Judith Kaufman. Brooch.
22k gold and fine silver,
tourmalines, Roman glass,
freshwater pearls,
rhodolite garnet. (1989)
(Photo by Ralph Gabriner.)

man's and no one else's. The texture is matte but smooth, unlike the work of both Coppelman and Fitzgerald, for example. And while the stones are prominent, they don't dominate the work but instead add their own elements of beauty to the mix. Whether she is using beryl, tourmalines, boulder opal, aquamarine, or even pieces of ancient Roman glass, Kaufman's painterly eye stands her in good stead. The colors and especially the shapes of the stones she chooses are totally integrated into the goldwork. The metalwork, in various colors and karatages of gold, harmonizes with the color and structure of the stones.

Kaufman's pieces, even when they employ wire work and high-karat gold, could never be mistaken for anyone else's work. Nor should the sense of primitivism in her designs be mistaken for carelessness in execution; she is totally in command of her method and materials.

The maturity of Kaufman's work is hard earned; she began making jewelry in high school and, with a two-week basic metalsmithing course under her belt, started selling jewelry to high school friends. She soon had four salespeople in different high schools taking orders for her jewelry.

Her "graduate" work stretched out over many years. For five years, she traveled around Connecticut and the Northeast, selling her work at small weekend craft fairs. A job doing "very basic chores" at a jewelry repair shop in Hartford followed, then another as both designer and saleswoman for another jeweler. In 1976, she opened her own studio at the Farmington Valley Arts Center, where twenty-three artists, including jeweler Vicki Eisenfeld, have studios. The Center was created from an old dynamite factory. This may be a mini-trend; Susan Sanders has her studio at the Torpedo Factory in Alexandria, Virginia, another artists' complex.

The craft shows Kaufman attends now are top rung: she has shown at Springfield on an almost yearly basis, twice at Baltimore, and twice at the small and select Smithsonian show in Washington, D.C. In 1990, she was one of the three Society of North American Goldsmiths winners, earning a space in the New Designer Room at the Jewelers of America show in New York.

Judith Kaufman. Earrings. 18k yellow gold, 14k pink gold. (1988) (Photo by Ralph Gabriner.)

Judith Kaufman. Brooch. Roman glass, indicolite, Biwa pearls, emeralds, green and yellow golds of 18k, 20k, 22k. (1990) (Photo by Ralph Gabriner.)

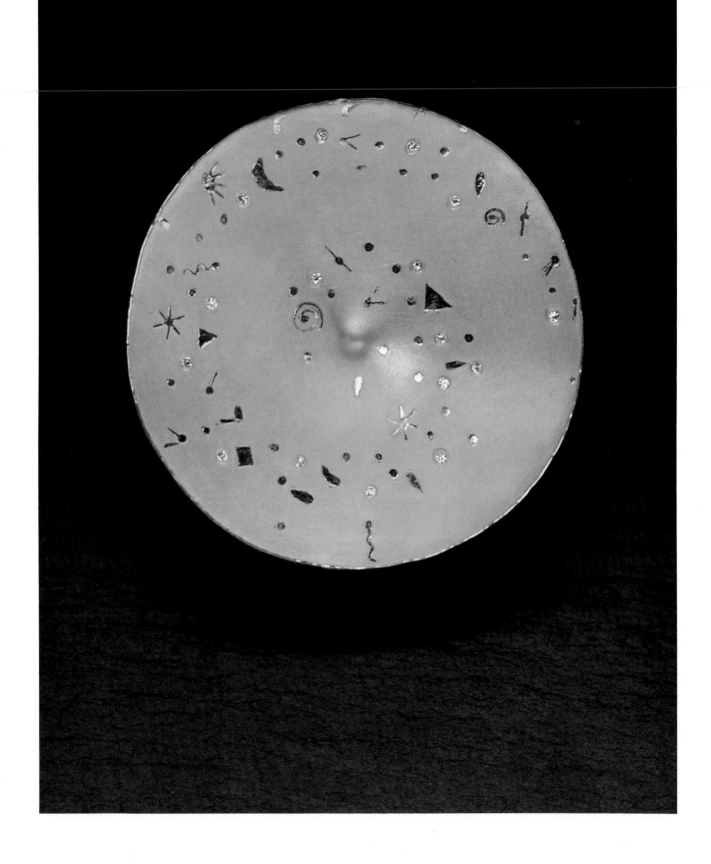

Chapter 9

Surfaces

It is useful to consider the look of commercial jewelry in order to understand and appreciate the varied surfaces created by the contemporary goldsmith. Traditional gold work is nearly all made by casting. When an element, or an entire piece, is removed from the mold, it is buffed or polished on a wheel to remove any roughness resulting from the casting process. The polishing also brings out the gleam of the metal. Fourteen-karat gold, the standard for most jewelry purchased in the United States, is a relatively hard alloy that permits the jeweler to buff the surface to a polish. The shiny, reflective look has come to be thought of as "real gold." But when a higher-karat gold is used, there is a lushness to the color of the metal that obviates the need for a bright surface. The higher the karat, the richer the yellow color, but the alloy is softer and less tolerant of polishing. For both practical and esthetic reasons, jewelers who work in high-karat gold often prefer to work the surface by a variety of mechanical and chemical methods. In the process, they achieve "signature" textures that can be read by those familiar with the work the way an art connoisseur can recognize the brush strokes of an Old Master.

These surface treatments are achieved by methods learned in the classroom and by freewheeling, ongoing experimentation by the goldsmiths. Some "pickle" the metal with chemicals to make it pucker; others roll a sheet of gold through a mill with a textured material to imprint the look of that texture. The material can be virtually anything that will fit in the rolling mill—fabric, window screening, coarse wrapping paper. Heat from a small torch will cause the surface to buckle in interesting ways, although the penalty accompanying this method is that the surface may simply melt into a puddle. Experience is the harsh taskmaster. While it is true that if you spoil a piece of gold you can always melt it to reclaim the metal, the sad fact is that many hours of

Facing page:
Barbara Heinrich. "Milky Way" brooch. 18k gold; matte surface with bright polish details; diamonds set flush. (1990) (Photo by Tim Callahan.)

*Stephani Briggs. Pin/
pendant. 18k, 22k golds,
tourmaline. (1988) (Photo
by Mark Rockwood.)*

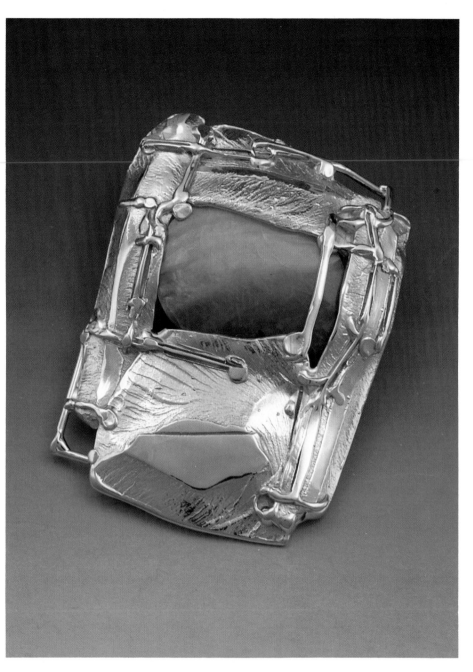

John Heller. Brooch. 14k gold, matrix opal. (1989)

work will be melted as well. Few surfaces are as intensely worked as
the tiny few square inches of a piece of gold jewelry.

Contemporary jewelers rarely use platinum in their work because
it does not readily lend itself to manipulation. Platinum's melting point
is so high that it requires completely different tools and torches. For
most jewelers, gold is the consummate metal. Jewelers who work in
high-karat gold often use lower karatages for the findings, a catchall
term for the joinings that permit jewelry to be worn (clasps, earring
backs, bails for necklaces, and the like). This puts the strength of the
lower-karat alloy where it is most needed, and out of sight, while the
beauty of the higher-karat gold remains on view.

BARBARA HEINRICH
Rochester, New York

One goldsmith who has found a unique way to bring out gold's innate qualities is Barbara Heinrich. Now living in the suburbs of Rochester, New York, Heinrich was born in Heilbron, West Germany. Her technical virtuosity was earned first in the demanding school in Pforzheim, followed up by a Master of Fine Arts at the School for American Craftsmen program at Rochester Institute of Technology (RIT), but she describes her design sensibility as American.

Her surfaces prove her claim—they are a personal expression, a dazzling combination of artistic freedom and technical perfection. Heinrich began to experiment with the roller-printing techniques she saw in use at RIT. "People were pulling different things through the rolling mills. I make my own templates of brass; the gold becomes the relief pattern." The sheet of metal and the brass templates are rolled through the mill together; the pressure imprints the design onto the gold sheet, raising it up into a miniature bas relief.

Heinrich also works the surface of the gold manually in a variety of ways that create subtle patterns on the relatively soft 18k gold. "Often I hammer the gold between paper. It takes on the soft surface. I brush it with pumice powder. Sometimes I use a fiberglass brush; it makes the surface rough and matte." These various techniques create the basic surface for her jewelry designs. She then adds elements of gold she has cut out and layers them on top, two, three, or four elements that she fuses to the surface. It is a look that evolved over time into the feeling of planned randomness she is known for today.

At this stage, the entire piece has a matte finish. Design elements

Barbara Heinrich. Brooch. 18k gold, diamonds, boulder opal. (1988)

Barbara Heinrich. Bracelet. 18k gold; bright and matte sections linked. (1990) (Photo by Tim Callahan).

need to be highlighted to create the desired contrast. "I burnish to get the high-polish areas. I never polish on a polishing wheel. I hand burnish everything with a little hand tool. That way I can get a varied finish on the surface of the piece. I can control exactly where it goes."

The seeming randomness of the design is an illusion. When she starts to work, Heinrich has a clear idea of the ultimate shape of the piece of jewelry from the sketches she does first. "I used to do more finished sketches, and I still do that for customers. Rough sketches are enough for me to visualize. I try out proportions on paper. I may draw it twenty times until I get to the finished shape."

Heinrich describes her attention to detail, both in the goldsmithing and in the trappings of doing business, as "the German side" of her personality. She is a precise and orderly artist. While most goldsmiths have a general idea of the number of pieces they make in a year, Heinrich says, "I like to make as many pieces as there are days in a year. We did exactly 365 pieces last year and are right on track this year [1990]."

Because there is a limit to the amount of work she can produce, even with the help of an assistant, Heinrich sells only through galleries, principally The Works, Quadrum, Aaron Faber, and Susan Cummins. Through Susan Cummins, Heinrich is also shown at the Navy Pier Show in Chicago each September.

Her feelings about where the work is sold perfectly reflect the continuing division between contemporary and commercial jewelry and is based on more than just intuition. In 1989, she participated in the, Jewelers of America show's New Designer Room, and once was enough. She says, "I don't want to get involved with jewelry stores. This work is totally handmade; I feel the galleries are a better showcase for that. The jewelry is made according to esthetic values. It does not go with commercial jewelry, which is sold by value and weight. The galleries are really doing a wonderful job. It's not looked at as just so much merchandise."

Barbara Heinrich. "Leaf" earrings. 18k gold, diamonds, pearls; matte surface with bright edges and veins. (1990) (Photo by Tim Callahan.)

MARNE RYAN
Philadelphia, Pennsylvania

The ability of jewelers to create signature looks springs from a genuine joy in working the metals. Marne Ryan, a veteran of both the commercial and the academic worlds, has created a niche in the field of handmade, contemporary jewelry with her own mix of textures. While it is the surface that catches the eye, her work is considerably more than one layer deep. Ryan's pieces are assembled in stages, beginning with the creation of metal collages that are eventually formed into rugged landscapes she calls "Geoscapes."

Ryan begins with various golds, 14k, 18k, 22k and 24k, then adds sterling silver. Using the heat process of reticulation, she causes the metals to interact, forming three-dimensional surfaces. The resulting combination is then bonded to a surface of karat gold by heating. "I don't solder my metals together; I fuse them. I like playing with the alloy."

This, then, becomes her own material, to be cut up and shaped into all kinds of jewelry. After the shape is established, Ryan forms frames by bending rectangular gold wire around the outside. The frame gives the piece added strength and durability.

The independent nature of her work is a reflection both of her own personality and her program of studies at Moore College of Art in Philadelphia, a women's school where she earned a Bachelor of Fine Arts in jewelry and metalsmithing. "My study was all independent," she says. "I had a tremendous amount of determination. What I did, I hadn't seen anywhere." That remains true more than ten years later. Other jewelers fuse metals together, the same metals in fact, but the results are totally different. Getting back to the Old Masters again, there's every reason why they should be different. Give the same oil paints to ten artists, and you get back ten different styles of painting. For jewelers, gold and silver are paint.

While her work is very complex in appearance, its creation comes out of Ryan's own clarity. Design ideas, she says, come very quickly.

Marne Ryan. "Landscape" series ring. Oxidized sterling silver, 18k gold. Set with topaz. (1988–1989)

Marne Ryan. "Landscape" series cuff bracelet. Oxidized sterling silver, 18k gold. (1989) (Photo by Jim Graham.)

Marne Ryan. "Landscape" series cuff bracelet. Oxidized sterling silver, 18k gold, pearls. (1986) (Photo by Peter Groesbeck.)

"When I do it, I am very clear in my thinking. There's a harmonious balance in my sensory input and output dynamics. It's not just what I see but what I feel, what it sounds like. I am using all my sensory awareness. When I am designing for someone else, I'm doing a reading off of them. When that matches, I have a very kinesthetic response." But once the piece is complete, whether for a commission or to put in her line, Ryan leaves all the intellectual discussion behind. "When I make a piece, I don't have cards explaining what the piece is. If it's a strong piece, some aspect of it will speak to people who are attracted to it.

"I think of myself as doing experimental research. I am really interested in what happens to the coloration of metal when it oxidizes. I like to leave something in its rawest possible state. I like the way the pieces have a look that's modern but also of antiquity. People say you can't tell when my pieces were made. That's what I like the most about my work."

Ryan also likes the fact that the work changes as it is worn. The patinas—the color the metals acquire as they react to the air and oxidize—change with the oils and acids present in the wearer's skin. Gold is inert, but the metals used to alloy it are not, and so some change occurs. But silver, Ryan notes, "is one of the most active metals. Silver will change from hour to hour. Depending on the wearer, it can become very shiny, polished, or very tarnished."

Working virtually on her own, Ryan produces about 300 one-of-a-kind pieces a year, a number she would like to reduce to no more than 150 to 200. About three-quarters of her sales are directly to clients who come to her through word of mouth, many of them for wedding rings. "Once a client who is a lawyer was in court, and after he won the case, the lawyer who lost the case asked about his wedding ring." There is no typical Marne Ryan customer. Businesspeople she knows always ask about her customer demographics, but there is no common denominator other than that they respond to her designs.

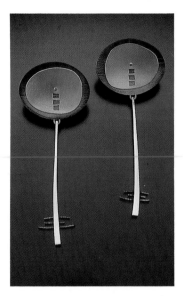

Tami Dean. Earrings. Sterling silver, gold, copper. (1988)

TAMI DEAN
Portland, Oregon

Bridging the worlds of surface treatment and patterning with a combination of reticulation and appliqué is Tami Dean, a jeweler who lives in Portland, Oregon. Although she works beautifully in both silver and gold, her heart is more with the silver. "I feel my silver work is more inspired than the gold. The graphic possibilities with silver are easier to achieve."

Using a variety of the reticulation process, she arrives at a moonscape kind of surface, full of craggy ups and downs. These rugged surfaces provide a background for her appliqués of gold and copper. Using a tiny jeweler's saw, she pierces the surfaces into specific patterns. "A lot of work I do involves rivets. I like the punctuation; I think they're a nice, clean-looking thing. They can be orderly or they can be functional, or spontaneous looking and purely decorative." The result is a look of architectural whimsey. Dean's "squiggles" are unmistakably hers, and this brings up the question of having a true artistic vision before sitting down at the bench.

When she does sit down at the bench, it's as a highly trained metalsmith in full command of both the techniques she learned and

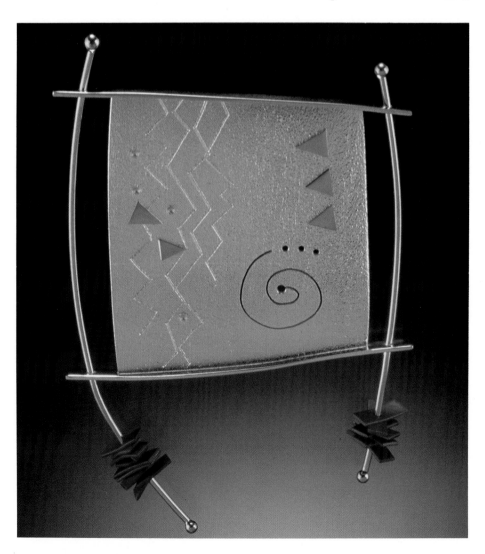

Tami Dean. Brooch. Sterling silver, gold, jasper. (1988)

those she has evolved. Dean describes her method of doing reticulation as "backwards." "I build up a layer of copper oxide firescale. Sterling silver oxidizes and really wants to form that firescale on the surface. I build up that layer until it's really black, and then I do the overheating process. The copper that's on the surface seems to protect the surface and buckles; the interior does melt. It allows me to get a finer grain texture than reticulation. Sometimes other jewelers think it's sandblasted because the texture is so fine. Then to get rid of the firescale, I go through the heating and pickling and brass-brushing process."

After preparing the entire surface, Dean selects the areas that are to be appliquéd and abrades them to give the solder a place to grab onto. Otherwise, she says, "with that surface, the solder really wants to crawl into that texture."

Dean lists several important influences on her as she was growing up, the kind of visual impressions that become part of a child's sensibility ready to be called upon by the adult. She was born in Los Angeles and raised in Pasadena; her father was a landscape architect, so ideas of form, volume, and symbols were ever present. She recalls clearly the house in which she grew up, "a magic old 1920s' Greene-and-Greene-style house, built by a decorative tilemaker." Those tiles, in the house and buried in the garden, had pre-Columbian motifs that remain with her to this day and helped shape her esthetic.

Following a college program of anthropology and linguistics, leading to her Bachelor of Arts degree from Portland State University, she embarked on a four-year course of study in the metals program of the Oregon School of Arts and Crafts, combined with an apprenticeship with Joe Reyes Apodaca. Both the anthropology and linguistics continue to make themselves felt in her jewelry designs. Motifs often refer to specific ideas well known in these fields; what keeps the jewelry from becoming so personal that it cannot be approached by customers is Dean's artistry. She interprets her influences and adapts them into fascinating, beautiful, and wearable jewelry. The jewelry is becoming to the wearer; the wearer is not merely a frame for the artist's canvas.

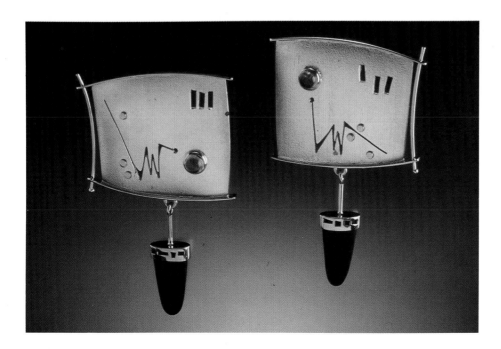

Tami Dean. Earrings. Sterling silver and gold set with amethysts and lapis lazuli. (1987)

JAN YAGER
Philadelphia, Pennsylvania

Surface treatments need not involve chemicals or layering of metals. In the commercial jewelry world, patterns are imprinted onto metals mechanically with the use of die-strike presses. This technique is used for large-scale production, for the most part, since the cost of making the die is considerable and the producer makes that investment only when he believes a particular design will sell in great numbers.

Jan Yager, however, discovered the mechanical possibilities of the machines while studying at Rhode Island School of Design in Providence and turned the method to her advantage, producing a line of embossed metal shaped into a very hands-on pillow form.

For Yager, the appeal of jewelry was tied up with its ancient role as talisman. She liked jewelry that was friendly to the touch, that could be handled with emotional attachment. And for that reason, she resisted hard-edged jewelry, even the craft jewelry that she describes as "cold and flat."

Jan Yager. Necklace. Five pillow forms in 18k gold with two Big Sur pebbles. (1988) (Photo by Marty Fumo.)

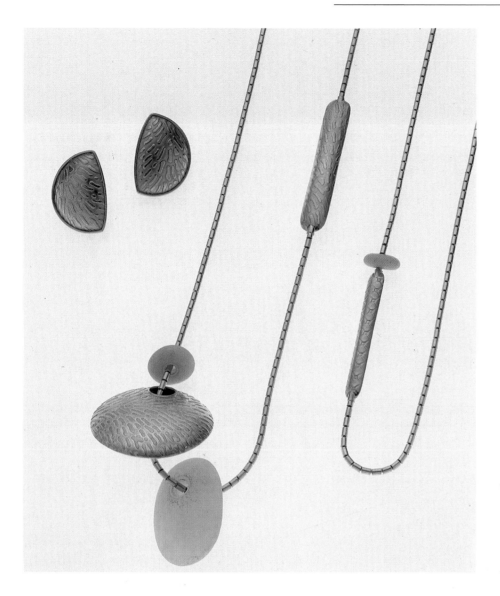

Jan Yager. Necklace. Three pillow forms in 18k gold with three white Cape May quartz rocks. Also shown, matching 18k gold earrings. (1987) (Photo by Michael Do'Bey.)

The ideal form, she decided, was a pillow—soft and inviting, " the complete antithesis of cold and angular machine-made 1970s jewelry." It began simply with a school assignment from her teacher, Jack Prip. "He had given us an assignment to do something with a company in Providence." When Yager opened up the Providence Yellow Pages, she discovered the world of specialists at her front door. "It was incredible to find out that there were people who did just etching, or just engraving, or stone setting." That led her to the drop-press machine.

Her patterns begin with photographs she takes herself or has seen in a book—often interesting walls. "I have always looked at texture and patterns, repeat images. When I moved to Rhode Island [from her home town of Kalamazoo, Michigan], the thing that was pretty powerful was all the stone everywhere, the cobblestone pavement and stone walls. That's when I started photographing walls." These visual ideas are absorbed and sifted by her own artistry and are transformed considerably by the time they are embossed into metal. But they are one of the most distinctive qualities about her work, the reason that it stands out so strongly from pattern work made by roller printing.

Chapter 10

Patterns

The goldsmith's ability to pattern and color jewelry takes many forms, limited only by the individual's technical skills and originality. Given the quality of today's goldsmiths, there seem to be no limits at all. Much of the work takes place at the bench, where the goldsmith hammers, heats, cuts, and pieces metals together. There is a quality of playfulness about this activity; one can see the child with scissors and paper, paint and paste. Goldsmiths often describe their way of working in joyful terms.

While traditional goldsmithing is as old as history, one might think that some of the more flamboyant and technically demanding techniques in use today are recent inventions. Many of these methods are equally venerable but were only brought to this country in modern times; what is new about them is the way they are adapted to contemporary jewelry. Here we look at the Japanese metalsmithing techniques of *mokumé gane*, *shibuichi*, and *shakado*.

Mokumé gane comes from the Japanese words for "wood-grained metal." The technique emulates the look of natural grains in woods and was originally created in Japan some three hundred years ago. Shibuichi and shakado are variations of the theme and refer to different combinations of metals. For our purposes, the term mokumé gane is used to describe the way metals are combined to create patterns and how those patterns are then used in jewelry.

*Facing page:
Gayle Saunders. "Secrets"
earrings. 14k colored
golds, 18k yellow gold.
(1986)*

In making a mokumé gane pattern, the goldsmith stacks layers of various metals one on top of the other and fuses them together with heat. These layers are very thin; dozens of them will be made into a sandwich, which is then worked as one metal element. Picture a hero sandwich with meats and cheeses piled up. Then cut through the pile to expose the layers. Cores are cut out from the stack to create holes. A cross-section view at this point looks like a mountain range in extreme miniature.

The laminated stack, with its hills and valleys, is rolled over and over through a rolling mill to even out the height. In the process, the metals become twisted or bent away from the original flat configuration. New patterns emerge, giving the goldsmith the metal equivalent of the dressmaker's paisley. Although the method involves a certain serendipity, in skilled hands it can be controlled quite vigorously, as may be seen in the designs of Terri Foltz-Fox, who explains the technique with the casualness of a cook sharing a recipe.

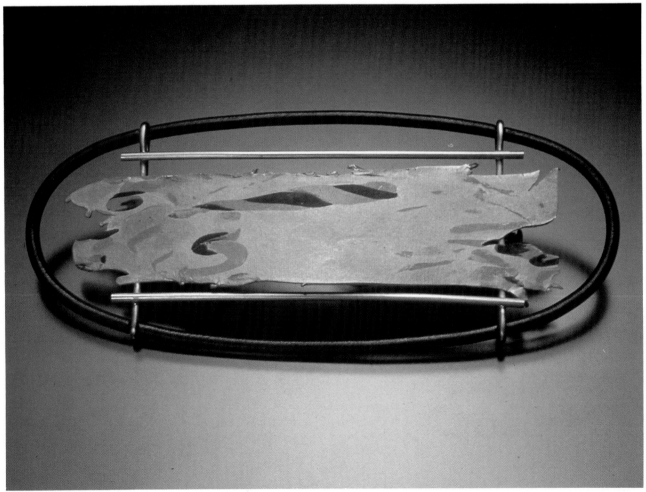

Gayle Saunders. "Setting Limits" brooch. 18k yellow gold, 14k colored golds, steel. (1982)

TERRI FOLTZ-FOX
Pasadena, Texas

"What I use most of the time is a variety of thicknesses. When I started, all the pieces were the same size; the regularity of that is boring. I started with fourteen and sixteen gauge metal; I'm using twenty and twenty-four gauge now. It's very thin, like a pencil line." Foltz-Fox explains that the higher the gauge number, the thinner the sheet. Roughly twenty to twenty-six layers equal an inch before the metal is milled down. As it is milled, it stretches, and the jeweler has a surface about double the size of the original block of metals.

The metals are fused together in a kiln. "The fusion process is a melting process; the temperature is such that the molecular layer from the outside of one sheet fuses to the next one. It's a very strong bond with no solder." Japanese copper alloys can be worked without much concern because they are not brittle. "When you start using brass or nickel silver, because of the hardness of the metal, you have to anneal as you go through the various processes. I use fine silver, nickel silver, copper, and brass. The patina I use on the brass is what oxidizes to black. Then I solder the laminated pattern onto sterling silver. That allows me to form the piece; the sterling back absorbs some of the stress."

The perfection in her work comes from "practice, practice makes perfect" she says with a laugh. Foltz-Fox began her jewelry-making education at Philadelphia College of Art, studying first with Olaf Skoogfors, and then Toni Schnieder and Robin Quigley. "I started out with married metals in 1977. I saw work that Gayle Saunders had done in my senior year; I had to do my senior thesis, and that's what my thesis project was. No one there knew much about it. It was a process of trying things, see what worked and what didn't. I learned the patterns on my own. I thought, this was what I was born to do, the geometric patterns. There was a fascination with colors and patterns of the metal."

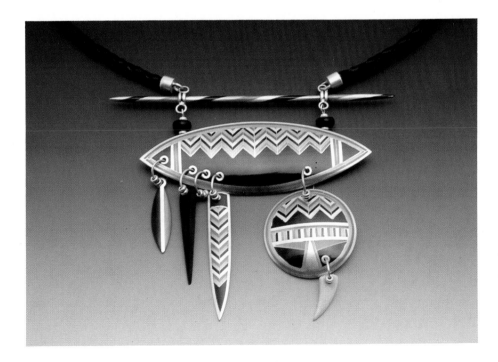

Terri Foltz-Fox. "Spirit Mask and Shield #1" neckpiece. Marriage of metals: sterling silver, copper, nickel, chemically oxidized brass. (1987)

"Then I took a workshop with Hiroko Pijanowski that led to mok-umé fusion. Instead of the metal controlling me, I wanted to control it. I wanted to stop with the geometric patterns; I wanted more than that." She also wanted to find a way to get the designs she envisioned without the extreme intensity of labor required; in one four-inch-long neck-piece, for example, in her loom series, there will be some two hundred pieces of metal married together.

The work from earlier years is excellent but doesn't have that distinctive signature we look for in the best metalsmiths. The abstract patterns reveal the hard-won technical expertise but not the dynamic personal expression that was still to come. She was searching, she says, "to create works with more input 'spiritually'—work that evokes a response from your heart and gut rather than just being pleasing to the eye." She embarked on a period of study and research.

"I studied works that I considered to possess the most magnetism and allure—the masks and shields of East Africa, the totems of the Northwest American Indian, the pottery and ceremonies of the Hopi and Pueblo tribes. I read all I could on African myths and legends and studied what I could about the ceremonies and customs of serveral North American tribes. The result was pieces which I think were more contemplative and celebrated the basics of life and the spirit."

The resulting work is all that she hoped it would be. The design, both of the patterned metals as well as the evocative images of the overall shapes, is a perfectly successful integration of tribal influence with contemporary metalsmithing.

Now when she works, the ideas come quickly, often evolving from

Terri Foltz-Fox. "Checks and Stripes" beads. Marriage of metals: sterling silver, copper, nickel, chemically oxidized brass. (1986)

Terri Foltz-Fox. Neckpiece, from the "Woven Image" loom series. Marriage of metals: sterling silver, copper, nickel, chemically oxidized brass. (1988)

a piece she is working on. "I sketch constantly. If I'm doing a series, I draw on the workbench when a piece is right there. I sketch on the table. The recent pieces take on the symbolism that are in the myths and legends." When Foltz-Fox and her husband, Bob, traveled to the Southwest, she says, "I was flabbergasted by the patterns. They had to make everything they utilize. I make it because I want to make it. They had to do it along with everything else in their lives. If I also had to produce the food, would I take the time to pattern a vessel?" But as I pointed out, no one needs to make patterns as complicated as hers, and she concluded that the Native Americans had the need to do their work as much as she has the need to do hers, no matter how demanding the method, no matter how busy the life.

PATRICIA DAUNIS
Portland, Maine

To the artist, the medium conveys the message. If Victor Vasarely had been a jeweler, instead of a painter—indeed, if he were a highly skilled jeweler—he might have expressed himself during the Op-Art period of the 1960s with pieces such as those created by Patricia Daunis. He was instead the inspiration for some of her most extraordinary pieces, work that she calls, quite correctly, a *tour de force.*

The wonder is in their construction, a refined expression of the marriage of metals technique that provides jewelers with "paint." This group of jewels derived from a holloware piece she made in 1980 called "Op Cube #1"; it was selected for the Young Americans show at the Museum of Contemporary Crafts that year. Here, in the demanding technique of marriage of metals, she recreates the undulating and visually baffling pulsations of the Op-Art that inspired her. There are no perfect squares in this piece; instead, each section appears to be pulled and stretched so that the corners are elongated or compressed, the straight lines bent into curves. The motion continues in a series of bracelets entitled "Diminishing Returns," "Optical Illusion," and "Undulating Checks."

Marriage of metals techniques are rarely pushed to this level. In this arena, the metalsmith cannot be separated from the artist, and the resulting work truly is "art to wear"—a term that is more often applied to work that isn't very wearable and sometimes not even particularly artistic.

The method is deceptively easy to describe: the metalsmith cuts out pieces of metal to emulate the design envisioned. More specifically, Daunis describes the process of making the optical illusion bracelet: "Each piece of metal [18k gold and copper] is individually cut out and soldered together, so there are hundreds of little pieces there." The cutting must be precise, exact. Even so, "When the pieces are soldered together, which is edge to edge, they never lie completely flat. They

Patricia Daunis. Two cuff bracelets, one of 18k gold and copper, and one of 14k gold and copper. (1981–1982)

*Patricia Daunis.
"Diminishing Returns"
cuff bracelet. Op-Art
marriage of metals
pattern: sterling silver,
copper. (1982)*

have to be filed, and this is what takes the most time—filing, smoothing, sanding, and polishing." The finished bracelet is smooth to the touch; it isn't possible to comprehend that this perfect flow of metal was once bits and pieces assembled at the bench. Such a bracelet takes three days to create.

This group of work Daunis calls high-tech/high art. Although she only made a handful of them, they provided the basis for the work to follow, pieces that could be made with the spirit of the cut-and-file work but at a price that brings them within reach of the average jewelry customer instead of restricting the pleasure of ownership to a discerning elite patron.

The first step in translating the work for a wider market while maintaining the integrity of the method involved the use of larger pieces of metal, thus reducing the number of inserts and shortening

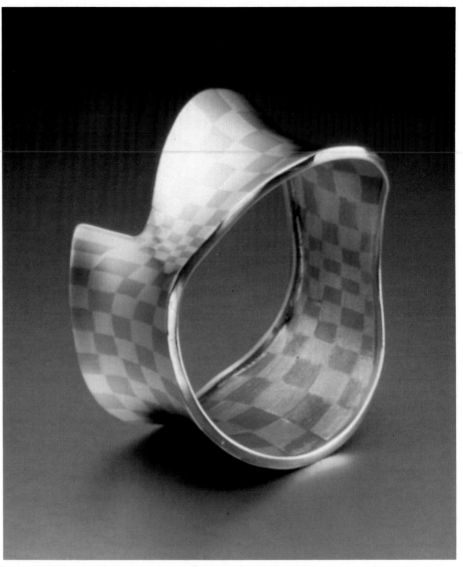

Patricia Daunis. "Undulating Checks" varied-width cuff bracelet. Marriage of metals in Op-Art pattern: sterling silver, nickel silver. (1982)

Patricia Daunis. Wide, open cuff bracelet. Marriage of metals in abstract pattern: sterling silver, brass, nickel silver, copper. (1982)

the time needed to finish the surface. Daunis's cuffs and earrings of that period express a softer version of the technique, offering the same feeling but with considerably less labor.

Whether using the marriage of metals techniques to the maximum or in modified form, Daunis was building on her very strong background as a holloware maker. She sees as her primary strength the ability to make jewelry that is strongly three dimensional. Indeed, because she saw jewelry as a "flat" medium, it never appealed to her as a metalsmith. Because most people sketch their designs, producing a two-dimensional drawing, she feels they are doomed to produce flat jewelry. And indeed, having judged a number of jewelry-design contests from sketches and then with the finished pieces in view, I can appreciate her conclusion. From drawings, it's always difficult to project just how rounded a design will prove to be. She sidesteps this process entirely.

When designing, she says, "I always start with metal. I take metals and I cut out things and I shape them and I make sketches in metal. They may be real rough, but that's how I sketch, rather than taking pen in hand." There is no gap, then, between thought and finished product, as there often is when the thought is not suited to the medium.

Ultimately Daunis's marriage of metals designs were translated into a production line. These pieces, in a technique of merged rather than married metals, were made in several series. Each piece began with a background metal—sterling or vermeil. Then a pattern of copper, nickel silver, brass, 14k rose gold, or a mixture of these metals was worked into the surface. The overlays were achieved by soldering metal wires to the background metal and rolling the mixture through a mill repeatedly until the overlays were perfectly imbedded into the background. This sheet of metal could then be cut and shaped as desired, much as cookies are cut from a sheet of rolled-out dough.

The three-dimensional quality of her work is also evident in the work that today accounts for a great deal of her true production line—a group of two hundred earring styles that are cast in gold, sterling silver, or vermeil. Within the jewelry world, these still stand out from conventional design. They have great volume with little weight. They turn and dance on the ear and are successful enough to be bought by five hundred stores all over the country. They have won awards from the "brand-name" type organizations such as Intergold and account for her success at the Jewelers of America show. But my heart is still with her marriage of metals work.

While Daunis and others, including Glenda Arentzen, have left their early marriage of metals work for more facile metal techniques, some few still labor in this demanding method. Tony Papp, as noted in the chapter on galleries, still makes pieces using the technique, although his designs now require fewer of the painstaking juxtapositions of metals.

Patricia Daunis. "Scales" limited-production collection. Fused metals: sterling silver, nickel silver. (1984–1987)

JANE MARTIN
Bainbridge Island, Washington

Somewhat less demanding technically, but liberating artistically, is a technique some call "collage." This version of marriage of metals, as described by Jane Martin, "involves the soldering of one color metal onto a base of another color [such as copper wire onto sterling silver sheet] which is then rolled." Once the sheets are prepared, Martin adds patinas to further enrich the patterns and colors of the finished pieces. "I don't like jewelry that's glorified technique. In mine, it's a very strong by-product. I like the pattern surface, I like working with beads; finding patterns that match my beads, and vice versa. I go back and forth, sometimes getting the pattern from the beads wherever I can get the color from. I love mixing the paint on the palette. That's what I like doing in metal; it's the color. In school, I liked mixing the paint more than the painting itself."

But Martin has added her own technical wizardry to the mix in the creation of her cubed beads. Making perfectly seamed metal cubes in jewelry was for her "a way of getting another dimension." It is an expression of her love of the metal itself. "I really like the feel of metal; it blossoms and grows."

Martin found the way to her signature look while attending the Philadelphia College of Art. Although, she says, "I loved being in that environment and trying new materials, I had a lot of resistance to my patterns from teachers who wanted the shiny surface. But I got support from the painting teachers. I wanted to combine the two." Martin has only praise for Robin Quigley, a teacher now at the Rhode Island School of Design, who, she says, "was wonderful. She was one of the newer generation and was very supportive." Although Martin was at Philadelphia during the reign of Olaf Skoogfors, he died during her sophomore year, before she could take a course with him. But Skoogfors's own teacher from the 1940s, Richard Reinhardt, came to the college to fill in when he died. Martin remembers him saying, "Something cannot be slightly precise. There are no mistakes, only opportunities."

Jane Martin. "Language" necklace. Marriage of metals with sterling silver inlaid with copper and brass; 1" cube beads; patinated; copal amber. (1988)

Jane Martin. "Picture Frame" earrings. Marriage of metals with sterling silver inlaid with copper; patinated. (1989)

Jane Martin. "Dice" necklace. Marriage of metals with sterling silver inlaid with brass, copper, nickel silver; beads; cubes are 1¼" square; patinated. (1988)

But the practical aspects of making a living from jewelry were not on the curriculum. "There was a real resistance to selling your work. I graduated in 1978, and you were supposed to teach." Martin, however, had been making jewelry since she was thirteen and had sold it while still in high school. The lessons she needed in business came, round-about, after she attended a class given by Helen Drutt for all the crafts departments. Martin went to work in Drutt's Philadelphia gallery for two years, doing everything and at the same time working on her own jewelry at night. "By then, [Drutt] was doing Olaf's retrospective. It was incredible being around her, talking with other artists, setting up shows. It was a business course." From Drutt, she says, she got a sense of the historic and academic documentation of work and how to place herself and her time within the history of craft itself.

Jane Martin. "Polka Dots" necklace. Marriage of metals with brass inlaid with copper and sterling silver; largest beads are 1¼" square; patinated. (1988)

Production classes with Thomas Mann at Peters Valley helped with some of the practical aspects of jewelry making. But it was when she sold her first "expensive" necklace directly to a customer during a jewelry show in Dallas that Martin felt "a wonderful feeling, a validation." The necklace cost five hundred dollars. Much more validation followed as she pursued the craft show marketplace, especially in being accepted to the prestigious Philadelphia Craft Show for three years. But after nine years, Martin packed up her life in Philadelphia and moved to Seattle, Washington. It was a decision several years in the making, one she says was really not a decision, but simply a process. "All I needed was new order forms and a rubber stamp [for the change of address]. It didn't affect my business at all." When I caught up with Martin again, in an independent show staged by a group of jewelers during the Baltimore Craft Fair in 1990, I could see that, indeed, the move had certainly not affected her work. It was as inventive and fresh as I remembered it to be.

Martin moved from one strong craft jewelry city to another. Seattle is home to a number of creative jewelers and boasts its own Seattle Metals Guild, started a few years ago by Micki Lippe. Today, it numbers one hundred members. The generous sharing of information is a hallmark of contemporary goldsmiths who know that it is not the technique but the jeweler that makes the jewelry.

MICKI LIPPE
Seattle, Washington

Micki Lippe's own pieces reveal a collage artist at work in metal. Combining sterling silver with 22k gold, copper, and shakudo, Lippe gives her metal surfaces such a soft appearance that they seem to be liquid. "I have always liked to affect the surface of the metal," she explains. "Just a plain buffed surface has never appealed to me." In order to focus on the surface, she found it necessary to limit herself to just a few basic shapes. "I was working one night, the pieces were getting fussier, and I wasn't happy. I decided I was going to limit myself to triangles, squares, rectangles, and circles. I set limits." She found that by giving herself visual goals, the work grew beyond anything she had made before.

"Just because the material is rigid," she says, "the work doesn't have to be rigid. For too long jewelry has been locked into this hard-edged, finished look." Being flexible was certainly a necessity for Lippe, who took her degree in commercial art. "There weren't advisors, or somebody would have told me 'You need to be in something three dimensional.' I tried pottery and weaving, and finally I found metal." Although she went to school at Washington University in St. Louis,

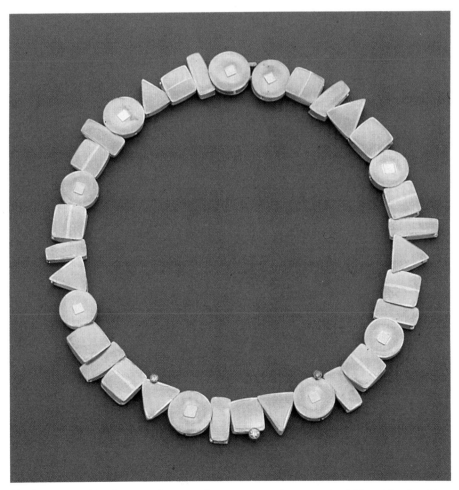

Micki Lippe. Neckpiece. Series of geometric elements in 22k gold edged in sterling silver, with yellow diamonds. (1989) (Photo by Richard Nicol.)

Micki Lippe. Brooch. 22k gold edged with sterling silver. (1990) (Photo by Richard Nicol.)

where Heikki Seppa teaches, the jewelry program didn't exist at the time she was there in the 1960s. But a jewelry course she took while in California opened her eyes to her future. "I said, 'this is it, this is what I should be doing'."

An amazing number of the woman goldsmiths I know are married to men whose work takes them to new cities every few years. This is the case with Terri Foltz-Fox and also with Micki Lippe, whose research scientist husband moved the family around to Charlottesville, Virginia, Yellowsprings, Ohio, and elsewhere, before arriving at their current and probably permanent home in Seattle. At each stop, Lippe looked around, found a place to work and to take courses, and managed to build a unique jewelry business, but the process was slowed down while she produced and raised her two children.

When she discovered jewelry she was making her living from commercial art, and so she made a deal with herself. "I said 'If I earned X amount of dollars from commercial art, I would give myself two months to do the jewelry.' I had to keep putting each workspace away in order to do the other. There wasn't room to keep out the equipment for both." At this point, her husband was in graduate school, and Lippe was the breadwinner. In later years, their roles reversed, and she gratefully says, "The luxury I have had is a husband; I could do new work," without being concerned as much about it selling.

Along the way she spent four years in Charlottesville, Virginia, where in the McGuffy artists co-op, she says, "I had access to other equipment and other people's esthetic values. A whole world opened up there; we moved there because of his work, but we stayed there because of McGuffy." The co-op housed forty-two artists in an old school

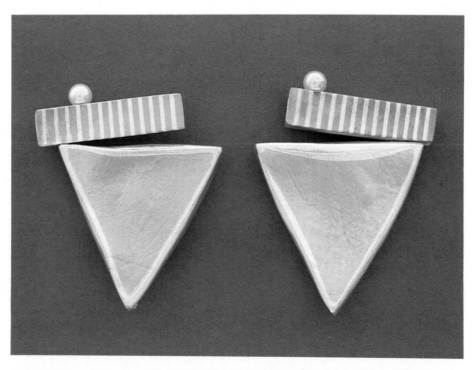

Micki Lippe. Earrings. Triangle shapes of 22k gold edged with sterling silver; bar at top of copper and 22k gold; pearls. (1988) (Photo by Richard Nicol.)

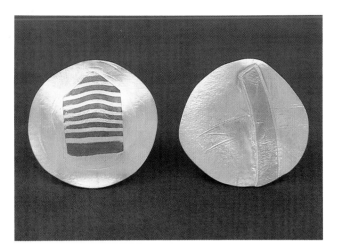

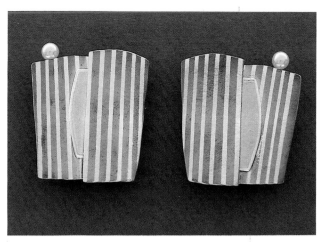

Micki Lippe. Earrings. Unmatched patterns of 22k gold, sterling silver, copper. (1988) (Photo by Richard Nicol.)

Micki Lippe. Earrings. 22k gold, sterling silver, copper, pearls. (1988)

building and was subsidized by the city. In return, the city ran school tours through the artists' studios. Artists had to give a certain number of hours of gallery duty and tours, and the city took a percent of the sales from the gallery.

Through the years, Lippe was limited to doing one craft show a year; that was all the time she could manage away from her home and children. "My first big show was in Connecticut. My children [now teenagers] said goodbye to mommy in the driveway, singing 'Make lots of money'." During this long apprenticeship, essentially forced on her by circumstances, Lippe's work matured.

This sense of growth over time is, I believe, one of the key elements missing from many of today's younger generation of metalsmiths. The fault lies largely with the marketplace, which no longer has any tolerance for experiment, for making mistakes, and for taking time to mature. The pressure to get into shows, and then to produce enough income to cover the expense of those shows, forces young artists to devise some kind of production line long before they are really ready. The result is a great deal of ordinary work, technically well executed but devoid of content. It is not far removed from the mentality of buying for weight that pervades the commercial jewelry market.

Lippe says, "Nobody should ever buy my work for the materials' value. You are buying the labor and the design. It's permanent. You have something to hand down to generations."

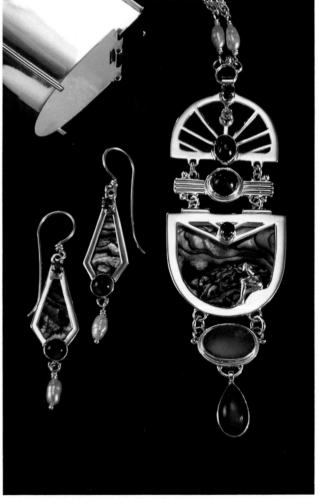

Epilogue

Jewel Box

The last word on originality in the making of contemporary American jewelry goes to Jane Campbell, a metalsmith who lives in Cambridge Springs, Pennsylvania. Campbell, who says she has always liked Fabergé eggs that came apart to reveal other treasures within, one day simply had a flash of inspiration. She was then making brooches, but says, "I knew I wanted to make something more elaborate." Suddenly she saw the brooch as the lid of a box. Everything grew from that thought. The brooch grew into a necklace with chain; studs that held the box together at either side became earrings. "If the box is a large oval, the entire bottom is a bracelet." That type of construction can take a couple of months. Somewhere within the construction a piece becomes a stickpin. The more elaborate pieces also include a "daughter pendant." Although Campbell has made three boxes in 14k gold for special orders, the silver sells the best. "What they want is the whole idea and the construction."

Whatever the metals and the methods used, these jewelers offer originality combined with technical excellence. That ultimately is the story of contemporary American jewelry: the whole idea and the construction.

Facing page:
Jane Campbell. Jewel box that disassembles to become earrings, pendant, and stickpin. Sterling silver, abalone shell, mabe pearls, tourmaline, opal. (1988) (Photos by Van Tuil.)

Appendix 1

Craft Galleries

A short list of galleries featuring contemporary American jewelry (by state).

Arizona

Joanne Rapp Gallery/The Hand
  and The Spirit
4222 N. Marshall Way
Scottsdale, AZ 85251
(609) 949-1262
Joanne Rapp
(Established 1972)

California

Concepts
6th and Mission Streets
Carmel, CA 93921
(408) 624-3688
Doug Steakley, Jackie Steakley
(Established 1977)

Susan Cummins Gallery
12 Miller Avenue
Mill Valley, CA 94941
(415) 383-1512
Susan Cummins, Beth
  Changstrom
(Established 1984)

Del Mano Gallery
11981 San Vicente Boulevard
Los Angeles, CA 90049
(213) 476-8508
Jan Peters, Ray Leier
(Established 1973)

HumanArts Gallery (formerly
  Running Ridge)
310 E. Ojai Avenue
Ojai, CA 93023
(805) 646-1525
Hallie and Stan Katz
(Established 1975)

Sculpture to Wear
8441 Melrose Avenue
Los Angeles, CA 90069
(213) 651-2205
Jan Ehrenworth, Samuel Zide
(Established 1986)

Connecticut

The Elements
14 Liberty Way
Greenwich, CT 06830
(203) 661-0014
Emily Toohey, Kay Eddy, Sunny
  Brown, Patsy Taylor
(Established 1973)

Maine

Etienne & Company
20 Main Street
Camden, ME 04843
(800) 426-4367
Etienne Perret
(Established 1975)

Massachusetts

The Artful Hand Gallery
Copley Place
Boston, MA 02116
(617) 262-9601
Joe Porcari, Mary Porcari
(Established 1985)

Quadrum
The Mall at Chestnut Hill
Chestnut Hill, MA 02167
(617) 965-5555
Cynthia Kagan
(Established 1978)

Signature
The Mall at Chestnut Hill
Chestnut Hill, MA 02167
(617) 332-7749
Arthur Grohe, Gretchen
   Keyworth
(Established 1987)

Michigan

Yaw Gallery
550 N. Woodward Avenue
Birmingham, MI 48009
Nancy Yaw
(Established 1962)

New Jersey

Sheila Nussbaum Gallery
358 Millburn Avenue
Millburn, NJ 07041
(201) 467-1720
Sheila Nussbaum
(Established 1982)

New Mexico

Handcrafters Gallery
227 Galisteo Street
Santa Fe, NM 87501
(505) 982-4880
Peter Kahn
(Established 1983)

Ornament
209 W. San Francisco Street
Santa Fe, NM 87501
(505) 983-9399
Sandy Polansky
(Established 1987)

Running Ridge Gallery
640 Canyon Road
Santa Fe, NM 87401
(505) 988-2515
Robert and Barbara Grabowski,
   Ruth and John Farnham
(Established 1979)

Santa Fe East
200 Old Santa Fe Trail
Santa Fe, NM 87501
(505) 988-3103
Gordon King, Alma King,
   Pierpont King
(Established 1980)

New York

Artium
730 Fifth Avenue, Suite 1710
New York, NY 10019
(212) 333-5800
Svetlana Dymski, Freddi Miceli
(Established 1989)

Clouds Gallery
1 Mill Hill Road
Woodstock, NY 12498
(914) 679-8155
Robert Ohnigian
(Established 1974)

Craftsman's Gallery
16 Chase Road
Scarsdale, NY 10583
(914) 725-4644
Sybil Robins
(Established 1973)

Helen Drutt Gallery
724 Fifth Avenue
New York, NY 10019
(212) 974-7700
Helen Drutt
(Established 1988)

Aaron Faber Gallery
666 Fifth Avenue
New York, NY 10103
(212) 586-8411
Edward Faber, Patricia Kiley
   Faber
(Established 1974)

Neil Isman Gallery
1100 Madison Avenue
New York, NY 10028
(212) 628-3688
Neil Isman
(Established 1974)

Gayle Willson Gallery
43 Job's Lane
Southampton, NY 11968
(516) 283-7430
Paul Willson, Gayle Willson
(Established 1981)

Pennsylvania

Helen Drutt Gallery
1721 Walnut Street
Philadelphia, PA 19103
(215) 735-1625
Helen Drutt
(Established 1974)

Gallery 500
Church and Old York Roads
Elkins Park, PA 19117
(215) 572-1203
Harriet Friedberg, Rita
   Greenfield
(Established 1969)

Langman Gallery
2500 Moreland Road
Willow Grove, PA 19090
(215) 657-8333
Richard Langman
(Established 1972)

The Works Gallery
319 South Street
Philadelphia, PA 19147
(215) 822-7775
Ruth Snyderman, Rick
   Snyderman
(Established 1965)

Texas

The Boardwalk Gallery
   Goldsmiths
5175 Westheimer, Suite 2350
Galleria III
Houston, TX 77056
(713) 961-3552
Rosemary Estenson
(Established 1977)

Appendix 2

Schools and Workshops

A short list of craft centers and colleges that offer jewelry and metal courses (by state).

California

California College of Arts & Crafts
5212 Broadway at College
Oakland, CA 94618
(415) 653-8818

Revere Academy of Jewelry Arts
760 Market Street, Suite 939
San Francisco, CA 94102
(415) 391-4179

San Diego State University
Department of Art
San Diego, CA 92182
(619) 594-6511

Colorado

Colorado State University
Art Department
Visual Arts Building
Ft. Collins, CO 80523
(303) 491-5895

Florida

Florida State University
Art Department
221 Fine Arts Building
Tallahassee, FL 32306-2037
(904) 644-6474

Illinois

Southern Illinois University at Carbondale
School of Art
Carbondale, IL 62901
(618) 453-3413

Maine

Haystack Mountain School of Crafts
Box 87A
Deer Isle, ME 04627
(207) 348-2306

Michigan

Cranbrook Academy of Art
500 Lone Pine Road
P.O. Box 801
Bloomfield Hills, MI 48013
(313) 645-3300

Missouri

Washington University
School of Fine Art
One Brookline Drive, Campus
   Box 1031
St. Louis, MO 63130
(314) 889-6500

New Mexico

Dunconor Workshop
Box 149
Taos, NM 87571
(505) 758-9660

New Jersey

Peters Valley Craft Center
Layton, NJ 07851
(201) 948-5200

New York

The College at New Paltz
State University of New York
New Paltz, NY 12561
(914) 257-3830

Craft Students League of the
   YWCA
610 Lexington Avenue
New York, NY 10022
(212) 735-9731

Fashion Institute of Technology
227 West 27th Street
New York, NY 10001
(212) 760-7665

Jewelry Arts Institute
2231 Broadway
New York, NY 10024
(212) 362-8633

Parson's School of Design
66 Fifth Avenue
New York, NY 10011
(212) 741-8910

Rochester Institute of
   Technology
College of Fine & Applied Art
One Lomb Memorial Drive
Rochester, NY 14623
(716) 475-2646

Skidmore College
Department of Art
Saratoga Springs, NY 12866
(518) 584-5000, ext. 2372

YM-YWHA
92nd Street "Y"
1395 Lexington Avenue
New York, NY 10128
(212) 427-6000

North Carolina

Penland School
Penland, NC 28765
(704) 765-2359

Ohio

Kent State University
School of Art
Kent, OH 44242
(216) 672-2192

Oregon

Oregon School of Arts and Crafts
8245 S.W. Barnes Road
Portland, OR 97225
(503) 297-5544

Pennsylvania

Moore College of Art
20th & The Parkway
Philadelphia, PA 19103-1179
(215) 568-4515

University of the Arts
College of Art & Design
Broad & Pine Streets
Philadelphia, PA 19102
(215) 875-4800

Tyler School of Art
Temple University
Beech & Penrose Avenues
Elkins Park, PA 19126
(215) 782-2828

Rhode Island

Rhode Island School of Design
Two College Street
Providence, RI 02903
(401) 331-3511, ext. 315

Tennessee

Appalachian Center for Crafts
Tennessee Technological
   University
Route 3, Box 430
Smithville, TN 37166
(615) 597-6801

Arrowmont School of Arts and
   Crafts
Box 567
Gatlinburg, TN 37738
(615) 436-5860

Washington

University of Washington
School of Art, DM-10
Seattle, WA 98195
(206) 542-0970

Appendix 3

Organizations

The American Craft Council and the Society of North American Goldsmiths are the principal organizations in the crafts field. Many fine metal guilds operate at the state level.

American Craft Council

Founded in 1943, the Council encompasses a museum, a library, a magazine, and a marketing group. The nature of the association and its relationship with these divisions as it heads into the 1990s is shifting, reflecting the dramatic changes that have taken place in the crafts field since it was founded.

- American Craft Museum
  40 W. 53rd Street
  New York, NY 10019
  (212) 956-6047
- American Craft Council Library
  72 Spring Street
  New York, NY 10012
  (212) 274-0630
- American Craft magazine (see Appendix 5: Publications)
- Guide to Craft Galleries & Shops, U.S.A.
- Sponsors "Young Americans," a periodic exhibition of works by craftspeople between the ages of 18 and 30.
- American Craft Enterprises (operates craft fairs around the country for both wholesale and retail buyers; see Appendix 4: Craft Shows)

Society of North American Goldsmiths
5009 Londonderry Drive
Tampa, FL 33647
(813) 977-5326

Organized in 1968 by a group of nine gold- and silversmiths to promote contemporary metalwork and jewelry, the Society publishes *Metalsmith* as well as the SNAG Newsletter; hosts an annual conference of speakers and technical demonstrations that is held at a different site each year; and sponsors exhibitions of contemporary metalwork. Membership is open to professional metalsmiths, students, collectors, gallery owners, and the general public.

The presidency is held for three-year terms and rotated among board members.

Appendix 4

Craft Shows

Craft shows may be found in major cities around the country, especially in the summer months and just before Christmas. Some shows designate the first days for wholesale buyers, followed by a weekend for retail customers. Others are open to either wholesale or retail buyers exclusively. Street fairs, as well as a number of shows held in the month before Christmas, sell retail only. A few longstanding events are listed. Extensive listings of current shows are published monthly by *The Crafts Report*.

American Craft Enterprises
P.O. Box 10
256 Main Street
New Paltz, NY 12561
(914) 255-0039

- Sponsors retail/wholesale events in Baltimore (February); Minneapolis (April); West Springfield, MA (June); San Francisco (August).
- Sponsors small, upper-market retail shows in Atlanta and New York, both in May.
- Participates in a wholesale-only gift show in Boston (March).

Buyers Market of American Crafts
3000 Chestnut Avenue, Suite 300
Baltimore, MD 21211
(301) 889-2933

- Sponsors wholesale-only shows, with shifting dates and venues. Currently, shows are held in Philadelphia (February); Boston (June); San Francisco (August); and Miami (September).

New Art Forms at Navy Pier, Chicago
c/o The Lakeside Group
600 North McClurg Court, Suite 1302A
Chicago, IL 60611
(312) 787-6858

• An annual retail show for galleries only, held in September. Craft-makers are invited to participate by gallery owners.

Roy Helms & Associates
777 Kapiolani Boulevard
Suite 2820
Honolulu, Hawaii 96813
(808) 836-7611

• Sponsors retail shows in southern California.

Crafts at Rhinebeck
Dutchess County Fairgrounds
Rhinebeck, NY 12572
(914) 876-4001

• A retail-only show held in June. Sponsor is the Fairgrounds, former site of the ACE "Rhinebeck" show. This event has no other relationship to that show.

Philadelphia Craft Show
Philadelphia Museum of Art
Parkway at 26th Street
Philadelphia, PA 19101
(215) 763-8100

• A 150-exhibit, upper-market retail show held in November at the Philadelphia Civic Center, sponsored by the Women's Committee of the Philadelphia Museum of Art.

Washington Craft Show
A & I 1465
Smithsonian Institution
Washington, D.C. 20560
(202) 357-4000

• A 100-exhibit, upper market retail show held in April, sponsored by the Women Associates of the Smithsonian.

Appendix 5

Publications

American Craft (formerly *Craft Horizons*)
72 Spring Street
New York, NY 10012
(212) 274-0630

A bimonthly publication of American Craft Council, this journal covers metalsmithing, ceramics, fiber, glass, and wood. It contains features on all craft media; an extensive calendar of exhibits; artists' retrospectives; and reviews.

The Crafts Report
P.O. Box 1992
Wilmington, DE 19899
(302) 656-2209

A monthly publication concerning the business side of crafts, featuring articles on marketing and management for professional craftspeople. News reports on craft shows and health and legal issues are addressed regularly in columns by experts.

Metalsmith
5009 Londonderry Drive
Tampa, FL 33647
(813) 977-5326

A quarterly publication of SNAG addressing philosophical issues pertinent to metalsmiths. *Metalsmith* profiles historical and practicing metalsmiths and reviews gallery shows and books.

Ornament (formerly *The Bead Journal*)
P.O. Box 2349
San Marcos, CA 92079-2349
(619) 599-0222

A quarterly publication covering ancient, contemporary, and ethnic objects of personal adornment.

Index

Italicized page numbers indicate photographs.